life with
SIR ALEX

A Fan's Story of Ferguson's 25 Years at Manchester United

WILL TIDEY

Published by Bloomsbury Publishing Plc
49–51 Bedford Square
London
WC1B 3DP
www.bloomsbury.com

First edition 2011

ISBN 978-1-4081-4951-5

A CIP catalogue record for this book is available from the British Library.

All cover images © Getty Images
Cover design by James Watson
Commissioned by Charlotte Atyeo
Edited by Sarah Cole

This book is produced using paper that is made from wood
grown in managed, sustainable forests. It is natural, renewable and
recyclable. The logging and manufacturing processes conform to the
environmental regulations of the country of origin.

Designed and typeset in 10pt Minion by seagulls.net
Printed and bound by CPI Group (UK) Ltd, Croydon, CR0 4YY

Picture credits: All photographs © Getty Images with the exception of the
following: Picture section page 12 (top) © Press Association

For Kendall and the boys

... And the old man, obviously

CONTENTS

PART THREE (2002/03 to 2010/11)

PREFACE

In the very top tier of the cavernous Camp Nou stadium sit a 47-year-old man and his 20-year-old son. The scoreboard reads Manchester United 0-1 Bayern Munich. The clock shows 90 minutes. Gloom hangs heavy in the balmy Barcelona air.

What seems like miles beneath them a bleached-blond midfielder in a bright red shirt scurries across to the corner flag. In comes the corner. Out goes the clearance. In comes a scuffed shot. Silence and the loudest noise you've ever heard both at the same time. Arms flailing; fists pumping; bodies crashing against each other in waves of euphoria.

Down below the bleached-blond one is taking another corner. In it comes. Near-post flick. A leg stuck out. Delirium. The men in red are still standing up. They won't sit down again. A man they've never met hugs the son, and then the father. Arms everywhere. Bodies everywhere. Noise everywhere. The father looks at his son. 'Just as well we didn't leave,' he says. 'Wouldn't want to have missed that, would we?'

And there it is. The story I'll tell at my dad's funeral. The story I'll tell anybody who's listening. It's not about a football match; it's about a shared emotional experience that touched on hope, despair and elation. It's about two men with a childlike love of the football team they grew up with. It's about what it means to be a lifelong football fan.

Or maybe that's just a load of sentimental rubbish. Of course it's about a football match – one that ended in the most dramatic way imaginable and sealed United their first European Cup in 31 years, and the Treble with it. One that will be talked about, and I quote Clive Tyldesley, 'forever and a day'. And one, most importantly, that signified the arrival to greatness of United's manager Sir Alex Ferguson.

The man who walked into Old Trafford from Aberdeen in November 1986 with little fanfare had transformed United from a lumbering, booze-addled relic to the greatest football team in Europe. He'd brought back the glory days of George Best, Bobby Charlton and Denis Law, and installed a new professionalism at Old Trafford that would see them surpassed. And fortunately for me, he'd done it all on my watch.

If the football team you support is a matter of luck and timing, then there are few luckier than the Manchester United fans who were born into my generation. I was eight when Ferguson got the job. In the 25 years since United have won twelve league titles, five FA Cups, four League Cups, a European Cup-Winners' Cup and two European Cups – a quite remarkable record of success. Little wonder they call us 'glory hunters'.

United fans my age or younger have known only Ferguson. There are blurry memories of the perma-tanned Ron Atkinson for the oldest of us, but they drift in and out. Ferguson was the headmaster during our school years, our lecturer at university and now he's our boss. He's the father figure to our football fandom. And he's never, ever, let us down.

This is the story of what it's meant to be a Manchester United supporter in the Ferguson era, told by a football fan first and journalist second. It's about the teams I grew up with, the players I've worshipped and the games that live on in my mind. It's about the effect United have had on every stage of my life, from the tears of a wide-eyed six-year-old to the groans of a 30-something with two kids and a mortgage.

I arrived at the United altar around the same time Ferguson arrived at Old Trafford. I was there when they ended their wait for a league title; I was there for Cantona's first goal; I saw the Fergie Fledglings in full fight. And I was there in Barcelona in 1999. I've been there all along.

I'm one of millions. And I'm beyond fortunate to have been given the chance to write about it.

INTRODUCTION

It was the afternoon of Saturday 18 May 1985. The strutting guitar riff of Dire Straits' 'Money for Nothing' was blasting from my parents' stack stereo system and there was an excitement in the air that felt like Christmas. It was FA Cup Final day, and for a six-year-old Manchester United fan it was the culmination of a new obsession. Music down, television volume up, it was finally time for the main event.

Standing before us, in bright red shirts and tight white shorts, were my original cast of heroes. Their leader was Bryan Robson, a swash-buckling midfielder who channelled the devil-may-care bravado of Han Solo. Robson could do it all, wash it down with ten pints, then do it again the very next day. He was the epitome of rugged, manly cool, and the best footballer in the country. His poster was already on my wall, and his No. 7 already on my back.

My next favourite was Jesper Olsen, a waifish Danish winger who flounced around like the lead singer in an indie band. I loved his left-footedness and the fact he wore his socks around his ankles – a fashion statement I've mimicked on the sports field ever since. They said he was more style than substance, and maybe they were right, but he was a maverick in the United mould and his legend lives on. Besides, the beautiful game, like life itself, needs its airy-fairy bit-part players just as much as its courageous do-or-die central defenders.

Then there was United's goalkeeper Gary Bailey, whose shock of blond hair gave him a passing resemblance to another prominent figure in my childhood, Luke Skywalker. That was reason enough to follow his progress and give serious consideration to whether he and Robson, given a Millennium Falcon, could take down the Empire

(Liverpool). Robbo would never have left Bailey to destroy the Death Star on his own, that's for sure. And he could have drunk Lando Calrissian under the table.

The two other hero crushes at the dawn of my United obsession were Mark Hughes and Norman Whiteside. Hughes had legs like torsos and they propelled him around the pitch and into the air like rocket launchers. They also came in handy when he was executing spectacular side-on volleys, which invariably fizzed into the roof of the net whenever United were in trouble. He was 'a scorer of great goals but not a great goal scorer', so went the oft-repeated tagline. Considering the vast majority of us aren't either of those things, I'd take that as a legacy.

As for Whiteside, he was but 20 years old and had already made a name for himself through youthful exuberance (Big Norm, as we later found out, specialised in exuberance). Aged 17 years and 41 days he broke Pele's record as the youngest player to play in a World Cup, when he turned out for Northern Ireland at the 1982 finals in Spain. The next season he became the youngest man to score in both an FA Cup Final and a League Cup final. That glorious day in 1985 he'd further his growing reputation with the most iconic contribution of his career.

United were up against Everton, the First Division champions and FA Cup holders, who under Howard Kendall were vying with Merseyside neighbours Liverpool for the title of best team in the land in the mid-1980s. Having already bagged the title and the European Cup-Winners' Cup, an unprecedented treble was theirs for the taking at Wembley, and most expected them to do it. They were favourites, and for an emotional six-year-old in the grips of an overpowering infatuation, tears before bedtime were a very real possibility.

What happened next represents the moment United took over my life. With just over ten minutes remaining and the score still goalless, United defender Kevin Moran slid in at the feet of Peter Reid. It was the kind of tackle that in today's game would warrant a straight red card and no questions asked. It would have ended Nani's career, put Didier Drogba in a coma and probably killed Cristiano Ronaldo outright. But these were hardier times; these were two of the hardest players around. And there had never been a sending off in an FA Cup Final.

Replays suggested that Moran had at least entertained the idea of getting the ball, but he'd also scythed Reid down and denied him the chance to win the game. After much confusion and waving of arms, referee Peter Willis sent him off. It was a shocking moment, and through my naive young eyes he could barely have been more evil had his head spun 360 degrees while he projectile-vomited ectoplasm.

Then came my affirmation. United held on with ten men to the final whistle and then for the first half of extra-time. They needed to survive just another 15 minutes and there would be a replay. It was terrifying stuff, ten times more frightening than the episodes of *Dr Who* or the bullying scenes from *Grange Hill* that saw me dive beyond the sofa or under a blanket. United needed saving; they needed a hero.

Enter Big Norm. After collecting a delightful outside-of-the-boot pass from Hughes he lurched his giant frame in from the right and made inroads towards the penalty area. 'Whiteside's onside,' said Brian Moore. We were up on our feet in the living room. The big man feigned to go to one way, made room for a shot and curled a sumptuous left-footed effort past the desperate clutches of Neville Southall and in off the post.

'A goal! That's incredible,' said Moore in that high-pitched nasal tone of his, before United's players descended on the bench to celebrate with the sunbathing Ron Atkinson. The red half of Wembley erupted in an explosion of flags and scarves, while the blue half sunk back into their seats. The contrast was stunning and the unexpected nature of United's winner made it all the more exhilarating to behold. It was positively the most overwhelming moment of my young life, and it changed everything. The second Whiteside's shot crossed the line I was an incurable Manchester United addict.

The celebrations seemed to last for ever. Robson, Hughes, Moran, Olsen, Gordon Strachan, Frank Stapleton, Mike Duxbury, to name but a few – all of them sporting sweat-drenched mullets and leaping around on the touchline like they were playing lead guitar for Van Halen (Google them, young people). Even my dad was in on the act, punching the air in celebration and jumping out of his chair to embrace the television set as if the box itself had scored United's goal.

The rest is history. United clung on for an improbable triumph and it was left to Robson to climb those famous Wembley steps and lift the FA Cup – suffice to say he probably led the revelry afterwards too. It was quite a crescendo to my maiden season as a Red, and it could only bode well for the future. If they could beat Everton with ten men, they could conquer the world. And this Atkinson guy is the best manager in football.

I re-enacted that Whiteside goal at least a hundred times that summer. And when I wasn't at school I'm not sure I wore anything but that 1985/86 United kit for months – sliding around in the garden to the imagined roars of 100,000 fans, pretending to swap passes with Robson. By the time the new season arrived there was no going back. I was a fully subscribed member of the religion they called Manchester United and the condition would impact on my happiness for the rest of my life. Team posters on the wall, fixtures list by my bed, United replica ball underneath it. Little else seemed to matter.

After a summer that seemed endless in my imagination, it was finally time to be reunited with my heroes. Atkinson's United got the season off to a stunning start – winning eleven games in a row and opening a comfortable lead at the top of the First Division. I felt like the luckiest new football fan in the country. The FA Cup triumph appeared to have galvanised his team and their flamboyant, preposterously bejewelled manager was on course to win United a first league title since 1967. History beckoned and having spent heavily on the likes of Robson and Strachan, Atkinson was starting to give United a return on their investment.

What happened next was as unexpected as Moran's red card and Stormin' Norman's Wembley wonder goal. It would usher in the central character in the next 25 years of Manchester United's storied history, and justify the existence of this very book. Little did I know it then, but my life with Sir Alex Ferguson was just around the corner.

PART ONE
(1986/87 TO 1994/95)

CHAPTER 1
NEW DAWN AT OLD TRAFFORD

Having started the 1985/86 season with eleven straight wins, Big Ron's United conspired to turn our hopes into despair. Knocked out of the FA Cup by West Ham and the League Cup by Liverpool, they were resigned to fourth place in the First Division and a depressing sense of déjà vu engulfed everybody concerned. This was not what I signed up for.

Liverpool's success heightened the pain. The goals of a young Ian Rush helped propel Kenny Dalglish's team to the Double, and their 16th league title served only to highlight United's barren run of 19 years without one. While Anfield laid claim to a dynasty, all Old Trafford could muster was a manager who looked like a fat J. R. Ewing from *Dallas*.

Liverpool fans were unbearable. In 1986 you could barely move for red shirts emblazoned with Crown Paints, they lurked around every corner and dominated every kickabout, in every playground and playing field in the country. Ray Houghton, Steve McMahon, Steve Nicol and Craig Johnston – the Australian with a comedy perm who would later give the world Predator football boots – provided the fizz in midfield that season, while fat genius Jan Molby served up all the ammunition they needed.

Every United fan had a Liverpool nemesis. Mine was a local lad named Ben Silk, and that Crown Paints shirt was practically glued to his back. He even had a Scouser perm, albeit a natural one, and he talked non-stop about winning titles, lifting trophies and dominating Europe. 'Rushy this, Rushy that; Kenny this, Kenny that'. He was a nice kid Silky, and a pretty decent goalkeeper too, but there were times when I wanted to rip that Liverpool shirt off his back and belt a half-volley into his face.

The 1985/86 Liverpool vintage were not even that special, but the fact they achieved what United had been clawing at since the days of Best, Law and Charlton said it all. Liverpool had a winning mentality, a clinical approach to the business of collecting trophies, and players who stood up to be counted from August to May, whatever the weather.

In contrast United were neither physically or mentally tough enough to sustain a challenge. Revelations to come would add fuel (and alcohol) to the fire, but even the most casual of observers could see United looked frail when the going got tough. They were a team of big names, with a larger-than-life manager, but they seemed to add up to less than the sum of their parts. And just when it seemed Atkinson had stumbled onto a way to get them winning, his team resorted to the frustrating inconsistency that had marked their underwhelming recent history.

The realities of United's predicament were starting to hit home, and there was more heartache just around the corner. Having survived a summer of speculation Atkinson somehow remained on his sparkly Old Trafford throne for the start of the 1986/87 campaign, but one of my original cast of United heroes, the indomitable Hughes, was gone. Terry Venables' Barcelona was his destination, with the fee £2 million and his wages about ten times what he was on at United. I remember worrying whether the millionaire superstar footballer Mark Hughes would be lonely in Barcelona. I pictured him arriving at Camp Nou like the new kid at school, with a boot bag over his shoulder and everybody making fun of that David Hasselhoff perm in a strange foreign language. Maybe if he hates it he'll be back I wondered. Hold that thought.

Things would get worse before they got better. United got off to a dreadful start. A 1-0 loss to Arsenal at Highbury was followed by consecutive home defeats to West Ham and Charlton. A 5-1 hammering of Southampton brought brief respite, before United lost another three league games on the spin – to Watford, Everton and Chelsea. Big Ron was on borrowed time and it was no surprise when United terminated his contract on 5 November 1986, the day after a humiliating 4-1 League Cup loss away to Southampton, and with United languishing second from bottom in the First Division.

There was little time for speculation. United's board had already decided on who they wanted to replace him and they acted quickly. At 2 p.m. that same day they placed a call to the manager's office at Aberdeen, where a fresh-faced Alex Ferguson excitedly accepted an offer to become United's new manager. He arranged to meet United chairman Martin Edwards, along with Bobby Charlton and a couple of United suits, at a motorway services in Lanarkshire at 7 p.m. that evening.

I've often thought it was a strange setting for a meeting of such magnitude, but logistically it must have made sense. Perhaps they ate at Wimpy that night, the leaders of the world's greatest football club. A few boiled sweets, chewable toothbrushes and a cup of weak tea later, they were off to their homes and the next manager of Manchester United was all but in his office. Little did the truck drivers and weekend warriors realise what they'd just witnessed.

Ferguson's contract was signed the following day, and a chain of events put into motion something that even the most wildly optimistic United fans could never have predicted. The greatest football club in the world had just appointed the man who would usher in the most prolific period of success in its glittering history. Ferguson would go from a seedy motorway services to Buckingham Palace and beyond in the next 25 years – winning enough silverware to fill the house he grew up in, and become one of the greatest managers of them all.

I'll admit it now. I was eight years old and had absolutely no idea who he was. Apparently Ferguson's track record north of the border was superb. That's what they kept saying anyway. Having led St Mirren from the Scottish Second Division to the First Division title in 1977, he joined Aberdeen in 1978 and achieved unprecedented success going head-to-head with the Old Firm. Ferguson took Aberdeen to three Scottish League titles, four Scottish Cups, a League Cup and the UEFA Cup-Winners' Cup in his eight years at the club. And did it all purveying an attacking, open style of play that was tailor made for Manchester United.

He also had a reputation as a hard taskmaster with a volcanic temper, who demanded the utmost standards of professionalism from everybody around him. With United's board well aware they had life-style problems to address within the club, Ferguson looked like just the personality to revive an underachieving operation. He was a headmaster type, ready to ride roughshod over the frailties at Old Trafford and give anybody who got in his way a good old-fashioned bollocking. You couldn't help thinking it was exactly what was needed.

But appointing Ferguson clearly carried a risk. There was a darker side to him that occasionally saw him lost in rage, and he was clearly not a man to back down in a conflict. 'Ferguson is a volatile, aggressive man. His relations with the press have been notoriously tense,' wrote Harry Reid in the *Glasgow Herald* on Ferguson's appointment. 'He loses badly… He is obsessive and temperamental; he has a tendency, normally well disguised, to paranoia. Yet he has a sweet affable side. He is fluent and persuasive; he can articulate the tension and traumas of football as few others can.'

Through the eyes of a young fan it looked as though United had sought out the anti-Atkinson. The pair could barely have been more different in appearance or public persona. In place of an exuberant showman with a mahogany tan and a penchant for garish suits, came a no-nonsense Glaswegian in grey. One seemed to represent the bloated excesses of the past, the other the stark realities of the present.

Atkinson's tenure at Old Trafford would be judged on his failure to build a team resolute enough to challenge for the title. He'd spent heavily, but left United no closer to Liverpool than they were when he arrived – and that was the only measuring stick that mattered. Two FA Cup wins were all well and good, but what United fans wanted above all else was a league title and a return to the heady European stage that saw Sir Matt Busby's team of the late 1960s immortalised. And they simply weren't going to get it under Atkinson.

United's drinking culture was arguably in part to blame. Edwards admitted as much to Ferguson in an early exchange, and when reports surfaced that several of the team were out toasting the departure of Big Ron on the Thursday night Ferguson signed his United contract, two days before his first game in charge, their new manager couldn't believe his ears.

Whiteside was the instigator and an account in his autobiography, the booze-sodden *Determined*, puts Robson, Strachan and Bailey at the scene of the crime in Rochdale – which we can only assume was at that time a metropolis of swaggering cool. All four were injured and out for the Saturday trip to Oxford anyway, so concluded the best option was to 'get stuck into the drink' and commiserate with their outgoing boss. It wasn't the best introduction to a new manager, and Ferguson reacted with a thinly veiled call for professionalism in his first address to the players the next day.

He also imposed a rule that forbade drinking within two days of a game or the night before training. That's how things had run at Aberdeen, and that's how they'd run at United. In time Ferguson rounded up the ringleaders – Robson, Whiteside and McGrath – and asked them to set an example. He knew he couldn't change United's social club mentality overnight, but with a new regime in place he hoped to instil a new ethos at Old Trafford. Ten pints in an afternoon might have been great for morale and the local economy, but it wasn't going to help United bring back the glory days.

Robson was the exception. He might have embarked on epic benders with the rest of them, but Ferguson never really worried about his drinking. The England captain was a 'miracle of commitment' and a 'human marvel' he said. Robson, like George Best in his heyday, was blessed with a metabolism that beggared belief in its capacity to withstand punishment. He was practically a walking tablet of Berocca and it only added to his legend.

Whiteside and McGrath were not so fortunate, and the latter ultimately fought a battle against alcoholism. But it's only fair to point out that United's drinking habits were not out of the ordinary for the time. The game was a far more relaxed place in the mid-1980s, and the media far less interested in what players did outside of their shifts on the pitch. Players also had a lot more time on their hands, with only a fraction of the media and commercial responsibilities that they have today. For United's boozy fraternity, what better way to while away the hours than on an all-day bender in the bars of Manchester?

Ferguson's first game in charge was a sobering 2-0 defeat to Oxford United. John Aldridge, who would later antagonise United in the colours of Liverpool, got the first goal of the Ferguson era from the penalty spot – albeit for the opposition. In many ways it was an apt setting for Ferguson to begin his reign. Manchester United, like the dilapidated Manor Ground, were a fading force in need of some desperate care and attention. A once-great football club had been ravaged by years of overachievement off the pitch and underachievement on it, and emerged on the other side a pale imitation of itself.

If you think I'm overstating the point, United's starting line-up that day says it all: Chris Turner, Mike Duxbury, Arthur Albiston, Paul McGrath, Kevin Moran, Graeme Hogg, Clayton Blackmore, Frank Stapleton, Remi Moses, Peter Davenport and Peter Barnes. Even allowing for injuries to Robson, Strachan and Whiteside, it was a United team that should have been playing for Bolton. And if Ferguson didn't appreciate the scale of his task before, he most certainly did now. United needed not only a new ethos of professionalism; they needed the genesis of an entirely new squad.

That summer Ferguson began making the team his own. He brought in Celtic striker Brian McClair for £850,000 and defender Viv Anderson for £250,000 from Arsenal. Stapleton, Siveback and Gibson were sold and goalkeeper Bailey released after a frustrating season spent managing a knee injury he picked up at the 1986 World Cup.

'Choccy' McClair hit the ground running. He scored 31 goals in all competitions in his first season at United and played a big part in helping Ferguson's men to a runners-up finish behind Liverpool in the championship. The winter signing of Norwich City defender Steve Bruce also proved a masterstroke. Bruce cost £825,000 and gave United a sense of assuredness at the back that they'd desperately lacked under Atkinson. There would be plenty of comings and goings in Ferguson's 25 years, but few departures would leave him as saddened as the day Bruce finally decide to walk out of Old Trafford at the age of 35. As a footballer, and as a person, he proved himself worthy of that transfer fee ten times over.

It was on Bruce's return to his former club that I got the first glimpse of my heroes in the flesh. Dad had planned the surprise meticulously. He even went so far as to cut the First Division fixtures out of the newspaper so I wouldn't notice United were in Norfolk the same weekend we were. That's Norwich City v United on same weekend we were visiting my Norwich City supporting grandparents and my grandmother's brother – the Norwich City season ticket-holder. I was nine years old and I clearly wasn't all that bright.

The game was highly forgettable, and desperately disappointing. United lost 1-0 and I walked away amid the celebrating Canaries with tears in my eyes. All that time waiting and Ferguson's team couldn't even put a show on for my surprise. Robson was low key, and Olsen didn't display style or substance that afternoon. But seeing the United players with my own eyes was worth the disappointment. And being part of a crowd of 19,000, albeit custard-loving pacifists, was as electrifying as anything I'd ever experienced.

That was March 1988, and United would not lose again that season. Ferguson delivered United's best league finish since 1980, and he added to his growing popularity by sealing a £2 million deal to bring cult hero Hughes back from Barcelona to Old Trafford in June. The thought of Hughes working in tandem with McClair was an exciting one for United fans, who in truth had never really taken to Atkinson's big-name signing Peter Davenport. Hughes and McClair, so went the thinking, could take United to the next level and finally bring the holy grail of a league title back to Old Trafford. 'I am delighted. It's been a long, drawn-out affair but worthwhile,' said Ferguson as United announced the club record deal to re-sign Hughes. They'd beaten off the challenge of Juventus, Bologna and Bayern Munich to make it happen, and ultimately got their man for what turned out to be exceptionally good value. Hughes' knack for scoring important goals, not to mention his support play and fierce desire, would play a key role in the evolution of Ferguson's team from also-rans to all-conquering force. Sparky would leave Old Trafford for the final time in 1995 with two league titles and his cult status secured forever. A lightning-fast teenage winger named Lee Sharpe was also among the arrivals that summer, along with Ferguson's former Aberdeen goalkeeper Jim Leighton – who replaced the departing Chris Turner as United's No. 1.

United had unquestionably done some good business in the transfer market, but the player Ferguson wanted most of all slipped through his fingers. That man was Newcastle United's Paul Gascoigne, a precocious young midfielder who could do it all. Gascoigne had two good feet, incredible close control and a reading of the game that belonged to a world-class player in the twilight of his career. He could score goals from anywhere, head the ball and dribble past opponents like they weren't there. He was a star in the mould of Best, and Ferguson knew immediately he was right for Old Trafford.

Gascoigne's genius set the First Division alight in the 1987/88 season, and Ferguson was blown away when he gave a virtuoso performance at St James' Park. In an interview with David Frost some years later, Ferguson talked of his astonishment at watching the swaggering Geordie dominate Robson, Whiteside and Remi Moses. 'He absolutely tore them apart,' he said. 'He nutmegged Remi Moses right in front of me in the dugout. And he went up to Remi and patted him on the head. After the game I went up to the chairman and I said, "Don't leave yet. Go and speak to their chairman about that boy, he's the best I've seen in years and years."'

When Gascoigne made a verbal agreement to join at the end of the season, Ferguson thought he'd got his man. But his summer holiday was interrupted by the shock news that Gascoigne had decided to join Tottenham instead. Spurs' offer to buy Gascoigne's parents a house had apparently swung the deal and Ferguson was left desperately frustrated at an opportunity missed. It was the first of many high-profile near misses in the transfer market for Ferguson at United, but you could argue the unravelling of Gascoigne's personal life in years to come softened the blow.

Whether moving to United could have helped Gazza avoid the pitfalls he later faced is up for discussion, but there's no question he would have been a beloved talent at Old Trafford. His instinctive brilliance would have seen him labelled the 'new Best', and a midfield of Robson and Gascoigne would have taken some beating – on and off the pitch.

Ferguson was left wondering in the worst possible way, as he led United through a hugely disappointing 1988/89 campaign. Dad took me to several games that season and the one that sticks out was against Wimbledon at Plough Lane, where we watched United escape with a 1-1 draw and their lives in a game of ludicrously contrasting styles. The Crazy Gang were ferocious beasts at that time, and in their claustrophobic home stadium were a force to be reckoned with. The physicality of their approach made it abundantly clear United needed to bulk up and add some bite if they were going to achieve consistency in the league.

I remember feeling genuinely worried for the safety of my heroes that day, as the likes of Vinnie Jones and John Fashanu carved into challenges and left their sharpened elbows hanging out to dry. United looked like a team of public schoolboys in comparison, sent out to take on the ruffians in the local park. They were happy to escape with a point and all their limbs intact.

United ended the season losing six of their last eight games and, having promised so much, Ferguson's men finished 11th in the First Division and once again without a trophy. But at least Liverpool didn't win the title. In the most exciting climax to a top-flight season you could possibly imagine, Arsenal went to Anfield and snatched a dramatic late goal to win 2-0 and win the championship on goal difference.

I slid on my knees when Michael Thomas grabbed the winner, embracing the burgeoning anti-Liverpool inside me and dancing around the living room to revel in their devastating disappointment. It wasn't a reaction rooted in deep-seated rivalry between two industrial cities, or the shipping canal that came between them. I was just a jealous football fan, sick and tired of Liverpool having the monopoly on glory.

CHAPTER 2
MARK ROBINS AND OTHER UNLIKELY HEROES

In the summer of 1989 I left the sanctuary of my village primary school for the big bad comprehensive five miles down the road. I arrived into a world of grizzled Norman Whitesides and my first term was not made any easier by United's woeful start to the 1989/90 season. A 5-1 mauling in the Manchester derby was the low point, in a game that would go down in City folklore as the 'Massacre of Maine Road'.

Ferguson had spent heavily for the new campaign, bringing in Neil Webb, Mike Phelan, Gary Pallister, Paul Ince and Danny Wallace for a combined £8.25 million. Strachan had already left for Leeds, with socialites Whiteside and McGrath following him out of Old Trafford before the new season. This was now very much Ferguson's team, but the results were some way from justifying his spending, or his reputation. Three years into his reign, United still hadn't won a trophy under their new manager. Understandably, calls for his head were growing louder by the day.

Webb seemed a curious signing. Even before he suffered a bad Achilles tendon injury, the midfielder looked barely capable of accelerating above walking pace, let alone marauding forward in attack. He was a languid, luxury player, who lacked the dynamism and fire Ferguson was going to need to end United's wait for a title, and he would be back at Nottingham Forest three years' later, having spectacularly failed to justify his £1.5 million price tag. Phelan was also an underwhelming acquisition, although you got the feeling he did the kind of work only those in the dugout can really appreciate.

By the time Christmas arrived the title was a lost cause. And with United already out of the League Cup there was only one piece of silverware left to fight for. Ferguson's job was on the line, and it was beginning to look as though the only way he could cling onto it was by winning the FA Cup. Chairman Edwards will forever deny it, but Ferguson took his team into a third-round tie against Nottingham Forest on 7 January 1990 a defeat away from picking up his P45.

United wore white that day, and having been given that strip for Christmas I felt especially ready to go to war with them. Before kick-off I went out into the garden and slid around in the mud as usual, tackling imaginary opponents and beating imaginary defenders with imaginary ease. Cue the heavy-breathed cheers that made me sound like an 80-a-day smoker in the grips of an asthma attack, no doubt prompting the neighbours to wonder why the strange boy next door didn't have any friends.

United were up against a Nottingham Forest side managed by the inimitable Brian Clough, who a few weeks earlier had spiced things up by saying Ferguson was out of his depth at Old Trafford. He might have been a football legend and a national treasure, but it was time for Old Big 'Ead to get knocked down a peg or two. It was time for a changing of the guard.

It was a scrappy game on a sticky pitch, and Forest deserved at least a draw. But a youth team graduate named Mark Robins took his opportunity to enter United legend as 'the man who saved Ferguson's career', scoring the only goal in a 1-0 win. Hughes was the provider, bending one of those trademark outside-of-the-boot passes behind the last man and inviting Robins to stoop and head home from near the penalty spot. United were far from convincing, and survived a controversially disallowed goal in the dying minutes, but Ferguson lived to fight another day. And for that we can all be eternally grateful.

'We've been playing well for the last few weeks, the only difference was today we got a wee break,' Ferguson said after the game.

'Our attitude was very, very good… I don't want to say whether this has been the break we've been looking for. We are an inspirational club and on Saturday we are going to have a huge crowd because of this. We are just going to go out and get on with the business.'

It was with great relief and excitement that I sprinted out into the murk of Sunday evening after that result, size four Mitre under my arm and the comic strip heroics of Robins my inspiration. I even managed to persuade Dad to join me, and had him crossing balls for a good half an hour in the cold while I threw myself on the ground recreating that diving header. Monday morning bragging rights would be all mine, and if we could beat cup specialists Forest, there was no reason we couldn't go all the way to Wembley and win it.

Ferguson's Robins reliance continued. The spritely ginger one scored at Newcastle, then snatched a dramatic extra-time winner in the semi-final replay against Oldham. It was as if United had genetically engineered an unlikely hero. Perhaps those experiments were the precursor to the ones that spawned the generation of teenage sensations to follow. Lo and behold, we were back at Wembley – for the first time since I'd taken United to my heart in the summer of 1985. And, for now at least, the pressures on Ferguson were off.

FA Cup Final day, Saturday on 12 May 1990, was hot and overcast, and the Wembley pitch was said by Bryan Robson to be in the best condition he'd ever seen. Friends and family gathered at our house and sat back expecting to watch United outclass the kick-and-rush of Crystal Palace comfortably. Steve Coppell's team had stunned Liverpool 4 3 in an incredible semi-final, but they wouldn't do it again… surely. Not at Wembley, not as underdogs against a United team practically frothing at the mouth to get the monkey off its back and win the club a trophy.

United were once again in white. Phelan and Wallace were sporting ridiculous moustaches and Ferguson looked seriously nervous in the dugout. Palace went ahead early, scoring all too predictably from a set piece. Robson equalised, before Hughes put United ahead in the second half in clinical fashion after the ball ricocheted to him just outside the six-yard box. Having come from behind United looked odds-on to add to their lead and the FA Cup was surely in the bag.

Enter the lightning fast, impossibly cocksure Ian Wright. The striker Palace had discovered playing non-league football, already in his 20s, was brought on as a second-half substitute and changed the game. Wright scored with almost his first touch to make it 2-2, then put Palace ahead in extra-time with a devastating far-post volley. Ferguson's hopes of securing his first trophy at United now rested on his team finding an equaliser. Another sliding doors moment in his career, and United's destiny, had arrived.

Cometh the hour, cometh the man as Hughes latched onto Wallace's through ball to score his second of the game and save his team from defeat. He sprinted off to the United fans to perform his trademark squat celebration, first clenching his fist and then pointing towards them with outstretched right arm. The FA Cup Final would go to a replay.

In the four days between the games, Ferguson made one of the most difficult decisions of his career. Fearing for the confidence of his goalkeeper Jim Leighton, who'd looked a touch suspect under the high ball, he turned to on-loan Les Sealey for the replay and dropped the man who'd been his No. 1 all season. It was as bold a statement of ruthless ambition as you can imagine from a manager, and proved as unpopular with fans as it was inside the United camp.

I was 12 years old and my moral compass almost cracked when I heard the news. Leighton wasn't cool and he wasn't a world-class goalkeeper, but he was still one of my United heroes. Ferguson's desperate drive for success had prompted a betrayal of somebody who'd stood loyally by his side – not just at United, but in a long and successful period at Aberdeen too. Leighton was as good as one of his children, yet he had cast him aside like a journeyman squad player. It was a decision that revealed a mean streak to the United manager we didn't yet know existed. We knew he was fiery and hot-tempered, but we didn't know quite how cold-hearted he could be in the heat of the battle.

It was a move that jarred with United players and fans alike, but history attests it was the right one. 'For what he knew was going to be a massive occasion, to change a player he had previously shown a massive allegiance to, showed that cold, cutting edge that all top managers need,'

Palace manager Steve Coppell would later reflect. Sealey was assured at Wembley and United won the replay 1-0. Lee Martin's rare goal, a barnstorming run and thundering shot into the roof of the net (set up by a pass from Webb no less), meant Ferguson finally got his hands on some silverware. The United manager jigged around Wembley like he didn't have a care in the world, and for the first time in his United reign he finally had some breathing space. Hughes' heroics were to be expected, but who'd have thought Robins and Martin would play such a pivotal role in keeping their manager in a job?

For the fans it was a triumph, but also an enormous relief. The players celebrated wildly, and we celebrated with them, but this success was as vital as it was enjoyable. Defeat to Palace was unthinkable and there was a sense that the blow to morale would have kept United in the doldrums for another five years. As with any recovery, the first steps are the most precarious and the most difficult to make. Perhaps that's why Ferguson did what he did to Leighton.

I often wonder if he felt any guilt as his team paraded the trophy that evening. He'd built a career on forming loyal bonds with his players, but he'd broken one that May. Leighton only played one more game for United, and he never spoke to Ferguson again.

CHAPTER 3
ONE STEP FORWARD;
TWO STEPS BACK

Italia 90 brought a new inclusivity to football. My mum and sister were among the millions converted by a World Cup that returned the sport to the very forefront of public imagination, and went some way to undoing the dark and troubled days of the 1980s. Pavarotti's 'Nessun Dorma' was the soundtrack, and delivered the message sublimely. Almost overnight, football's cultural significance entered unchartered territory. Highbrow intelligent types were writing about it, talking about it and taking notice like never before. Suddenly, it was OK for posh blokes to like football again. In fact, it was pretty much essential.

England's campaign was once again fired by the goals of Gary Lineker, who won the Golden Boot as the tournament's top scorer. Bobby Robson's side reached the semi-finals, but lost on penalties to West Germany in a game made famous by the yellow card that meant Paul Gascoigne would have missed the final. The Germans, driven by the barnstorming Lothar Matthäus in midfield and the goals of Andreas Möller and Jürgen Klinsmann, deservedly went on to win it. England cried along with Gazza. And after all that heartache set to opera, it was somewhat of a relief to return to the business of United.

For the 1990/91 campaign Ferguson's squad was bolstered by the arrival of Denis Irwin, an intelligent two-footed full back who had impressed him at Oldham and played his part in the epic FA Cup semi-final battle between the two sides the previous April. Irwin would go on to win seven league titles, three FA Cups and a European Cup in 12 years of glittering success at Old Trafford. He was a low-key acquisition, and an understated personality, but the diminutive Irishman would prove to be a brilliant signing by Ferguson.

Irwin cost just £625,000, but left Old Trafford having made over 500 appearances and earned a reputation as one of the most reliable and complete full backs in English football. Ferguson hailed him as Mr Consistency, and considers him one of the best value-for-money buys of his career in management. 'Sometimes players get overlooked. It has happened to quite a few in my time, especially the quieter ones,' Ferguson said of Irwin's role in bringing the good times back to United. 'Denis Irwin gave me eight or nine out of ten every week but he never had the celebrity status of people like David Beckham or Eric Cantona.'

It would also be the season in which a teenager named Ryan Giggs would take his first elegant strides on the way to becoming a United legend. Giggs was the latest name to be weighed down by the tag of the 'next George Best', and Ferguson saw something truly special in him. The United manager had seen him glide past his most experienced players on the training ground enough times to realise he had a genuine talent on his hands. What he also had was a young player with a remarkably calm and mature approach to the business of realising his dream. He was brilliant, hard working and grounded – a once-in-a-generation talent. 'He floated across the ground like a wee cocker spaniel chasing a bit of silver paper in the wind,' Ferguson would later reflect.

When Giggs made his debut against City, and scored, I took great delight in telling everybody I'd already seen him in action. As Ryan Wilson he'd turned out for England Schoolboys in 1989, and my local junior side had run a trip to Wembley to watch the game. Naturally I boasted I'd seen enough that day to know he was the next big thing, but in truth I barely remember noticing him. The young Wilson could well have been appalling, but I suspect he was probably brilliant.

The 1990/91 season proved another disappointment domestically for United. But there were still moments to cherish. Like Choccy McClair kicking chunks out of Arsenal's Nigel Winterburn at Old

Trafford in an incident that erupted into a full-scale brawl that later saw both sides deducted points. Or Lee Sharpe's brilliant League Cup hat-trick at Highbury, celebrated with exuberant knee slides and somersaults.

Sharpe was now a United regular, and a genuine teen idol. The ebullient winger with a Hollywood smile was box office, and as the game entered a new era of pop star footballers Sharpe's celebrity grew with every game – and every night out. Playing for my local junior side it was now Sharpe I channelled, not Robson. I wanted to go past defenders, turn on the tricks and celebrate goals with hip-swinging tributes to Elvis. I bought United's blue shirt after his hat-trick at Highbury. I even began favouring my left foot and asked to play on the opposite wing.

But Sharpe's enthusiasm was not enough to get United firing. A 4-0 battering at Anfield coupled with a League Cup final defeat to Sheffield Wednesday prompted yet more questions about Ferguson's aptitude for the task in hand.

Thankfully his team were on course for a glorious return to Europe. With the ban on English clubs lifted, United were back on the continental stage in the Cup-Winners' Cup. After they dispatched Pesci Munkas, Wrexham, Montpellier and Legia Warsaw (you might say a path of little resistance), Ferguson's team were bound for a final showdown with the mighty Barcelona.

The final was on a Wednesday night and there was even less chance than usual of any homework getting done in the Tidey house. United were wearing white, and up against a Barca team boasting the likes of Ronald Koeman and Michael Laudrup. Johan Cruyff's men were Spanish champions and very much the favourites. But we had Hughes, and he had a score to settle. After a year being teased for that Bucks Fizz perm at the Camp Nou, Sparky exacted his revenge with both goals in a 2-1 win.

The first wholly contradicted his reputation as scorer of spectacular goals. After Bruce met Robson's flighted free-kick, Hughes snuck in for a one-yarder that had goal-snatcher written all over it. Normal service resumed for his second. Captain Marvel was once again the provider, releasing Hughes on the break with a dinked pass over the top. Hughes slalomed the goalkeeper, but his touch was heavy and left himself an extremely tight angle for the finish. He shot instinctively, with power and precision, and the ball fizzed beyond the despairing lunges of the Barca defenders.

Koeman got one back, embarrassing Sealey at his near post from fully 30 yards, but United held on. Ferguson had brought them a first European triumph in 23 years and he was giddy with excitement. Watching on, I remember scenes of him conducting the United fans in their celebrations, looking for all the world like a drunk uncle on New Year's Eve. He was dazed, delirious even. And the relief of a season salvaged was writ large across his face. 'It's the biggest moment in my career, a fairytale moment,' said an ecstatic Ferguson afterwards. 'It's a wonderful day for the club, having waited 23 years since our last European trophy.'

It was a night that brought home everything we'd been missing during the ban on English clubs in Europe. As cameras swept around the Feyenoord Stadium flares burned bright and fans of two of the world's great football clubs took their passion and mutual respect to a global stage. This was where United belonged. For too long they'd been purveyors of a mediocrity that betrayed the club's romantic past, and it was time for Ferguson's red and white army to re-conquer the continent. After watching them beat Barcelona that night it felt like it was a matter of when, not if.

A league title would surely come sooner rather than later, and the following season they were very much on course when I made my first pilgrimage to Old Trafford – in the company of Dad and his cousin PJ, an ardent Red who was so entrenched in the scene he knew just about everybody in and around the stadium. PJ lived and breathed United. He would later name his two sons Ryan (after Giggs) and Joe Ole (after Solskjaer), and probably would have named a daughter Eric. Family life would ultimately put paid to those long Saturdays driving to and from Old Trafford, but during the 1990s he moved hell and earth to be there. He was just the man I needed to further my United obsession. And fortunately enough he was willing to take me under his wing.

Dad picked quite a fixture for my Old Trafford baptism. It was a horribly wet and cold Tuesday night in Manchester. But it was derby night and you could sense the atmosphere a mile away from the stadium. Our first stop was the Manchester Sheraton, where we met a friend of PJ's who had managed to secure us tickets. He was studying at Manchester University and clearly moving in the right circles. It was buzzing. Almost everybody in the hotel foyer was either going to the game or trying to get tickets. Everybody was talking about the game, and most of them were talking about Giggs.

The rain eased slightly as we made our way to the stadium and PJ insisted we eat at Lou Macari's fish and chip shop on Chester Road. He ordered me cod, chips and mushy peas and we weaved through the crowds with the smell of tobacco, beer and mystery meat thick in the damp, cold air.

The United fans were in buoyant mood. We were top of the league and in Giggs had unearthed a precocious talent who was the envy of every team in the country. Ferguson had also improved his squad defensively by adding Peter Schmeichel and Paul Parker. Both had quickly made themselves indispensable. United were beginning to look like the genuine article. Meanwhile City were undergoing something of a revival. Under Peter Reid they had finally found some momentum, with the goals of David White propelling them into the top half of the table en route to a fifth-placed finish.

I was desperate to get inside the stadium. There was still an hour to go before kick-off, but I'd waited a long time to see it and didn't want to wait any longer. So Dad and I went ahead, squeezed through the turnstiles, and climbed several flights of stairs to find the level that matched our ticket. We were inside the womb of Old Trafford now. 'If you lose me we're in the South Stand, about halfway up, next to the United fan in the red shirt,' Dad said. 'Here's your ticket, whatever you do, don't lose it.'

The moment you walk out into the stadium proper never gets old for me. It's the best 'reveal' in the business. From the dark underbelly of concrete nothingness we emerged to a shimmering green carpet under brilliant white floodlights. The possibilities were endless. It was about the most exhilarating sight I had witnessed. I took my seat in stunned silence. 'Not bad seats, are they,' Dad said, ever the master of understatement. 'I'm not sure there are any bad seats in here,' I thought.

When the teams were announced my excitement grew further. Giggs and Sharpe would start on the flanks. United's electric boy wonders deployed in tandem on a slick surface would be quite a sight. Robson was injured (again), but otherwise United were close to full strength and there was every reason for optimism. In the warm-up Giggs and Sharpe whet the appetite with some sumptuous skills and effortless cross-field volleys to one another. 'United! United! United!' came the rousing chant from the Stretford End. PJ and the ticket master took their seats, and we were ready for the main event.

United started well and went ahead midway through the first half in some style. Sharpe clattered into United hate figure Steve McMahon (Liverpool and City in one career suggests he felt the same way) and won the ball deep in the United half. He found McClair, who made yards down the touchline before setting the ball back to Hughes. Hughes in turn spread the play to Giggs who, cutting in from the right, drove a low shot into the bottom corner from 25 yards. What. A. Goal!

Any United goal would have done. But to witness a goal like that, from the most talked about player in the game, was quite an introduction to the Theatre of Dreams. I leapt out of my seat and punched the air as the swaying bodies rubbed and jarred against each other in celebration. 'F**k off you City scummers,' barked the man next to me. 'Giggsy f**king mugged you off like children.' That he had, but the 'City scummers' fought back, and equalised from the penalty spot after Bruce chopped down White when he should have stayed on his feet.

White later missed a glorious chance to win it, so it could have been worse, but a 1-1 draw was not what United need to press home their title advantage. They were still runaway favourites to win the league, however, and on the evidence of that first-half display I felt certain they had enough in the tank to bring it home. Bitter rivals Leeds United were in pursuit, but with six games remaining it would take something of a catastrophic collapse to deny United their first championship success since 1967.

It was at this time United suffered, you guessed it, a catastrophic collapse. They drew with Luton and lost to Nottingham Forest, West Ham and, of all teams, Liverpool. The only conclusion you could possibly draw was that they'd choked and Leeds were handed the title. As Jim White wrote in his excellent book, *Manchester United: The Biography*, 'During the final six games of the 1991/92 season United went from racing certainties to deadbeats.'

It was a sickening end to season that promised everything. And all too predictably questions were raised over Ferguson's leadership in the run-in. Did he get his selections wrong? Did he lose the dressing room? Was he really the right man to bring the league title back to Old Trafford?

Twelve months later we would have the answer. And ironically Leeds would help provide it.

CHAPTER 4
THE KING IS BORN

September 1992: Nirvana's *Nevermind* was crackling from every Walkman on the school bus and grunge was taking over, Doc Martens, dirty hair and fuzzy guitars were de rigueur and the world was suddenly starting to open up before my 14-year-old eyes. They said Ferguson was under pressure at Old Trafford. But there is no pressure like being a teenager.

Dad and PJ were both with me at the Goldstone Ground when United took on Brighton & Hove Albion in the second round of the League Cup. It was a nothing game really. Danny Wallace scored a decent goal and United left with a 1-1 draw to take to the second leg. We were sat among the Brighton fans, which made for a subdued night for everybody concerned. But in years to come I realised we'd witnessed a major milestone. Aged 17, a midfielder named David Beckham had made his United debut as a substitute that night. He wouldn't play for the first team again that season, but as the world knows only too well, he'd make a significant contribution to the cause in years to come.

United had made only one major signing that summer, bringing in striker Dion Dublin from Cambridge United for £1.1 million. After his fleeting heroics in 1990, Mark Robins had faded into the background and was sold to Norwich City. On paper Dublin was a strong replacement. He offered Ferguson new tactical possibilities and the promise of goals. He also seemed like the kind of character who'd light up the dressing room and lift the entire mood after the disappointment of the season before. The deal went some way to appeasing Ferguson's bitter frustration at missing out on Alan Shearer. The Southampton and England striker looked for a while to be Old Trafford bound, before the intervention of Blackburn Rovers owner Jack Walker convinced him to move to Ewood Park for a British transfer record of £3.6 million instead. Dublin was wanted by Chelsea and Everton, but this time Ferguson got his man. 'The boy has made a decision which pleases me immensely,' Ferguson said. 'He is a good finisher. If we had scored a few more last season we might have won the league.' On two legs the big man could have helped United to the title, but he broke one of them horribly in September and didn't play again that season. It was a cruel twist of fate, but it ultimately ushered in the man many regard as the greatest United player of them all, Eric Cantona.

It's a story every United fan knows. In November 1992 Ferguson was shopping for strikers when Leeds called to enquire about Denis Irwin. Martin Edwards said no immediately, but Ferguson was in the room at the time and he handed the United chairman a piece of paper asking him to enquire about Cantona. Incredibly Leeds wanted to sell, and the fact United bartered them down to £1.2 million makes it arguably the greatest transaction in the club's history – perhaps the greatest in the Premier League era of English football.

Just like that, Eric was a Red. But it didn't make any sense whatsoever. Leeds were champions, and Cantona was among their most influential players, so why on earth did they let him leave for their fiercest rivals for less than United paid for Neil Webb and Danny Wallace? In today's game it would be the equivalent of Wayne Rooney signing for Arsenal, for £5 million. Unthinkable.

The rumour circulated that Cantona was having an affair with Lee Chapman's wife – cue the timeless chant 'He's French/He's flash/ He's shagging Leslie Ash/Cantona'. But the real reason for his exit, according to Leeds manager Howard Wilkinson anyway, was simply that Cantona was too focused on Cantona and not on the good of the team. The fact was that he'd been dropped and had told Wilkinson that he didn't understand how he could possibly consider Chapman a better option. He probably had a point, but Wilkinson was looking for unity and that show of dissent put him off the Frenchman for good.

Ferguson didn't care; he knew a Manchester United player when he saw one. According to Philippe Auclair's book *Cantona: The Rebel Who Would be King*, Ferguson's excitement was only heightened when he took Cantona for the customary stroll onto the Old Trafford turf. 'I wonder if you're good enough to play on this ground,' Ferguson asked. 'I wonder if Manchester United is good enough for me,' Cantona replied. Priceless.

On 6 December Cantona made his United debut as a substitute in the derby at Old Trafford. Chest puffed, collar up, he exuded a swagger and supreme confidence United fans had not seen since Best, maybe not ever. Here was a footballer with an almost unearthly belief in his powers – for whom the concept of nerves was as alien as that of doing anything other than putting on the Lord Mayor's show every time he crossed the white line. That said – his debut was fairly innocuous.

Two weeks later, PJ called. He had tickets for Chelsea away and wondered if we'd like to view this mythical beast Cantona in the flesh. 'You've just got to see him out there,' he said. 'It's like time stops when he gets the ball and speeds up when he does something with it. He makes football look easy. The United fans love him already. He's a god.'

With that build-up we could hardly refuse. And so, on a bitterly cold Saturday in late December, we drove through heavy Christmas traffic to within a mile of Stamford Bridge. United shirts well hidden, the three of us made our way gingerly to the stadium, choosing our route carefully to avoid the attentions of Chelsea's, how shall I say this, 'spikier element'.

The atmosphere was tense and threatening to erupt. After finding shelter amid a group of United fans we were herded aggressively by police on horseback. Bodies began to press tightly against bodies. It was a frightening experience and there was a real possibility the more antagonistic United fans would make a charge on the authorities.

It soon became clear what the police were up to. A few hundred yards away the Chelsea swarms began emerging into the open and making their way to the stadium. You could feel the potential for violence in the air, and for all I know it may well have been realised after the game. But thankfully the three of us avoided a kicking. As we were funnelled into the away end I was more than slightly amused to be the subject of a police search – the fight-shy 14-year-old picked out for special attention as the gnarled masses strolled through unnoticed. 'They must think you're going to kick off in there,' PJ said, trying to keep a straight face. 'I hope you left your blade in the car.'

It was packed on the terraces. The swaying crowds in Father Christmas hats fighting for vantage points as their United heroes took to the field for the warm-up. United's starting line-up that day was as follows: Schmeichel, Parker, Irwin, Bruce, Pallister, Phelan, McClair, Ince, Sharpe, Hughes and Cantona. They'd won four on the spin, but Chelsea were also in the grips of a strong run.

All eyes were on Cantona and he didn't disappoint. Dropping into midfield he moved attacks forward at will and brought a new incisiveness to United with his reading of the game. He was upright and strong, and a good deal quicker than we'd been led to believe. To the fans' delight, in the hateful atmosphere of Stamford Bridge, he positively thrived. After United fell behind their new talisman opened his account with a swivelled finish from a tight angle, pointing to the sky in celebration as his new disciples sang his name. 'Ooh Ah Cantona,' was a chant borrowed from the Leeds fans, but like Cantona himself, it was just too good to pass up. Leeds were in giving mood that Christmas, little did they know they'd practically handed the title to their most hated rivals.

The game finished 1-1 and we drove home talking of Cantona. PJ was among the growing number of fans who'd already flicked their collars up to mimic the Frenchman's style (a fashion that lives on AC – 'After Cantona') and we were all agreed that United had found a cult hero for the ages. Goals in his next three league games multiplied the Cantona love-in, and by the time United visited Queens Park Rangers on a Monday night in January he was firmly on his throne as the King of Old Trafford.

Monday night football was a new commodity that jarred with old-school sensibilities. Rupert Murdoch's Sky Television had paid

£191 million for the rights to live football, the First Division was now the Premiership and football was on its way to filling the whole week. It was a brave new era for the game in England, and its practices felt rooted very much in the American school of sport as entertainment.

Dad and I were in the very front row at Loftus Road and suffice to say we both sat open-mouthed when the dancing girls took up their positions before kick-off – just a few feet from our seats. Simple Minds' 'Alive and Kicking' was Sky's new soundtrack to football, and as fireworks exploded from the middle of the pitch, shimmering cheerleaders performed their eye-popping moves for the television cameras. 'It's all a bit much, isn't it,' Dad said, the glimmer in his eye betraying his every word. 'Isn't the fact United are the best team in the country enough to get people excited these days? Who needs dancing girls when you've got Bruce and Pallister?'

As it turned out, United put on an all-singing, all-dancing display of their own. With Cantona missing, Ferguson turned to Giggs up front and on his prompting United cut through QPR with an exuberance that matched anything the cheerleaders could muster. Giggs latched onto a ball over the top to get the first, with Ince delivering an acrobatic overhead kick for the second, and Kanchelskis notching the third in a confident 3-1 win.

United played with searing pace that night, on a slick surface that was made for their bold counter-attacking and players with speed to burn like Kanchelskis, Giggs and Sharpe. They were positively fizzing with enthusiasm, and it nearly boiled over when former QPR man Paul Parker was stamped on right in front of us. Ince, as ever, was the first man over and he wasted no time in addressing the home fans. 'I'll take every f**king one of you,' he said. It wouldn't be the last time.

Ince was growing in influence in the United midfield, and his marauding performance at Loftus Road was typical of the exuberance he was now bringing to United's play. United suddenly seemed to be playing a more confident, dynamic game and they looked fitter than every side they came up against. With outlets like Kanchelskis, Giggs and Sharpe they were devastating on the break, and could get men forward from midfield in support in a matter of seconds. When

Cantona played he brought a calm sense of assuredness that only added to their potency.

'Vision. All the best players in the world have imagination,' Ferguson said of his footballing revolutionary that January. 'They can see a picture that no one else can quite make out. Eric can see those things. His head's up, you know? The point is anyone who comes to this club must cope with the expectation. Some players haven't done it, unfortunately – good players at their last club who couldn't quite handle it because the stage can be a bit frightening. Eric's attitude is, "This is where I should be". It's more a question of us having to tailor the expectation to suit him.'

A league victory against Nottingham Forest came next, and United were now unbeaten in 12 and looking every bit like champions. Cantona had still to lose in a red shirt. But the familiar doubts came flooding back in March, with a loss and three draws in the space of three weeks. Aston Villa and Norwich City were the teams in pursuit and United's floundering had opened the door for a challenge. Ferguson's team needed a show of strength; they needed to make a statement of intent.

As a fan I remained quietly optimistic. United had imploded the previous spring, but this time around they had Cantona and he seemed to have imparted a new belief on everybody around him. The pressure on Ferguson and his team to finally deliver a title was immense, but you could only hope the experience of 12 months ago would avoid a similar disaster.

Their next game was Norwich away on Easter Monday, and to say they flew out of the blocks at Carrow Road would be doing United a disservice. There have been emphatic endings aplenty for Ferguson's teams over the years, but has there ever been a more devastating beginning to a game than the one his team delivered on 5 April 1993? Here's how I remember it.

Schmeichel throws to Sharpe. Sharpe evades a tackle, cuts inside and finds Cantona. Cantona, as ever in space, waits for Giggs to time his run and sets him away through the middle with a weighted pass. Giggs rounds the goalkeeper and scores: 1-0 United.

Pallister clears from inside the United box, Kanchelskis cushions a volley to Ince in midfield. Ince finds Giggs, who lays the ball back to McClair, who releases Kanchelskis down the right with a wonderful first-time pass. Kanchelskis scampers forward then squares to Cantona: 2-0 United. Ince intercepts a Norwich throw-in, drives past one tackler, beats two more, and keeps going. Faced with Norwich goalkeeper Bryan Gunn, he flicks the ball to his right for Kanchelskis to tap in from five yards: 3-0 United. Game over. Inside 20 minutes.

Reports the following day lauded United for their devastating display. 'All guns firing', 'United burst back in champion style', 'Eric Idol' and 'Nerves of steel' were some of the headlines. It was an exhibition performance that said everything about what Ferguson was trying to achieve. Here was his United team as he imagined them, true to the club's romantic heritage as an expression of pure footballing joy. At their hub was Cantona, orchestrating the soaring tones of Giggs, Sharpe and Kanchelskis as if he'd played alongside them his entire career.

In goal Schmeichel was not only a commanding presence, physically and vocally, and a superb shot stopper, but he was also United's time signature. When urgency was needed he delivered it, hurling the ball like a fizzing Viking spear to a red shirt with unerring accuracy. And if calm was called for he held the ball so tight you thought it might burst. No wonder Cantona took to the great Dane. The pair shared a fiery emotional make-up that could occasionally isolate them, but was integral to their relative powers. They shared a passion above all others.

At the back Bruce and Pallister had developed an understanding that makes you wonder why they were never paired together for England (Bruce, remarkably, never played for his country). Aerially they were peerless, and both were confident ball players who could bring the ball out of defence and launch an attack. Pallister had a stuttering start to his United career, struggling to justify his transfer fee, but the fans had long since been won over. Alongside them, in Parker and Irwin, United had arguably two of the best full backs in the division. With six games left, the title was now United's to lose.

The following Saturday we boarded a ferry to France at four o'clock in the afternoon. A group of 20 of us, family and friends, were off on a week's skiing trip to Italy and spirits were high. The only problem was how Dad and I would keep up with United's all-important (is football ever anything less?) home game against Sheffield Wednesday. My portable radio was never going to get any reception in the choppy waters of the English Channel and the world barely had the Internet, let alone 3G phones to use it with. So we were wholly reliant on the ferry having a TV, and that TV being on BBC One for the full-time results at 4.45 p.m. If that failed, we wouldn't know the score until we picked up a paper the following day.

We were in luck. In the corner of the main bar a small screen hung on the wall, around which sat a group of dishevelled men in football shirts nursing beers and saying nothing. Usually the English would never engage in conversation in such a social situation, but there is one exception, one question an Englishman can always ask. 'Excuse me, mate, what's the United score?'

'They're losing 1-0 at home to Wednesday, mate, five minutes left,' came the gruff reply. Stunned silence. Suddenly the enjoyment of a week's holiday rested on the result of a football match I couldn't see. The BBC's Videprinter was now in control of United's destiny and we sat praying 'Manchester United 1-1 Sheffield Wednesday (Cantona 90)' would flicker across the screen to keep our title hopes alive. Even that might not be enough.

Goal United! Straight to Old Trafford, where Bruce had headed a dramatic equaliser at the death. What's more, there were still six minutes of injury time to play – thanks to a hamstrung referee and the time it took to replace him. Hang on a second... Back to United! Bruce again. Ridiculous! United had won it 2-1.

When I looked back at the highlights of the game during my research for this book they made the hairs on the back of my neck stand up. Bruce not even breaking stride to steer the winner into the corner with his head; Ferguson and Brian Kidd leaping like 80-year-old Bruce Springsteens onto the turf in euphoric celebration; Barry Davis doing what Barry Davies does best in the commentary box. 'They've come back from the dead in this one,' he proclaimed. 'At Easter last year it went away. At Easter this year Manchester United may have started the final move to end their search. Six minutes of injury time and Steve Bruce has the freedom of half of Manchester... What a match!'

United were almost there. Wins against Coventry and Chelsea put them on the verge and we had tickets for Crystal Palace away. After 26 years the title was in touching distance and the atmosphere around Selhurst Park that Wednesday night was charged with a heady lager-fuelled excitement, as thousands of travelling United fans descended on the bars in celebratory mood. 'Take it over, take it over, take it over Selhurst Park,' came the chant as we walked from the train station to the stadium. That we had.

The first half ended goalless, but the atmosphere in the United end was buoyant with the news that Aston Villa were losing 3-0 at Blackburn. With Norwich out of the race, Ron Atkinson's team were the only thing between United and the title. If they lost, United could seal the championship with victory at home against Blackburn that weekend.

Ferguson's men, well aware of events at Ewood Park, came out firing in the second half. Cantona, in particular, was majestic, crossing superbly for Hughes to smash home a trademark volley just after the hour mark. United wore the green and yellow shirts that gave a nod to their inception as Newton Heath, but they were on the verge of making history of their own. Ince settled it. Released by Cantona, he drove powerfully into the box and shot across the goalkeeper and into the net. It was a fitting crescendo to a night that was over a quarter of a century in the making.

'We're gonna win the league/We're gonna win the league/And now you better believe us/And now you better believe us/And now you better believe us/We're gonna win the league.'

By the time United took to the field against Blackburn the title was won. Villa had slipped up against Oldham and the race was over. Ferguson was playing golf with his son Mark when he heard the news. They hugged and immediately made their way off the course, stopping only to tell a group of Japanese golfers the good news. 'I noticed that one of them had the name of our sponsor, Sharp, on his golf cap,' Ferguson wrote in *Managing My Life*. 'He must be a United fan, I told myself, and informed him with great pride, "United have won the League."' Unlike the rest of the country, the man had no idea what Ferguson was talking about.

At Old Trafford, on Bank Holiday Monday, United fans were treated to a performance to fit the occasion. Blackburn were swept aside 3-1, with Pallister helping himself to his first goal of the season – much to the delight of his manager. It was left to Bruce and Robson, captains both, to lift the Premiership trophy and the celebrations began in earnest. 'You strive all your life to get a feeling like tonight, to experience an atmosphere like tonight,' Ferguson told Sky TV. 'I've never seen anything like it.'

There was still one game left, away at Wimbledon – who had by this time left their Plough Lane dog track and set up home at Selhurst Park. Dad, PJ and I had tickets and were looking forward to seeing United smash in a few goals and parade the Premiership trophy. It should have been a glorious afternoon for a United-mad 14-year-old, but it didn't get off to a great start. The night before I'd been to a football club dinner in honour of the senior team for whom I was playing. I had duly made myself acquainted with some potent export lager.

The next morning I spent two hours throwing up, before sitting in heavy traffic for four hours, then walking through heavy crowds to the stadium. Everybody around us smelled of booze, and it wasn't long before United fans trapped on the terraces began urinating there and then and letting their work trickle down the concrete steps. It took everything I had to stop myself vomiting again, and as a hangover cure I wouldn't recommend it. But it was worth it.

Eventually the fresh air started to take effect. And everything was right in the world by the time Robson scored United's second to seal a 2-0 win. Captain Marvel had been ravaged by injury and his powers were on the wane, but he deserved his moment as much as he deserved credit for helping United win the title. He'd be back next season, but it felt like his swansong that day. It felt like the crowd were saying goodbye to a legend. It was time for Robson to pass the baton.

As we headed home the chant of 'Championes, Championes, Olé, Olé, Olé' was ringing around Selhurst Park and the drunk tanks were getting ready for a busy night. Twenty-six years of frustration had been put to bed and United fans would drink to every single one of them. I, on the other hand, vowed to never drink again.

CHAPTER 5
RAMPANT REDS

By the time the 1993/94 season came around a 21-year-old midfielder named Roy Keane had signed for Manchester United. Ferguson paid £3.75 million to Nottingham Forest for the Irishman, whose swash-buckling midfield play drew natural comparison with Bryan Robson – the very man he had been bought to replace.

The talk among United fans was of Keane's remarkable engine, his rampant all-round game and, most of all, his endless potential. Here was a born winner, a player with sheer will to burn. With Robson now 36 and no more than a bit-part player, Keane was the man Ferguson tasked with driving United forward and making them a dominant force for a decade. It proved another masterstroke.

By the time the fiery Irishman stormed out of Old Trafford in 2005 he'd dragged United by the scruff of the neck to seven Premier League titles, four FA Cup wins and a European Cup triumph – and lived every single minute in a red shirt on his own terms. In the Ferguson era, surely only Robson bears comparison in the field of blood-or-guts commitment. 'Roy Keane's fantastic – he's the best player I have had here and I have some great players,' Ferguson said in 2003. 'It's his authority, his play, it's everything he does.'

When PJ and I went to the Charity Shield at Wembley in early August, we both expected Ferguson to field a weakened side. It wasn't a major trophy and we thought he'd resist showing his strongest hand until the Premiership court was in session. As it turned out the starting

XI he picked against Arsenal that day went down as the first truly great team of his reign.

It's a team that played together 13 times and won every game. One that nearly every United fan in the country would have sent out given the resources available that season. And one that any United fan worth their salt could recite in their sleep. McClair, Robson and, in particular, Sharpe played their roles that season, but this is the XI we all remember: Schmeichel, Parker, Bruce, Pallister, Irwin, Kanchelskis, Ince, Keane, Giggs, Hughes and Cantona.

The Charity Shield finished 1-1, with Ian Wright volleying a spectacular equaliser past Schmeichel. But United's goalkeeper would have the last laugh, saving David Seaman's penalty in sudden death to see his team into the season proper with confidence soaring. Debutant Keane scored in the shootout, as did Cantona – who nonchalantly flicked the ball into the bottom corner like he was passing it back to a ball boy in the warm-up.

How I wished for Cantona's confidence. I was 15 years old and about to start my GCSEs. Life was suddenly very complicated. Kissing girls and being cool were the benchmarks of success, and it turned out not being a football-obsessed weirdo was of paramount importance to both. It was time to take down the United posters that had adorned my bedroom walls since I was six, time to hide my autograph shrine, and time to stop heavy breathing the crowd chanting my name at Old Trafford. The day had come to eschew my real identity and pretend to be the teenager everybody else was. Goodbye Jesper Olsen; hello Pamela Anderson.

The autographs were hard to lose. In the mid-to-late 1980s I'd written to every single member of the United squad asking for a signed picture. That they all wrote back with signed prints told me two things. One, footballers are ultimately good people who care about their fans and realise how important they are to the people who worship them. And two, their egos are so inflated even Peter Davenport could believe he was a fan's favourite player (and Chris Turner, and Arthur Albiston, and Clayton Blackmore… I could go on).

But not everything about supporting United was at odds with the demands on a teenager to be cool. Cantona was football's counter-culture equivalent to Kurt Cobain – a supremely gifted artist who adhered to his own moral code. Everybody was talking about him, and everybody seemed to have an opinion. He transcended football and engaged the dinner party set like no player before him.

Cantona was a genius, but he was also a philosopher and an eccentric. England had never seen a sporting personality like him, and we've not seen another since. Whether you loved him or loathed him, you were fascinated by him. And for United fans, as Jim White put it best, 'The King made it fine to be a fan'. He made United the coolest team on the planet. Ferguson called him 'Mon genius', and the accolades poured in practically every time Cantona took to the field. 'I'd give all the champagne I've ever drunk to be playing alongside him in a big European match at Old Trafford,' said the late, great George Best. 'A player like that only comes along once or twice in a lifetime,' added Sir Bobby Charlton, who's seen a player or two in his time at Old Trafford. 'He paints beautiful pictures on football pitches,' gushed French international Jean-Pierre Papin. And as football fell in love with Cantona, so the Frenchman returned its affection.

There was also the pop star duo of Giggs and Sharpe to consider. In football's new age of celebrity the players had become pin-ups. Giggs and Sharpe were sportsmen, but they may as well have been movie stars or DJs. It was a trend that would usher in the so-called Spice Boys at Liverpool, and served to bring a new sex appeal to the game generally. Men idolised them, women fancied them. And it meant people were talking about football like never before.

United started the new season with five wins and a draw, Keane opening his account with a brace against Sheffield United at Old Trafford. They looked lean, hungry, and ready to go to war. In Schmeichel, Bruce, Ince, Keane, Hughes and Cantona, United had a formidable spine of fierce competitors who were not afraid to mix it. Out on the flanks Giggs, Kanchelskis and Sharpe were running on rocket fuel, and in Robson and McClair, Ferguson had plenty of experience to turn to.

Bring on Europe. For the first time since 1969, when Sir Matt Busby's team qualified as champions, United were back in the European Cup. And if United fans are completely honest, despite UEFA's rules at that time limiting Ferguson to three foreigners, we half-expected Cantona and co. to waltz all the way to the final and win it.

First up were Kispest-Honved of Hungary, who were dispatched with relative ease, 5-3 on aggregate. Then came the draw Ferguson, and the rest of Europe for that matter, dreaded. In the second round United were to face Galatasaray of Turkey. And after escaping with a 3-3 draw in the home leg at Old Trafford, Ferguson took his men into a cauldron of hate like no other. I still remember the footage from the airport. United were met by banners depicting skulls and crossbones and reading 'Welcome to Hell'. This was a new level of fervour, a frighteningly raw and vivid experience for Ferguson and his team. Among their number were emerging young players like Nicky Butt, Gary Neville and David Beckham. It must have been quite an awakening.

United were beaten by the crowd that night. Ince (taking a night off from Guv'nor duties) was captured in a press photo smiling in bemusement at the ferocious chanting of the home fans, and even Keane looked taken aback by the primitive atmosphere. Take Liverpool away and multiply it by ten. A scrappy 0-0 draw saw United out on away goals, and ended with a frustrated Cantona sent off and he and Robson being struck by police batons in the chaos that ensued after the final whistle. 'The return leg in Istanbul exposed us to as much harassment and hostility as I have ever known on a football expedition,' wrote Ferguson in *Managing My Life*.

Out of the frying pan and into… a slightly less hot frying pan. United's next game was at Maine Road in the televised Sunday afternoon slot, against a City side who were going well under new manager Brian Horton. Perhaps still reeling from the devilment and disappointment of Turkey, United were breached twice during the first half – derby specialist Niall Quinn heading both past Schmeichel, both times due to lax defending.

They needed a response and predictably it arrived in the guise of Cantona. United's No. 7 got one back with a composed finish, then equalised at the far post to finish a move he started with a swaggering display of kick-ups on approaching the City box. The momentum was with United, and it was no surprise when Keane motored in at the far post to finish Irwin's superb curling cross and give his side all three points – and the perfect pick-me-up for their European hangover. That was early November and the start of a fine run of form.

United travelled to Anfield in January 1994 unbeaten in 17 league games and sitting pretty at the top of the table. In contrast Graeme Souness's Liverpool were languishing in ninth, 21 points behind United and in the grips of a spiralling fall from grace. United's great rivals had not won a title since 1990 (still they wait) and, much to the chagrin of their fans, were quite clearly treading water as the balance of power shifted east.

Homework once again avoided I sat down with Dad and a plate of fish and chips to watch the game. United went ahead when Bruce headed home Cantona's cross at the far post. Then Giggs chipped Bruce Grobbelaar from outside the box to make it 2-0. Then, after Neil Ruddock smashed into Keane to concede a free-kick, Irwin curled a shot into the top corner from 25 yards to make it three. Twenty-four minutes on the clock, 3-0 United. They looked set to get six or seven.

But Liverpool dug deep. A minute later Nigel Clough beat Schmeichel from fully 30 yards to get one back, and the son of Brian helped himself to another before half-time, drifting all too easily inside the United box to wrong-foot Schmeichel and make it 3-2. The comeback was complete on 78 minutes, when Ruddock leapt above Pallister, like a ferocious fat salmon, to head Liverpool level and send Anfield into raptures.

'At 3-0 down Liverpool went kamikaze,' Ferguson said after the game, admitting he was 'bloody raging' at losing a three-goal lead. 'They charged in for every tackle, ran a yard faster and a yard harder every time. The crowd had them at fever pitch. As a game it will take some beating.'

According to an account in Patrick Barclay's *Football – Bloody Hell: The Biography of Alex Ferguson*, the manager singled out Schmeichel for the hairdryer treatment and accused his goalkeeper of letting the team down. 'The big Dane responded in kind,' Barclay wrote, 'questioning Ferguson's qualities as a manager and a person and feared Ferguson might well react by throwing a cup of tea in his face.' The pair soon settled their dispute, which was nothing more than symptomatic of having so many ferocious winners in one dressing room.

It would have been a frightening place to be if you weren't armed with fierce convictions, which was exactly how Ferguson wanted it. As a fan I've often imagined myself on the end of one of those hairdryers, and I'm pretty certain I would have curled up into a ball in the corner of the room and rocked back and forth until it stopped. A fired-up Ferguson must be a terrifying proposition, and there are plenty of self-styled hard men who've been left shaken by his rants over the years. Maybe when he retires he can offer his services to the parents of unruly children.

United's next game was away at Sheffield United in the third round of the FA Cup. PJ, Dad and I made the trip on a freezing cold Sunday in January and we definitely got our money's worth. After scoring the only goal with a classy finish to a neat team move, Hughes played vigilante and sought retribution for the rough-handed treatment he'd received from Sheffield United defender David Tuttle. Tuttle had been indecently tight on Hughes the whole game, clinging to his shirt and attempting to nullify his threat by any means necessary. A man of Hughes' experience should have known better, but as Tuttle walked away from yet another bristling challenge Hughes snapped. He threw a boot from behind his man and caught the defender square in the unmentionables. A straight red was the only option and the game finished with tensions very much flared.

As we left the stadium I witnessed the only example of fan violence I've seen to this day. Two opposing fans were arguing over the relative merits of United's victory when a heated debate escalated into a fistfight. The only problem both men had was the crowded nature of the stairwell leading out of the stadium. Neither could retract their arms enough to throw a decent punch, and the surrounding fans, fortunately, appeared to have no interest in joining in. Both thrashed around wildly like stranded fish desperate to escape the net. 'I'll have you mate,' said one. 'Like f**k you will,' replied the other. But both were saved any embarrassment as the crowd swelled further at the bottom of the stairs, leaving the pair separated by 30 or 40 bodies. Still they shouted back and forth, ever more violently, but they did so safe in the knowledge that a fight was not going to happen. Pride retained, no blood spilled. Everyone's a winner. Except Hughes, who received the wrath of Ferguson and a ban.

At least in private he did. Publicly, Ferguson stayed loyal and defended him to the hilt, blaming the red card on poor refereeing and citing intense provocation. As ever, his was a blinkered take that perfectly served his aims of harnessing a 'them-against-us' mentality at United, and focusing the attentions away from the wrongdoer. 'Tuttle went right through him and the ref did nothing about it,' he said. 'They gave Mark a lot of abuse, and I think he will be terribly disappointed by the lack of protection he got out there.'

The Hughes incident was a rare example of a footballer actually turning to outside-a-pub-style violence on the pitch, instead of merely threatening it for effect. Football is never short of push-and-shove pseudo aggression, but it's a rare spat that translates into a full-on ruckus. Most of the time neither antagonist actually wants to fight, they simply want to give the impression they're ready to. There's an unspoken code in such encounters where both players know an actual fight is not on the agenda. I've done it myself many times, got up from a challenge and given my opponent a push in the chest followed by the classic 'Come on then!' I suppose there's a vague risk of being punched, but most likely both men are just waiting for their teammates to prise them apart so they can get on with the football. Only once have I seen it go beyond that in the amateur game, and that was when my uncle took a sabbatical from rugby and brought an altogether more manly code to the occasion. He got pushed. He pushed back, and then some.

Like good old Uncle Bill, when it came to physical confrontation, Ferguson's United of 1993/94 needed no pretence. In *Managing My Life* he refers to the 'warlike' members of that squad, being most notably Cantona, Keane, Ince and Hughes – who were so full-blooded and potentially unhinged they needed reigning in on a regular basis.

Cantona was sent off twice in three days in March – prompting his manager to deliver a rare roasting to his favourite Frenchman. The first came at Swindon, where he stamped on a prone John Moncur in a heated encounter that ended in a 2-2 draw. Keane had steam coming out of his ears that afternoon after a couple of tasty challenges, and Hughes was treated to a bit of afters from a spectator after being clattered into the stand during the first half. Cantona extracted revenge on their behalf. And at Highbury the following Tuesday he saw red again, this time for two bookable offences.

The Cantona backlash was gathering momentum and United fans were facing a moral dilemma. Should we defend him and justify his mistakes as the by-product of the same impassioned personality that made him a genius? Or accept that the self-destructive tendencies he'd displayed earlier in his career would unravel and ultimately bring down the King of Old Trafford?

The media's kneejerk reaction was largely to opt for the latter. Having built him up during the season he brought United a long over-due title, it was time to deconstruct the Cantona myth. 'Crazy Cantona' and 'Eric le Terrible' were among the headlines, and he was vilified as aggressively as he'd been lauded just a few months before. He'd been through the cycle before, and he'd go through it again. Opposing fans followed suit, but the harder they came down on our hero, the more I wanted to defend him.

He was a flawed genius, but he was our genius. And what he delivered in the 1992/93 season was enough to put most United fans in forgiving mood for the rest of his career. Even Moncur was forced to admit the majesty of the greatest footballer in the country. 'Cantona stamped on me, I have the marks to prove it. But I'd still vote for him as Player of the Season,' he said.

Maybe the black kit had an effect on him? Was it a coincidence that United were wearing black for Cantona's two reds in three games? There's no science to back it up (at least, there may well be but I haven't gone looking), but you wonder if the players let the menace of their strip infiltrate their personalities in that all-black ensemble. Cantona certainly had an interesting time in a black shirt, especially when you consider the events that were to follow in January 1995 at Selhurst Park. And watching Ince and Keane pillage in that strip really was a sight to strike fear into the opposition. They were like rampaging dervishes.

United were now a physical specimen ready for a back-alley brawl with any team in Europe. Having taken over a team of booze-addled underachievers Ferguson was now watching on as his ferocious warriors went to battle for him. His players would miss chances and make mistakes, but they would never give him anything less than a win-at-all-costs mentality. With Keane on board he'd taken his title winners from 1992/93 and made them bulletproof.

Naturally United's public image suffered as a result. They were no longer the lovable relics of a wistful bygone age, purveying attractive football for the mutual benefit. They were hard and fast gunslingers, and the new mentality applied on and off the pitch. Old Trafford had been developed and a new megastore opened to capitalise on the club's new success. United were also successfully branching out their business globally, taking advantage of avenues Liverpool had seemingly ignored during their years of dominance. Add to that a new breed of snarling, ultra-competitive players, and it's easy to see why United were becoming popular hate figures during the early months of the 1993/94 season.

The media accused officials of giving them bias, and at times they were justified – Cantona's FA Cup assault on Norwich City's Jeremy Goss witness for the prosecution. Cantona should have got a straight red for a crazy lunge, but he escaped with a booking and scored in a 2-0 win. He also got the benefit of the doubt from his manager, who had only truly vented his anger at the Frenchman he held dear above all others for the first time after the donkey kick at Swindon's Moncur. For Cantona, it seemed, a different set of rules applied and, as the wins kept coming, so blind eyes turned.

With Cantona in the cockpit United were flying. On-course for an unprecedented domestic Treble, they travelled to Selhurst Park to take on Wimbledon in the fifth round of the FA Cup. It was a Sunday afternoon and time to get out my new edition yellow and green United strip for the occasion (Santa Claus clearly had no problem with United's burgeoning corporate empire and the club's penchant for cashing in).

Cantona got things going with a goal only Cantona could have scored. Cushioning a clearance with one touch, he volleyed instinctively into the top corner with his next to put United ahead in sumptuous fashion. It was one of the great United goals and those who were there to see it knew they'd witnessed something special. Some may argue they were treated to an even better one before the afternoon was out – Irwin finishing off a slick seven-man move that had the purists purring. United looked unstoppable. Selhurst Park had once again proved a venue of celebration.

For Ferguson, a swaggering victory over a physical Wimbledon team billed as 'arch party-poopers' served to illustrate just how far United had come during his reign. In 1988 I'd been in the crowd at Plough Lane when Wimbledon's Crazy Gang gave them a brutal lesson in thuggery – and practically chased them off the park. Six years' on and United, hardened of body and spirit, were not for the bullying. All too predictably Vinnie Jones did his best to unsettle Cantona, but ultimately was taught such a lesson he resorted to a ridiculous tackle that should have earned him a straight red card.

When Ferguson took his team to Wembley for the League Cup final at the end of March they'd lost just once in their last 39 games. Up against him that day in the manager's dugout was none other than Ron Atkinson, the man he'd replaced at Old Trafford nearly eight years before. The script was waiting to be written and football delivered it. Atkinson's Aston Villa outplayed United and won 3-1, with Kanchelskis sent off late on for deliberate handball. Dreams of the Treble would have to wait.

Two weeks' later Ferguson was back at Wembley for an FA Cup semi-final against Oldham, and with a minute left, and his side 1-0 down, it looked like the Double would go the same way. But United kept on pressing and when Hughes stole in on the shoulder of his marker to volley a dramatic equaliser Oldham may as well have conceded the replay. They were swept aside 4-1 at Maine Road and the Double loomed large.

Sparky was marking himself out as Ferguson and United's Cup saviour. His equaliser had saved them from defeat to Crystal Palace in the 1990 FA Cup Final, his two goals had won them the Cup-Winners' Cup a year later and now his spectacular goal saved them from defeat against Oldham. It turned out he was not only 'a scorer of great goals', but also a 'great scorer of important goals' too. He was also a great servant of the greatest football club in the world. But journalism lecturers will warn about the overuse of the word 'great', so I'd better stop there.

United wrapped up the title with a 2-1 win against Ipswich Town on 1 May 1994. The Double followed all too easily, with a 4-0 defeat of Chelsea in the FA Cup Final. Cantona celebrated being named PFA Players' Player of the Year, presumably benefiting from Moncur's vote, by scoring twice from the penalty spot. United's 1993/94 vintage had brought the club a ninth league title and its first Double. And on this evidence they would do it all again next season. They were rampant and irresistible, the epitome of everything Manchester United stood for.

Ferguson dedicated the success to the only United manager now worthy of his comparison – the great Sir Matt Busby, who had passed away four months earlier at the age of 84. The Double was a fitting memorial to Busby, and it strengthened Ferguson's resolve to win the only prize that now eluded him. Without matching United's 1968 European Cup win, he could never consider himself a worthy peer to his fellow Scot. The quest had become an obsession, and United still seemed some distance away from achieving it. To do it Ferguson would have to conquer the likes of AC Milan, whose 4-0 hammering of Barcelona in the 1994 Champions League final he called 'magnificent' and 'frightening'.

And he'd have to do it without the great Bryan Robson, who had announced his plans to take over as player-manager at Middlesbrough. The only remaining representative of my original cast of heroes, Robson had been there since the start with Ferguson. He'd lived through the revolution and stuck around long enough to celebrate the coup. But his epic, heroic United journey had come to a natural conclusion.

Ferguson was sad to see him go, but not sad enough to give him a spot on the bench for the Cup final. That went to McClair, with Ferguson deciding to go with the man who would be alongside him next season. It was a decision typical of his clinical approach and, unlike the one he made to drop Jim Leighton in 1990, he regrets it.

Robson, above all others, deserved a swansong.

CHAPTER 6
I AM NOT A MAN...
I AM CANTONA

The summer of 1994 was a low point for British music. For two weeks in May United and Status Quo topped the charts with their FA Cup Final single 'Come on you Reds' – backed by a squirm-inducing video of the unlikely collective in the studio. Mike Phelan, the least rock 'n' roll footballer you ever saw play, could not have looked more awkward if he'd tried. Mark Hughes and Denis Irwin didn't fare much better. And Steve Bruce, yet again, was in one of those oversized caps that belonged to an 80-year-old American in a Florida golfing community.

Only Lee Sharpe and Brian McClair, sporting some gruff rock star stubble for the occasion, appeared to be enjoying themselves. Brandishing unplugged guitars they played the role of pop stars with an appetite that suggests both would have enjoyed the real thing. Sharpe, as we know, was pretty much living the lifestyle already. But not even he could appear cool singing along to these lyrics:

Busby Babes they always made me cry,
Thinkin' 'bout the teams of years gone by:
Charlton, Edwards, Law and Georgie Best.
We're United, you can keep the rest.

Schmeichel, Parker, Pallister,
Irwin, Bruce, Sharpe and Ince,
Hughes, McClair, Keane and Cantona,
Robson, Kanchelskis and Giggs.

Come on you Reds, come on you Reds,
Just keep your bottle and use your heads.
For ninety minutes we'll let them know,
Who's Man United, here we go.

Phelan had good reason to feel awkward. He and Clayton Blackmore were asked to sing along with a verse listing all the key members of the United squad, 14 of them in total – and neither of them got a mention. It was left to Scottish crooners Wet Wet Wet to knock United and the Quo off the No. 1 spot, and their ubiquitous cover of 'Love Is All Around' was still top of the charts by the time the 1994/95 season kicked off.

At least it didn't have Phelan on backing vocals. He and Blackmore would never go into the studio for United again. The pair joined Robson and Dion Dublin as the big-name departures from Old Trafford in the summer of 1994. FA Cup Final hero Lee Martin also said his goodbyes, with Blackburn Rovers defender David May the club's only major signing – joining for £1.2 million to provide Ferguson some much-needed cover in central defence.

The United manager saw no need to wade any further into the transfer market. The precocious crop of youngsters who had won the FA Youth Cup in 1992 were reaching maturity, and Ferguson was almost ready to blood them. 'In all my managerial career I've never been as excited about a group of young footballers as I was about those who were coming through as teenagers at Old Trafford at the beginning of the 1994/95 season,' he wrote in *Managing My Life*.

Nicky Butt, Paul Scholes, David Beckham, Keith Gillespie, Chris Casper, John O'Kane and the Neville brothers were among that brood. But of them only Gary Neville and Butt would make a telling contribution to the 1994/95 campaign. The others would continue their incubation, and it was not until the following season – made famous by Alan Hansen's suggestion that 'you'll never win anything with kids' – that the 'Fergie Fledglings' would make good on their manager's optimism.

The 1994/95 campaign should have given them another lesson in well-oiled success – an opportunity to watch on as the dominant force in English football reach new highs and finally delivered on the European stage. Instead it delivered a nightmarish blend of chaos and failure.

Ferguson's team were knocked out of the Champions League in the group stages, humbled 4-0 by a rampant, Hristo Stoichkov-inspired Barcelona on the way. The foreigner players rule meant Ferguson opted for Gary Walsh in goal that night, sacrificing Schmeichel to use his quota in the outfield. Walsh had a night to forget and Ferguson was heavily criticised for the decision. But while the Barca battering was a brutal blow to Ferguson's pride and yet another crushing disappointment for United's fans, there were long-term benefits to the footballing masterclass dealt out that night at the Camp Nou. 'The defeat in 1994 was a great occasion for us in the sense of realising how important it is to retain the ball,' Ferguson said in 2008. 'In terms of the quality and possession of the football, Barcelona were far better than us, so it was a good lesson.'

The death of the European dream put domestic matters at an absolute premium. January 1995 arrived with United, seeking a third successive title and a back-to-back Double, locked in a tight battle at the top of the table with Kenny Dalglish's Blackburn Rovers. United's Lancastrian neighbours had been bought by industrial tycoon Jack Walker in 1991 and spent heavily in the transfer market to arrive almost overnight as genuine contenders. Walker was desperate to bring the club their first league title in 80 years, and a runners-up finish to United in 1993/94 proved they were getting close.

In an attempt to keep pace with the free-scoring Rovers' strike force of Alan Shearer and Chris Sutton, the so-called 'SAS', Ferguson broke the British transfer record in January to bring Andy Cole to Old Trafford – United parting with £6 million and the young winger Gillespie to get the striker from Newcastle.

Cole started in a 1-0 win against their title rivals on Sunday 22 January, but it was Cantona who got the all-important winner. It meant United arrived at Selhurst Park for a midweek meeting with Crystal Palace three days' later in optimistic mood. Palace were on their way down and had been swept aside 3-0 at Old Trafford early in the season. It should have been a routine victory – it should have been another Selhurst Park celebration.

For once we weren't there to see it. I was playing myself that night and it wasn't until Dad put the radio on in the car going home that we had an inkling of what had happened. At first it didn't seem particularly serious. They were talking about Cantona having had an altercation with a fan. It sounded like the kind of thing Cantona might get involved in, and we thought he'd probably lost his head and been sent off. The assumption was the fan had attacked Cantona. Such was the hate campaign against the Frenchman it wouldn't have been all that surprising, but the truth was a good deal more shocking.

Twenty-four hours later the footage was inescapable. Cantona had been sent off for kicking out at Palace defender Richard Shaw. United's No. 7 was not happy with the decision, but after straightening his collar and taking a moment to survey his surroundings with hands on hips, he left the field with a minimum of fuss and headed for the dugout. Assuming Cantona's part was played out, the cameras diverted their gaze back to referee Alan Wilkie. First Irwin protested, then Cole even more violently. Largely predictable stuff from teammates trying to save their friend.

Then suddenly attentions turned to a flurry of black on the side-lines, where we saw Cantona launch himself right-foot first into a Palace supporter who had walked down to the edge of the hoardings to tell him to 'F**k off back to France' and called him a 'French motherf**ker' or something to that effect – accounts vary, but the xenophobic sentiment is clear. Cantona's attempted kick caused him to fall backwards, but he lurched back with his right fist flailing. United's kit man intervened, as did the police – rushing in to separate players from fans. Chaos ensued.

It was left to Schmeichel to guide Cantona down the tunnel, taking all manner of abuse on the way. The big goalkeeper gave sweep after sweep of his right arm in protest to the home fans, keeping his left around Cantona to ensure his friend didn't make a U-turn back to the action. 'You dirty northern bastards,' sang the Palace fans. Back at the scene of the crime, Cole and Paul Ince were leading the aggression against an enemy 5,000 strong. Ince allegedly offered to fight every one of them. But it was too late – the damage was already done. Cantona had ventured into infamy.

The fan was 20-year-old Matthew Simmons, a self-employed glazier who, perhaps mercifully for Cantona, had a criminal record and links to the BNP. He was sentenced to seven days in jail and had his season ticket revoked by Palace for his aggressive and threatening behaviour. In an interview for *Cantona: The Rebel Who Would Be King*, Simmons said he greatly regretted acting like a 'cretin' that night, and had paid a high price. He struggled to find work for years after the incident and found himself regularly abused or ignored by people who knew what he'd done.

But while it was wholly wrong, Simmons' abuse was not extraordinary in Cantona's world. Like Shaw's uncompromising physical approach on the pitch that led to Cantona's sending off, it was simply a facet of the environment a professional footballer works in. He had surely heard worse on his return to Leeds and in Galatasaray in the months before, and not once launched into a karate kick into the stands. And the anti-foreigner stance came with the territory of playing in front of English crowds. Why should this be any different? What triggered the most notorious incident in English football history?

The truth is Cantona's crime had no deep-seated psychological justification. 'I am not a man. I am Cantona,' he famously said, and therein lies all the explanation we should need. In that moment, for whatever reason, he felt compelled to react – just as Zinedine Zidane would do over a decade later, when he head-butted Marco Materazzi during the 2006 World Cup final. Nothing would stop Cantona being Cantona. 'A young man has a right to be a rebel,' he said. The philosophy that made him great also made him flawed, but he embraced it and we loved him for it. He later said his only regret was not kicking Simmons harder.

The media reacted with outrage and demanded a lifetime ban. Cantona's behaviour was 'a new low for player behaviour' wrote Trevor Haylett in the *Independent*. 'Shocking', 'shameful' and 'unforgivable' were the adjectives dominating the front, middle and back pages of every newspaper in England. The BBC called it 'the ten seconds that shook the English football world'. Even Gordon Taylor, the chief executive of the Players' Union, couldn't escape the fact that Cantona – the reigning PFA Player of the Year – was 'in deep trouble'.

In Scotland the *Daily Record* printed a huge picture of a Nike football boot, under the headline 'Lethal Weapon'. One newspaper went with 'Le Nutter'. Cantona's past troubles gave the media the perfect narrative. Here was a stereotypically strong-willed Frenchman who had acted outside the law his entire career. A player who'd courted controversy in the colours of Auxerre, Montpellier, Marseille, Nimes, France and now Manchester United. What happened at Selhurst Park was the inevitable culmination of Cantona's self-destructive personality. Obituaries to his career were coming thick and fast.

United fans responded by embracing the cult of Cantona with even greater ferocity. T-shirts in support of the Frenchman were everywhere at Old Trafford and his plight was read as that of the persecuted genius, misunderstood everywhere but in the bosom of the United faithful. The more the media and the public chastised him, the more vehemently we came to his defence. He was a spectacularly flawed genius, but he remained – for now at least – our genius. And there was no crime he could commit to cheapen the wealth of riches he'd already brought to our door.

Ferguson and the United board knew they needed to act quickly. They held an emergency meeting and decided to fine Cantona two weeks' wages and banned him until the end of the season. Ferguson has always maintained they decided on his sentence on the advice of the FA, who agreed it was a fair punishment and said they would take no further action if United took the initiative. It that's true, then football's governing body reneged spectacularly – and had an almost immediate change of heart. They called a hearing and extended Cantona's ban by a further four months. Ferguson was outraged, claiming the FA had been 'dictated to by the media'. But United accepted the judgement immediately. This was damage limitation, and the more Cantona's crime was discussed the worse things were going to get.

Then there was a hearing at Croydon Magistrates Court to negotiate, which unsurprisingly overshadowed Ferguson's trip to Buckingham Palace to collect a CBE. Cantona and Ince both faced charges of common assault, and the pair were mobbed on arrival at the court. Ince was later cleared, but Cantona was found guilty and sentenced to two weeks in jail. 'Ooh ahh prisona,' led the *Sun* the following morning. 'Frog off,' said the ever-PC *Daily Star*. His French lawyer Jean-Jacques Bertrand immediately appealed the decision and a second hearing saw his punishment commuted to 120 hours of community service, to be spent coaching football to children in Manchester.

Having stayed tight-lipped throughout, Cantona took the press conference afterwards as his opportunity to respond. Surveying a room full of journalists who had spent the last three months baying for his blood, he leant back and gave a wry, knowing smiling. This time the story would be told on his terms. 'When the seagulls follow the trawler… ' he began, before taking a sip of water as punctuation, flashbulbs flickering wildly, '…it is because… they think sardines… will be thrown into the sea. Thank you very much.' And with that he got up and left the gathered media to stare into their laptops.

His metaphor that the press were no more than scavengers, with Cantona the all-powerful force that kept them alive, was hardly advanced in the philosophy stakes. But this was football, where clichés speak louder than words and players are barely expected to string a sentence together. Yet from the man they called a heathen came the most eloquent attack on the media in British football history. It was brilliantly conceived, apparently with the help of United staff in a London hotel room, and it only enhanced Cantona's legend – that and his earning potential as a counter-culture god.

The big question now was whether Cantona would repay the faith of the football club who had stood by him, and return to the field in the colours of United. It seemed unlikely. His FA ban ran until 30 September 1995 and the speculation was very much that he'd take the opportunity to move abroad, most likely to join Inter Milan in Italy, and leave the media circus behind. 'Eric's love affair with England has been affected by all of this,' his lawyer Betrand told the *Independent*. 'It will never be the same again because of what has happened. Can you blame him?'

Conventional wisdom suggested he'd leave, but Cantona was never one for convention. Having served out his community service, which more or less consisted of him talking about football and having the odd kickabout with fans who worshipped him, he appeared to have come upon a new sense of purpose. And to the huge relief of everybody at Old Trafford, El Nutter decided the best way to make things right was to return to the red No. 7 shirt and make his next statement of intent with a football at his feet – rather than a Crystal Palace supporter.

Perhaps watching the unbearably tense culmination of the 1994/95 season helped made up his mind. United entered the last game of the Premier League season two points behind Blackburn, with the leaders away at Liverpool and Ferguson taking his team to face West Ham at Upton Park. United were relying on their bitter rivals to do them a monumental favour, and Liverpool fans played on the suggestion their team would roll over by booing them when they walked out – then cheering King Kenny and his men. Of course, Roy Evans' team would do anything but that.

Ferguson controversially left Hughes out of his starting line-up, opting to go into a must-win game with Cole as a lone striker and United set up in a cautious 4-5-1 formation. He justified the decision afterwards by saying he wanted 'to take the wind out of West Ham's sails in the first half', and had always planned to bring him on later. When Hughes replaced Butt at half-time, United were 1-0 down to a fine finish from his namesake Michael. Meanwhile Blackburn were a Shearer goal to the good at Anfield and seemingly cruising to the title.

Things were about to get interesting. McClair headed home Gary Neville's free-kick early in the second half to bring United level, then John Barnes delivered an equaliser for Liverpool. The news quickly reached the United fans at Upton Park and they erupted in celebration. All they needed now was for United to find a winner in the remaining

26 minutes and Liverpool to hold firm or better at Anfield. But try as they might, United shot blank after blank. Cole was denied by a fine save and then missed a glaring chance after being set up by Scholes. Hughes headed over. The game finished 1-1.

'We did more than we needed to win the game but maybe fate was against us,' Ferguson reflected afterwards, but he knew only too well his team had simply failed to take their chances. And while United were left to ponder what could have been, Walker's nouveau riche Blackburn joyously celebrated the title at Anfield. Liverpool had beaten them 2-1, but to the great relief of their supporters this would not be remembered as the day they handed the enemy the biggest prize in English football. Unsurprisingly they joined in the party.

Cole in particular was singled out for criticism for United's profligacy at Upton Park. United's big money signing had scored an impressive 12 goals in 17 Premier League appearances since his arrival, but he'd also missed a hatful. PJ and I were there when he scored five at Old Trafford in a ridiculous 9-0 win over Ipswich, and it was typical of his United career that we left talking about whether he should have got ten. That's the twisted mind of a football fan for you, and you almost wonder if Cole would have garnered greater acclaim had he scored a third of his goals, and missed a third of his sitters.

That 9-0 made for an interesting first game for PJ's wife Tracie. Having kept a healthy distance from her husband's obsession for years she was finally talked into making a pilgrimage for that one. Naturally PJ decided afterwards she'd have to come to every United game for the rest of his life if she had that effect on the team, but I'm not sure she ever went again. One man's 9-0 is another woman's 0-0 I suppose you could say. Perhaps she knew she'd seen the perfect performance and it could never be beaten. Perhaps she'd simply seen enough.

Goal king Cole was cup-tied for the FA Cup Final against Everton the following weekend. United were up against Everton in a reprisal of their 1985 Wembley showdown, and this time it was the team in red who arrived as favourites. Everton had spent the early part of the season near the foot of the table and eventually finished a disappointing 15th. But manager Joe Royle had cultivated a team of footballing

Orks who scrapped for everything and nobody expected them to go quietly. Royle called them his 'Dogs of War'.

Cantona was there for the occasion, but even his aura could do nothing to stop United suffering a second crushing disappointment in the space of a week. Paul Rideout's first-half goal was the difference, with Everton's veteran goalkeeper Neville Southall putting in a virtu-oso performance to keep United at bay. A double save from Scholes' efforts was particularly impressive, along with a full-stretch dive to hold a Pallister header. The game finished 1-0 and United's miserable campaign was complete.

It felt as if United's luck had run out. In the previous two seasons Ferguson had masterminded the coup of Cantona's signature and watched on as time and again his team hit the right notes exactly when he needed them to. There was the late Bruce show against Sheffield Wednesday in 1993 that spurred them to a first title, the Hughes equaliser against Oldham in the 1994 FA Cup semi-final, the brilliant comeback win against City at Maine Road. But for whatever reason Ferguson's team were short on magic at the business end of the 1994/95 season.

Ferguson was livid. A season that began with United as all-conquering Double winners ready to dine out like never before had ended with a paltry UEFA Cup spot. It was a monumental comedown for the club and their fans alike, and the gut reaction was to point towards Cantona's absence as the defining factor in the failure. He had been the catalyst for United's success, so it stood to reason his suspension had prompted their failures. Ferguson was unequivocal, 'The Cantona situation cost us everything,' he said.

Of course, the 'Cantona situation' encompassed a whole lot more than the loss of the Frenchman on the field. It was an all-consuming soap opera that followed United wherever they went in the second half of the 1994/95 season – a football story that served rolling sports news like no other before it and was fed to those ravenous seagulls on a daily basis in one form of another. No matter what happened at Upton Park and Wembley, that January night in South London would always have defined United's campaign.

Thankfully for Ferguson and United, his return would define the next one. But this time three members of Ferguson's first great team would not be joining him. In what looked from the outside a shockingly ill-conceived yard sale, Ince, Hughes and Kanchelskis were all sold before the 1995/96 season came around, and nobody brought in to replace them. It was a curious move that had United fans wondering if our club were in financial difficulties or the manager gone mad.

Ferguson knew exactly what he was doing.

PART TWO
(1995/96 TO 2001/02)

CHAPTER 7
THE KIDS ARE ALRIGHT

For most of us the late teens and early 20s are spent drinking heavily and avoiding responsibility. Sometimes it was a genuine effort to get up in the morning, let alone get through a day's work. You've got to wear the right clothes, like the right music and go to the right places. And with all that to worry about, the rest of your life can seem an unwelcome distraction.

I spent the summer of 1995 having a good time and working the occasional part-time job to justify my existence. Oasis and Blur were the new musical superpowers and they were on heavy rotation in the cars and bedrooms of the next generation up and down the country. Britpop had arrived and many hours would be whiled away debating which band was superior – the snarling Mancunians or the chirpy Southerners. They might have been United-hating City fans, but it was still Oasis every time for me.

For Paul Scholes, Nicky Butt, David Beckham, John O'Kane, and Phil and Gary Neville, however, there was no time for such distractions. On 19 August 1995 all six were in United's squad for the season's opener against Aston Villa. It was a remarkably bold show of faith by their manager, who sent out a team of unprecedented youth and inexperience in a competition he and United's fans held above all others. To no one's surprise, the kids were schooled. They were beaten 3-1, with Beckham scoring the consolation with a dipping drive late on.

Andy Cole, Steve Bruce and Ryan Giggs (still only 21) were all out injured, but that didn't stop Alan Hansen famously pointing out the inadequacies of Ferguson's squad on *Match of the Day* that night. 'The trick is always to buy when you are strong,' he said, '… You'll never win anything with kids.' It was a piece of punditry that has been widely ridiculed ever since, but on the evidence of that afternoon's fragile performance at Villa Park, Hansen had a point. What he didn't know was just how good these 'kids' were. And just how much they wanted to prove him wrong.

United responded. Ferguson welcomed back his captain Bruce and they won their next four league games on the spin – beating West Ham, Wimbledon, Blackburn and Everton. Cole returned with a goal at Wimbledon, and Giggs came off the bench to score at Goodison Park. Beckham, Scholes, Gary Neville and Butt kept their places in the starting line-up and it appeared that with a little experience around them United's fledglings could get the job done. Whether they could win the title was another question entirely, and I have to say I didn't fancy their chances.

Serious doubts remained over United's transfer policy. After protracted negotiations Andrei Kanchelskis finally joined Everton for £5 million. In the summer Paul Ince had left for Inter Milan for £6 million, and Mark Hughes said goodbye to United for a second time to join Chelsea for £1.5 million. These were three players who'd starred in Ferguson's first great team, the 1993/94 Double winners, and there was unsurprisingly some scepticism surrounding his decision to sell them.

Ince's departure had been coming. Ferguson called him a 'fucking bottler' after United were ripped apart by Barcelona at the Camp Nou, and he blamed him for giving the ball away to Everton's Dave Watson in the FA Cup Final, a mistake which led to their winner. Ince was a big personality, the self-styled 'Guv'nor' of the United dressing room, but Ferguson was beginning to sense he was acting on his own authority. Moreover, with Butt, Scholes and Beckham in the ascendancy, he saw the offer from Inter Milan as seriously good business for United.

The fans, myself included, didn't agree. We'd seen Ince rampaging through midfield in the formidable 1994 side and saw no reason why he couldn't do it again. He had fine technique and he was one of those players fans instantly relate to – a wild-eyed swashbuckler who gave the impression he was ready to fight everybody in the world when he put on the shirt. United fans respected that. We'd respect him less when he later joined Liverpool, but that's another story.

There's no question United lost a unique character when Ince left the club. Only recently a story came to light of him bringing an air rifle to United's training ground after Ferguson had given him the famous 'hair-dryer' treatment. 'He must have had something about him to threaten Fergie with a gun,' Steve Bruce told the *Daily Express*. 'We saw him do it. He poked the gun through the door and he was only 22 at the time.'

Ince was an exaggerated version of a personality who has inhabited every football team you've ever played for. If you've known the game, you've met him. I've played school football, Sunday football, non-league football, park football, street football, beach football, even a bit of football in America, and he's always there.

He's the man who sees himself as an entertainer, the people's champion and somewhat of an anarchist to boot. He shouts louder and lives louder than anybody else in the dressing room, and he desperately needs you to know it. A psychologist would say underlying insecurities are the catalyst for such behaviour, which is maybe why he spends every waking hour seeking to appear as emboldened and confident as possible. Part of that make-up made Ince a world-class midfielder; the other part made him an infuriating man to manage and, at times, a loose cannon. Ferguson had seen enough of the latter.

But as one larger-than-life personality left United, so another returned to the fray. Just over eight months after launching his right Nike boot into an abusive Crystal Palace supporter at Selhurst Park, Cantona was available for selection again. And typical of the great man's sense of timing, he would make his comeback at Old Trafford in the televised Sunday afternoon clash with Liverpool on 1 October 1995. 'I've been punished for my mistakes,' he said in a brilliant Nike advert to coincide with his return. 'Now it's somebody else's turn.'

The hype machine was in full flow. 'Liberation day for the French enigma,' read one headline. 'Return of the prodigal son,' said another.

Even the *Washington Times* in America picked up on the story. 'Return of the banned,' came the opening refrain in their article, which pulled together the fates of Cantona and Diego Maradona, who was set to return the very same weekend for Boca Juniors after serving a drugs ban relating to the 1994 World Cup. 'To loving fandom Maradona, Cantona back in action', read the headline in the *Rocky Mount News* – a local title on America's East Coast. It was the biggest story in world sport. It was inescapable.

Cantona would start. Ferguson had seen enough in training to justify the decision and in Scholes and Beckham he had two willing substitutes ready to fill in if the Frenchman faded in the second half. United were second in the league but they needed a lift, having been knocked out of the UEFA Cup midweek by unfancied Russian side Rotor Volgograd. Who better to deliver it than their talisman in exile returned to his adoring masses? The footballing Count of Monte Cristo was ready for his revenge.

It took Cantona two minutes to demonstrate to United's fans and their manager what they'd been missing. Having collected possession in an advance position on the left he picked out Butt with a wonderful clipped cross, and the young midfielder took the ball in his stride with one touch before ramming it past David James to put United 1-0 up. Things could have got even better when Butt laid on a great chance for Lee Sharpe, but he shot straight at the goalkeeper with his unfavoured right foot when he should have scored.

Life was good. The sun was shining on Old Trafford and the prodigal son was back in business, but Robbie Fowler was about to crash the party. First he smashed an unstoppable shot past Schmeichel from a tight angle to bring Liverpool level, fizzing a drive with such power that it hit the net before United's keeper could even get his hands up. Then, early in the second half, he held off the challenge of Gary Neville to advance into an almost identical position. This time Schmeichel rushed out to close him down, but Fowler reacted with an exquisite curled lob into the far corner to put Liverpool 2-1 up.

This was not in the script for Cantona's return. But there was still time for United's No. 7 to ensure his name dominated the headlines the following morning. The opportunity arrived on 70 minutes, when Jamie Redknapp was adjudged to have tripped Giggs and referee David Elleray pointed to the penalty spot. Up stepped Cantona, with the ball under his arm and his collar standing to attention with the 35,000 fans inside Old Trafford (the stadium was under development at the time). He placed the ball down calmly, walked back to his mark and after a brief hesitation passed it calmly to the bottom right-hand corner as James dived to the left.

'You can't save a penalty from a brilliant penalty taker and Eric Cantona was the best,' James would admit later in his career. 'His technique was so good it was a joke. After he retired I found out his secret, he was watching the keeper. As soon as the keeper's knee went, Cantona took the ball the other way and left him stranded. For any keeper a bent knee is a point of no return.'

The game finished 2-2, but United almost won it with what would have been one the great Old Trafford goals. Substitute Beckham clipped a ball in towards Cantona on the right edge of the box. The Frenchman dummied and let it run to Giggs, who cushioned it back into the path of his run. Cantona was now inside the box and with Liverpool's defenders expecting a shot he stubbed a disguised cross to Cole on the penalty spot. The striker launched instinctively into an acrobatic overhead volley and the ball bounced just wide of the upright.

Cantona was back, still some way from his imperious best, but his mere presence had a galvanising effect on United. The younger players, Beckham especially, idolised his professionalism and the way he approached his craft. His habit of staying late on the training ground rubbed off on the next generation, and his example helped foster a work ethic at United that Ferguson had been trying to develop since taking over in 1986. It's ironic when you consider his disciplinary problems, but Cantona was in many ways the ultimate role model.

With their talisman alongside them, Ferguson's young guns continued to ram Hansen's words down his throat in the run-up to Christmas. Scholes scored a derby winner against City, then a brace in a 4-1 win against Chelsea at Stamford Bridge. He got another in a 4-1 defeat of Southampton, with Giggs providing a double. Then

Beckham got his third of the season in a 1-1 draw with Chelsea at Old Trafford, with another superb strike from outside the box. Meanwhile Gary Neville and Butt continued to command their places, with the younger Neville, Phil, usually lurking on the bench.

But defeats against Liverpool, Leeds and Tottenham meant 1996 arrived with United some distance behind league leaders Newcastle United – who under Kevin Keegan were playing some breathtaking attacking football. The Toon Army had Peter Beardsley and Les Ferdinand doing the business up front, with their very own French maverick, David Ginola, producing flashes of inspiration from midfield. Ex-United winger Keith Gillespie was also making a contribution, having joined in the deal that saw Cole move to Old Trafford.

Newcastle were the people's team that season. Keegan's philosophy was to attack in numbers and let the scoreline look after itself, and it was working. They were scoring goals for fun at St James' Park and seemed intent on delivering blockbuster entertainment every time they played. In the cynical new age of the Premier League, Keegan's men were an ode to how the grand old game could still be played. In their naivety, lay their appeal. And by comparison United were cast as a cynical, corporate machine intent on global domination at any cost. It was good vs. evil, and good was romping away with it.

All United could do was win their games and hope Newcastle came unstuck. It was time for Cantona to come into his own, and when he scored the winner in a fiery 1-0 victory against West Ham on 22 January it proved a sign of things to come. Between the Upton Park game and the FA Cup Final at Wembley in May he would score 14 times, with six of those the decisive goals in 1-0 wins. It was as if he felt he had a debt to repay to the fans, and to the manager who'd stuck by him throughout. Once again he was the difference.

The two title rivals met at St James' Park on 4 March, with Newcastle four points ahead and a game in hand. Keegan gave debuts to water-carrying midfielder David Batty and Colombian Faustino Asprilla, a striker of outrageous potential who could score from 40 yards in one mood and miss an open goal from two in another. The hope was the new additions to his squad would see his side to the title, but they didn't get off to the best of starts – thanks largely to the brilliance of Schmeichel in the United goal.

The Dane gave a blockbuster performance that day. Newcastle were rampant in the first half, but time and again Schmeichel was on hand to deny them a deserved lead. Twice he thwarted Les Ferdinand from close range, diving directly at the striker's feet then reacting brilliantly to parry his shot. He was quite simply immense. Ferguson later said the 1995/96 season was when Schmeichel persuaded him he was the best goalkeeper he'd ever seen. There was no better example of his influence than the display that took United into the break level at St James' Park when they could easily have been 3-0 or 4-0 down. 'If you've ever seen a team hammered 0-0 that was it,' said Keegan afterwards.

Dad and I were watching the game at home and seriously concerned. United were being out-played and the fizzing attacking football we'd grown accustomed to from the men in red was being produced almost exclusively by the opposition. The 'Anyone but United' brigade were no doubt watching in raptures, and we could only hope they'd be deflated by a smash-and-grab second half from the champions. But the way it was looking, it would take another 45 minutes of 'Super Schmeichel' to escape with a point, let alone three.

In his half-time talk Ferguson asked his team if they wanted the title as much as Newcastle. He got the desired reaction and suddenly United began to play with the confidence and movement we knew they were capable of. Soon enough they went ahead, when Cantona volleyed home Phil Neville's cross at the far post, and for Newcastle there was no coming back. United had snatched another 1-0 win and regained the momentum. 'It's a race now,' said a flushed Ferguson afterwards. 'It's going to be one incredible finish.'

The Newcastle game had been billed as the showdown that would define the season, but as it turned out that honour went to a comical verbal exchange between Ferguson and Keegan a month later. Ferguson had just watched his team battle to a 1-0 win at Old Trafford, against a dogged Leeds who despite being reduced to ten men fought for everything and provided fierce resistance, when he took the chance to make a very public point. 'You think for some of these teams it's more important to get a result against Manchester United and stop them winning the league than anything else,' he said. 'To me they're cheating their manager. Of course, when it comes to Newcastle you wait and see the difference... you know?'

Ferguson maintains that it was never his intention to antagonise Keegan, just to send a message to their upcoming opponents, but the Newcastle manager was beyond furious. What he did next would come to define his career in management. After his side beat Leeds 1-0 at Elland Road thanks to a headed winner from Gillespie he took the chance to respond in sensational fashion on live television. 'I think you've got to send a tape of this game to Alex Ferguson, haven't you? Isn't that what he asked for?' he began. And he was just getting started.

'That sort of stuff, we're better than that... I've kept really quiet, but I'll tell you something. He went down in my estimation when he said that. We have not resorted to that. But I tell you... you can tell him now if you're watching. We're still fighting for this title. And he's got to go to Middlesbrough and get something. And I'll tell you honestly... I will love it if we beat them. Love it.'

The nation watched on in astonishment. Newcastle's manager had unravelled on live television and handed Sky Sports the kind of global PR you simply can't buy. Cantona had gifted them the kung-fu kick in 1995, now Keegan delivered the manager breakdown. It was like the moment Michael Douglas gets out of his car in the film *Falling Down*. In those gigantic Sky headphones he suddenly looked like a small boy whose emotions had got the better of him. Sitting at home, Ferguson said he felt a tinge of guilt.

Some have argued it was a watershed moment for the psychological battles to come. Keegan may have been an easy victim, but Ferguson was all too aware of the effect he'd had on his main rival that season. With just a few well-chosen words he'd brought about a show of weakness that sent a transparent message to the players and fans of both clubs. It was no surprise when United eased to a 3-0 win against Middlesbrough to seal the title, while Keegan's team could only draw their remaining games against Tottenham and Nottingham Forest.

United went to Wembley for the FA Cup Final with a historic second Double in their sights, to face a Liverpool side they'd drawn with at Old Trafford and lost to at Anfield – a Liverpool who had more motivation than most to deny Ferguson and his team the perfect finale to a superb campaign.

The big news before the game was the ridiculous Liverpool attire. Roy Evans' team were bedecked in cream Armani suits as they strolled out onto the Wembley turf. The so-called 'Spice Boys' of James, Redknapp and Steve McManaman, Stan Collymore and Jason McAteer were described by Ferguson as looking like 'a squad of bakers'. His team, in contrast, wore business-like dark suits and were left to focus on the business of winning the FA Cup. That and laughing at Liverpool's ridiculous clobber obviously.

The game was a largely forgettable affair, with Liverpool failing to do those flamboyant suits justice when they changed into their equally appalling green and white away strip, and United not much better. Beckham had a good shot saved by James in the first half and Cantona was denied by a sharp stop at the near post in the second, but that was about it. The newly crowned Footballer of the Year was captain for the day in Bruce's absence, but far from his influential best for most of the game.

Then, with five minutes left, came the moment Cantona's script demanded. Beckham swung over a cross from the right and James stretched to punch clear. There waiting just outside the box was Cantona, who adjusted his stance in a split-second, let the ball drop just in front of him and volleyed it through a sea of Liverpool defenders and into the net. 'What a fairy story for Eric Cantona,' came the commentary. And with the final whistle Cantona's redemption was complete.

United became the first club to win the 'double Double', and the celebrations began in earnest when Cantona walked the Wembley steps to collect the famous trophy. 'Now we can go on a nice holiday,' he said afterwards. When asked how the experience contrasted with the misery of Selhurst Park and all that came with it, he simply shrugged his shoulders. 'That's life,' he said. It may not have been as profound as his 'Seagulls follow the trawler' speech, but Cantona could now let his football do the talking, and that was just about the most eloquent prose in the business.

But to make the 1995/96 season solely about Cantona is an injustice to the contribution of his superb teammates, and in particular the young players whose readiness for the task had been widely doubted at the outset of the campaign. United's next generation, of Beckham, Butt, Scholes and the Neville brothers, had played a key role in the success and Ferguson's faith in youth had been spectacularly affirmed. Like Sir Matt Busby before him, Ferguson had countenanced that age is no barrier when the players in question are blessed with the requisite talent and belief in their abilities. For the Busby Babes, read the Fergie Fledglings.

Panning around Wembley the cameras picked up on a fans' banner that summed it up perfectly: 'You don't win 'owt with kids do you Mr Hansen?' it read.

CHAPTER 8
COMING OF AGE

The summer of 1996 was a celebration. United had just done the 'double Double', Euro 96 brought football home for the first time in 30 years and I'd finally finished my A-levels. In light of having no idea what I wanted to do, I decided to put off university, opting instead to go 'travelling' around Europe in the autumn with my best mate Ben. With no responsibilities to distract me, I was free to concentrate fully on the football, and the revelry, at hand.

Terry Venables picked both Neville brothers in his England squad, which was captained by Arsenal's Tony Adams and leant heavily on the man at the top of Ferguson's wanted list that summer – Blackburn Rovers' free-scoring striker Alan Shearer. Shearer was partnered in attack with Tottenham's cultured forward Teddy Sheringham, and he furthered his reputation by finishing as the tournament's top scorer with five goals.

In the group stages, England got my 18th birthday off to a cracking start with a rousing 2-0 win against Scotland. Paul Gascoigne scored the brilliant second, outrageously chipping the ball over Colin Hendry before crashing a volley into the bottom corner. It was the perfect aperitif to the house party my parents unwisely let me host that evening, which ended with unfamiliar bodies strewn across their lawn and unfamiliar stains on the carpets. Fourteen years on, they're still finding beer bottles and cigarette butts in the hedges.

Three days later, with the smell of bleach still thick in the air, Dad and I sat down to watch Venables' team rip Holland to shreds. Shearer and Sheringham both scored twice and I'm not sure England have surpassed the performance since. The 5-1 win against Germany in Munich was clinical, but this was England playing a breed of flowing, swaggering football that we didn't know was possible from a group of men born of our shores. It really was like watching Brazil.

I watched the penalty shootout victory over Spain in the quarter-finals from behind my hands and punched the air ferociously with Stuart Pearce as he faced the demons of Italia 90 like a man possessed. But it proved only a brief respite from the spot-kick agony we've come to expect. England drew 1-1 with Germany in the semis and after the first four penalty takers scored, Gareth Southgate took his place in England's hall of shame by missing the last. Typically, the Germans went on to win the final.

By the time the tournament was over Ferguson was more determined than ever to put Shearer in a Manchester United shirt. United put in a formal bid of £12 million the day after the final, but Blackburn turned it down. Just over a week later Kevin Keegan's Newcastle entered the race with a bid of £10 million, but they too were rebuffed.

Then came the farcical news that United had listed Shearer in their party to travel for a pre-season friendly against Inter Milan. The hoax was down to an employee at their travel agency, but it nonetheless served to rile Rovers, who felt United were approaching the Shearer situation too aggressively and issued a 'hands off' warning. In reaction Rovers faxed a £4 million offer for Eric Cantona to Old Trafford – knowing full well they wouldn't have sold him for five times that amount.

What followed were lengthy discussions between Shearer and Ferguson, Shearer and Keegan, and Shearer and Jack Walker, Blackburn's millionaire owner. The story seemed to run and run. Until finally, in late July, the England striker made up his mind. He would go to Newcastle for a world-record fee of £15 million. For Keegan, after the embarrassment of his televised unravelling, it represented a major public victory. Ferguson was disappointed, but he took the opportunity to state Newcastle were now clear favourites for the title.

'He's a crafty old so-and-so,' was Keegan's response. 'It's exactly what I would say if I had just won the Double. Please God he's proved right.' He wasn't.

Despite missing out on Shearer, United still managed to bring in a host of new players that summer. On the strength of their performances at Euro 96, Ferguson signed Czech international midfielder Karel Poborsky from Slavia Prague for £3.5 million and Johan Cruyff's son Jordi from Barcelona for £1.5 million. The international shopping spree also took in the purchases of Norwegian pair Ronny Johnsen and Ole Gunnar Solskjaer, and Dutch goalkeeper Raimond van der Gouw.

As the new players flooded in, so some of Ferguson's old guard sensed the time was right to drift downstream. To his manager's great sadness veteran Steve Bruce ended his glorious United career to join First Division Birmingham on a free transfer. Paul Parker also left on a free, to Derby County, while Lee Sharpe made the move to Leeds for around £4 million. All three had begun to doubt their claims to a regular first-team spot, and the new arrivals wouldn't help their cause.

Bruce had been invaluable to Ferguson. If Cantona was the inspiration for United's return to prominence, then Bruce was the foundation that allowed the Frenchman to flourish. Nobody could forget the late goals he scored against Sheffield Wednesday at Old Trafford, or his unflinching commitment to the cause whenever he put on the shirt. He made over 400 appearances and left Old Trafford with three league titles, three FA Cup wins, a League Cup triumph and a Cup-Winners' Cup medal – that and the admiration of every fan who saw him play. 'It's a terrible wrench leaving United,' he said.

Sharpe was simply desperate for regular first-team football. He'd spent the summer watching Euro 96 and wondering how he might win his England place back without playing every week. There was no question Giggs and now Beckham outranked him in the Old Trafford pecking order. Injuries and a bout of viral meningitis had cost him vital ground during Ferguson's reign, and he wanted a fresh start. Sadly, his time at Leeds would be blighted by more injury problems and his career would never recapture the highs of the pop star years he spent marauding down United's left flank.

After all the transfer shenanigans with Shearer, it was ironic that the world's most expensive player would make his competitive debut for Newcastle against the team he spurned, in the Charity Shield at

Wembley. The Toon Army came for a coronation, but the day belonged to Ferguson's Double winners, who played brilliantly to win 4-0 and make a sizeable statement of intent ahead of the season proper. Cantona calmly slotted the first, with Nicky Butt, David Beckham and Roy Keane completing the rout. Cantona also gave a glimpse of his fiery temper, when he threw compatriot Philippe Albert to the ground in the second half. The nature of the contest meant he escaped with a yellow card.

United's opening league game would see the Frenchman return to his old stamping ground, Selhurst Park, but this time the headlines belonged to the man who idolised him, David Beckham. The 21-year-old with his floppy hair, movie star jaw line and that Hollywood smile had made huge strides in the 1995/96 campaign, but on Saturday 17 August 1996 he sent his star into the stratosphere.

With United two goals to the good and the clock running down some of the fans began to filter out of the stadium – among them my good friend John and his young son, making their first United pilgrimage. They'd seen goals from Cantona and Irwin and three points come easily to their team that afternoon. Why not make early strides to beat the traffic?

But as they made their way down the stairwell and away from the ground towards the train station a huge roar served to tell them they'd missed something special. 'No big deal,' John said to me later that night. 'Probably just the best goal of the season and one of the most iconic football moments of the decade.'

Beckham had collected the ball inside his own half, looked up to see Wimbledon's keeper Neil Sullivan off his line, and floated a miraculous shot over his head and into the net. The young starlet turned to the crowd with his arms outstretched and accepted their exultation as if he'd been readying himself for it his whole life. It was still only August, but Ferguson hailed it as 'the goal of the season', and wasted no time in suggesting his young charge was ready for international recognition under England's new manager Glenn Hoddle. Beckham had begun his heady rise to becoming the most famous footballer on the planet.

Hoddle reacted by including him in his first squad for a World Cup qualifier in Moldova on 1 September, and showed his faith by immediately thrusting him into the starting line-up in midfield alongside Paul Gascoigne, Paul Ince and Andy Hinchcliffe. England won 3-0, with Beckham involved in two of the goals, and United's sparkling new star was on his way to collecting a record-breaking 115 caps for the national side.

But Beckham could do nothing to stop United's mini-collapse in October. First came a humiliating 5-0 hammering at the hands of league leaders Newcastle, which predictably saw Shearer on the scoresheet. David Ginola was inspired at St James' Park, weaving in and out of despairing United tackles and scoring a sublime second goal past Schmeichel. The goalkeeper's miserable night was rounded off by an audacious chip by Albert – which made for quite a contrast to the contest six months before when he had kept Newcastle at bay with one of the best displays of his career.

Further embarrassment was just around the corner. A 6-3 away loss against Southampton made for a second humiliating trip to The Dell in successive seasons. Towards the end of the 1995/96 campaign Ferguson and his team had been widely ridiculed after blaming their short-lived grey away strip for a dire first-half performance. The players came in at half-time 3-0 down and apparently complaining they couldn't pick each other out against the backdrop of the crowd. Ferguson ordered them to change shirts, but it didn't prevent a 3-1 defeat. Sceptics should note United lost four of the five games they played in that strip – which was officially retired two days after the Southampton debacle.

This time there were no such straws to grasp at, only the heels of Matt Le Tissier as he inspired the Saints to a thrilling victory, treating Schmeichel to another stunning lob along the way. United wore white and blue, but it was another grey day on the south coast for Ferguson and his men.

October's slump continued with a Champions League group-stage defeat to Turkish side Fenerbahce at Old Trafford, which remarkably represented United's first home loss in Europe. It 'put a blot on my career that I had always dreaded', Ferguson wrote in *Managing My Life*. A few days later came a 2-1 home defeat to Chelsea in the league, which made it three Premiership defeats in succession to an aggregate score of 13-4.

As Ben and I made final preparations to hit the railways of Europe, United were in the grips of a worrying slump. Bookmakers had slashed the odds to 3-1 that Ferguson would be gone by the end of the season and, ridiculously for a team who'd just won the Double, United were only 100-1 to get relegated. The newspapers rounded on Ferguson's young team and speculated they had run dry of inspiration. Jordi Cruyff didn't help matters when he told the *Independent*, 'When you've been losing like this it eats away at you.'

All attentions were now focused on whether Ferguson could get his team into the knockout stages of the Champions League. A home loss to defending champions Juventus in November didn't help, and progress rested on the final round of the group stages on the evening of 4 December. United had to go to Rapid Vienna and get a result, while relying on Juventus to beat Fenerbahce. To Ferguson's great relief, United and Juve both won 2-0, and both progressed to the quarter-finals.

Meanwhile, Ben and I were touring the football stadiums of Europe. We took in the San Siro in Milan, the Olympic Stadium in Rome and, most impressive of all, the Camp Nou in Barcelona. Museums and art galleries could come later in life we reasoned. And who's to say football stadiums aren't as culturally relevant as ancient monuments and historic churches?

At the Camp Nou we made a financial decision typical of our truncated adventures. Our three-day stay coincided with a Cup-Winners' Cup meeting between Barcelona and Red Star Belgrade, and for the price of a week in a decent hotel we were offered a pair of tickets. This was the Barcelona of Hristo Stoichkov, Luis Figo, Ronaldo and Pep Guardiola, managed by the great Bobby Robson. The credit cards came out and the cheeky tout who saw us coming soon had his reward.

Barca won 3-1 and we were left wondering how United could ever hope to win the Champions League if a team as good as this weren't even in it. Figo and Ronaldo were sensational, and Stoichkov made a cameo appearance from the bench that gave the impression his left foot was a golf club. Add into the mix a few flares thrown in our direction from the visiting Red Star fans and it was truly a night to remember – well worth sacrificing the entire cultural offering of Barcelona for. Thankfully, I'd be back.

By the time we returned from our travels, United were speeding down the road to recovery. After losing at home to Chelsea at the start of November they went unbeaten in the league until the following March. The goals of Solskjaer played no small part in the revival, and the Norwegian would end his first season as United's top scorer with 19 goals. Cantona scored 15, with Beckham chipping in with an impressive 12 from midfield. Andy Cole missed the first half of the season after Neil Ruddock broke both his legs in a reserve match, but he still managed to score seven times.

Ultimately, United coasted to the title, finishing seven points clear of Newcastle, Arsenal and Liverpool. Arsenal, under new manager Arsène Wenger, had led the table briefly early in the season and were beginning to look like serious contenders. Wenger was orchestrating a cultural revolution at the north London club, and his success was destined to usher in a new rivalry at football's top table. The Frenchman had Ferguson and his side in his sights.

But while United's fourth title in five years paid tribute to Ferguson's mastery of the domestic stage, his team was once again found wanting in Europe. Having reached the semi-finals courtesy of a devastating 4-0 defeat of Porto at Old Trafford, United stood one tie away from a final in, of all places, Munich. Bearing in mind the club's tragic association with the German city, there was a romantic pull to the European quest that served only to exaggerate Ferguson's desire for success.

It was now 29 years since the generation of Best, Law and Charlton swept aside Benfica 4-1 at Wembley to bring United its first and only European Cup triumph. Ferguson knew to be considered alongside the great Sir Matt Busby he had to end the wait, but to his eternal frustration his team could find no way past Borussia Dortmund in the semi-finals. United lost 1-0 in Germany and by the same scoreline at

Old Trafford, missing what Ferguson called a 'barrowload' of chances along the way.

United had a ridiculous number of attempts on goal in the home leg, but no matter what they tried, the Germans somehow kept them at bay. It was like a cruel joke designed for the amusement of everybody who wanted Ferguson's team to fail. 'I've never seen a team defend like Dortmund for so long and be fortunate enough to keep us out for the entire match,' wrote Brian McClair in his book *Odd Man Out*. 'It just wasn't to be.'

Ferguson's team would come again in Europe, but they would do so without their captain and talisman Cantona. A matter of days after United wrapped up their season with a 2-0 victory over West Ham at Old Trafford, Cantona called a meeting with his manager at the Mottram Hall hotel. He told Ferguson he was retiring from football and there was no chance of anybody changing his mind. He'd become tired of United's rampant commercialisation and the club's unwillingness to invest in high-profile signings. The fire inside him had gone out, and Ferguson knew straight away there was nothing he could do.

He was resigned to losing the player he credited above all others with bringing the good times back to United. He was 'as talented, exciting and productive a footballer as I have ever imagined,' Ferguson wrote in *Managing My Life*. But he was more than that. He was the strutting embodiment of absolute, unflinching belief, and his unerring confidence rubbed off on everybody around him. To his teammates he was a role model, and to the fans he was nothing short of a god.

When Cantona arrived United were eyeing a return to former glories. By the time he left they'd become the dominant force in English football. 'I am not a man, I am Cantona,' he had said. You couldn't help but agree.

The King was dead. Long live the King.

CHAPTER 9
OUT-GUNNERED

When Alex Ferguson arrived at Old Trafford in 1986, Liverpool were the all-conquering force in English football. They'd been champions in eight of the previous 11 seasons and won four European Cups in the space of a decade. Under player-manager Kenny Dalglish they'd just won the Double and with it a record 16th league title. Meanwhile, United were stuck on seven and hadn't graced the biggest European stage since the late 1960s. Ferguson captured the mood of every United fan in the country when he said he wanted to 'knock them off their f**king perch'. He was good to his word.

By the time the 1997/98 season kicked off Liverpool had gone seven years without a title, their longest barren patch since the late 1960s. They'd also not won an FA Cup in five years and were on their third manager since Dalglish resigned in February 1991. Some pointed to their failure to adapt to a changing football landscape, and a business model that was stuck in the 1980s. Others blamed the management of Graeme Souness. There was also the suggestion that the club had never really got over the 1989 Hillsborough disaster, which had deeply affected Dalglish and played a big role in his decision to leave the club.

But while United's return to prominence was arguably greased by Liverpool's decline, it was hard to prove that Ferguson's team had been the main reason. The re-emergence of United had simply coincided with a dip in fortunes at Anfield, who had finished outside the top three in all but one of the seasons since Ferguson won his first title in 1993. In United's first four championship-winning seasons under Ferguson, Liverpool had not once provided a genuine threat to their challenge in the second half of the season.

But as one great rival lay prone on the canvas, so another stepped into the ring, and with them a manager who would go head-to-head with Ferguson like no other before him. The 1997/98 season would be remembered as the making of Arsène Wenger, who heaved his Arsenal side up from distant second to champions, and won the Double. In just his second campaign in English football, the Frenchman did to Ferguson what the United manager had become accustomed to doing to others.

United made three major signings in the summer of 1997. Nobody could replace Eric Cantona, but the 31-year-old Teddy Sheringham offered his own brand of guile and vision to United's forward line. The England striker had handed in a transfer request at Tottenham and, with most reports suggesting he'd go abroad, possibly to Italy, United made a surprise move for his signature. An offer of £3.5 million was accepted and, having missed out twice on Alan Shearer, Ferguson had lured his international brother-in-arms to Old Trafford.

Sheringham said he left Spurs because he wanted to win trophies, but after a disappointing first season he'd be mocked ferociously for timing his move to coincide with a season that saw their great rivals Arsenal fill their cabinet. 'Oh Teddy Teddy, he went to Man United and he won f**k all,' came the famous refrain.

Ferguson's two other major signings were Erik Nevland and Henning Berg, who joined Ole Gunnar Solskjaer and Ronny Johnsen to take the quota of Norwegians in the United squad to four. Nevland was a teenage striker who'd impressed on trial at United, while Berg had been a key member of Blackburn's championship-winning side under Dalglish. The defender, who arrived with 44 international caps under his belt, cost United £5 million and signed a five-year contract.

The season began with Ferguson still fuming from England's decision to play David Beckham and Gary Neville in a four-team international tournament in Paris. 'Le Tournoi' was organised as a rehearsal for the World Cup the following summer, and the United manager was adamant his players should be rested following an exhausting season in which they'd both started over 40 games. 'You have to take a long-term view with young players,' he said. But the FA didn't listen and both players featured as England beat Italy and France, then lost to Brazil, on their way to winning the trophy.

Beckham and Neville were still suffering the effects when the Charity Shield came around in August, and as a result were eased into the season by Ferguson. United drew 1-1 with Ruud Gullit's Chelsea at Wembley and won on penalties.

The league campaign got off to a fine start. United travelled to Leeds having won five and drawn three of their opening eight games, and with doubts over how Ferguson would cope without Cantona beginning to fade into the background. Sheringham had opened his account in a 2-0 win against Everton, and Solskjaer and Andy Cole had both been in the goals too. Meanwhile, new club captain Roy Keane had set the example from midfield with two goals and some typically dynamic performances.

With Cantona gone, Keane was now the focal point. Ferguson identified him as United's most influential player and relied on him above all others to drive his team to further success. Keane was a remnant of the snarling 1994 Double winners, and he was ready and willing to go to war for United every time he crossed the white line. But with one innocuous flick of his boot at Elland Road, his season was over.

Keane was making a trademark run into the Leeds penalty area when Alf-Inge Haaland did exactly what you'd expect him to. He ran across Keane and put his body between the United midfielder and the ball. Keane flung a leg out and Haaland went to ground, but while the Norwegian was quickly back on his feet, Keane remained down, writhing in pain. Haaland gave him a volley of verbal abuse for his troubles, but was quickly ushered away by his teammates. The incident would come back to haunt him four years later, when Keane exacted a brutal revenge.

But for now Keane was left with torn cruciate ligaments and the diagnosis he wouldn't play again that season. Having lost Cantona, Ferguson was now robbed of the man he'd chosen to replace him as captain. It was the worst possible news, made all the more unpalatable by the fact United lost 1-0 at Leeds and surrendered their unbeaten record.

The onus was now very much on Beckham, Butt and Scholes to fill the void in midfield, but there was a genuine concern that United would be lightweight in mind and body without Keane. Ferguson's new signings Cruyff and Poborsky offered little in terms of physicality, and all three of the aforementioned fledglings were wiry, inexperienced and a long way from imposing. 'No team is quite the same without its best players, but when Roy's not in the United side there's something more than just his ability as a player that the rest have to do without', wrote David Beckham in *My Side*. 'For leadership and drive there's nobody who can touch him.'

I was seriously worried for United without their captain, but the mood was recovered somewhat with a trip to see Oasis at Earls Court that same evening. Touring their third album, *Be Here Now*, the Gallagher brothers were by now the most powerful force in British music, and the performance was a snarling celebration of everything that put them there.

Oasis were so influential that Noel Gallagher had been invited to spend the afternoon with new Prime Minister Tony Blair a few months earlier. They were also ardent City fans, who loved nothing more than announcing United's misfortune from the stage. It didn't stop United's players loving their music, but when Ryan Giggs requested tickets to a show at Maine Road some years later he was flatly refused. 'There's no way he's ever going to get them, he scored against City on his debut,' Gallagher said.

United returned to action the following Wednesday. Juventus were the visitors to Old Trafford and they went ahead inside a minute when Alessandro Del Piero brilliantly turned inside Berg, left Schmeichel for dead and passed the ball into an empty net. It was hardly the start Ferguson wanted after seeing his side fall at Leeds and his captain ruled out for the entire season, but you couldn't help but admire the skills of the diminutive Italian.

Watching on I feared a rout, but United equalised when Giggs burst down the left and picked out Sheringham at the far post, and gradually grew in confidence. Then, after Didier Deschamps was harshly sent off with 20 minutes left, Paul Scholes rounded the goalkeeper to put the home side 2-1 up. A superb game was rounded off with two great goals, one from either side. Giggs fired home from a tight angle to make it 3-1, before Zinedine Zidane curled a sublime free-kick past Schmeichel for a late consolation.

The win represented a notable scalp for United, who'd lost home and away to Juventus the previous season. Marcello Lippi's team had won the Champions League in 1996 and been runners-up in 1997. Ferguson saw them as the benchmark for European success, with their combination of immaculate technique and fierce competitiveness, and he was thrilled to have overcome them that night. 'The 3-2 victory was proof we could flourish in the most elevated company,' he wrote in *Managing My Life*.

United carried their momentum through the whole of October, beating Feyenoord home and away, and battering Barnsley and Sheffield Wednesday in the league at Old Trafford. The goals were flowing, with Cole bagging two hat-tricks and Sheringham helping himself to five in six games. So much for United missing Keane and Cantona.

A 3-2 loss to Arsenal at Highbury was no more than a blip. Wenger's team proceeded to lose their next three league games and United remained firmly in command at the top of the table. United pressed home their advantage through the winter months and at one point extended their lead to 11 points. With ten games left in their season Fred Done bookmakers were so convinced of the outcome they famously decided to pay out on United winning the title. They would end up paying out twice.

Those ten games saw United lose twice and draw three times. Meanwhile, Arsenal summoned a remarkable streak of victories to overtake them at the top, and ultimately sealed the title with a 4-0 victory against Everton in the first week of May. The turnaround was so dramatic that Wenger's men could even afford to lose their last two league games and remain a point clear.

Dennis Bergkamp was their inspiration, their Cantona if you like. The Dutch forward had taken time to settle in England, but in the 1997/98 campaign he delivered a masterclass. He scored a collection of brilliant goals and was named PFA Player of the Year and the Football

Writers' Player of the Year for his efforts. Arsenal's defence of Lee Dixon, Martin Keown, Tony Adams and Nigel Winterburn also earned acclaim, as did the midfield combination of Patrick Vieira and fellow Frenchman Emmanuel Petit.

Arsenal's season was topped off with a 2-0 defeat of Newcastle in the FA Cup Final, and United fans were left wondering what had hit them. Wenger had taken just two seasons to achieve the Double and towards the end of the campaign his team were irresistible. If Ferguson had knocked Liverpool off their perch, was Wenger about to do the same to United? Unlike the fleeting challenges of Blackburn and Newcastle, Arsenal looked capable of mounting a long-term threat to United. Wenger had his side playing expressive, exciting football and they'd produced a clinical finish to the season that suggested it was under-pinned by a fierce mental resolve. Arsenal's was a dramatic rise, and it had United fans seriously worried that their team would be left behind.

To compound the disappointment, United's European dream had perished in the quarter-finals. After a 0-0 draw in Monaco, Ferguson's team went into the home leg without Schmeichel, Giggs and Gary Pallister. They fell behind to a thunderous shot from David Trezeguet, and despite equalising through Solskjaer simply could not summon the inspiration to find a winner. Ferguson took his anger out on Nicky Butt in the dressing room after the game, blaming the young midfielder for the mistake that led to Monaco's goal. 'I'm out of the f**king European Cup now, Butty, and it's your f**king fault. What were you f**king doing?' he said.

The United manager's frustration had got the better of him. It was now 30 years since United had lifted the European Cup and in four attempts Ferguson had failed to get further than the semi-finals. Galatasaray, Borussia Dortmund and Monaco were hardly footballing superpowers, but all three had got the better of Ferguson in the knockout stages. And the group stages exit in 1994/95 could have been avoided had United not crashed 3-1 to Swedish side Gothenburg.

The success of United's legendary 1968 vintage loomed larger than ever. And Ferguson was left with much to contemplate as footballing attentions turned to the 1998 World Cup finals in France.

CHAPTER 10
STAND BY YOUR MAN

David Beckham's trajectory had been steep and uninterrupted. He'd established himself at the club he loved, broken into the England squad and was engaged to a world-famous pop star. And he was still only 23 years old. There was a Willy Wonka flavour to the Beckham story that appealed to every schoolboy in the country. With a right boot for a winning ticket he'd won a Bobby Charlton Soccer Skills challenge at the age of 11 in front of 40,000 fans at Old Trafford. A decade later he was covering the same turf, before the same fans, with Charlton watching on in the stands. Neither club nor player could have scripted it better if they'd tried.

Beckham's dad was from East London, the archetypal 'cockney Red', and he bred his son on stories of the Munich air crash and the Busby Babes of Best, Stiles, Charlton and Law. The moment Beckham junior was spotted by United scout Malcolm Fidgeon playing for Waltham Forest, there was only one possibility worth considering. He wore his hair spiked like Gordon Strachan and Bryan Robson was his hero. When Alex Ferguson called David and his parents in for a meeting on 2 May 1988, all three Beckhams wanted the same thing.

Beckham had a six-year offer on the table from Tottenham, but he desperately wanted to go to United. Even if they'd offered considerably less money he would have taken it, and his parents would too. But he needn't have worried. Ferguson said United would match Spurs' offer and Beckham didn't need to hear another word. 'I want to sign,' he said. And that was that. 'I'd been ready, waiting to say those words, for the best part of ten years,' he wrote in *My Side*.

Beckham impressed Ferguson and his staff with his dedication, reading of the game and technical ability. He was part of the 1992 side that won the FA Youth Cup and spawned the Fergie Fledglings, captained by Ryan Giggs and boasting the likes of Nicky Butt, Paul Scholes and Gary Neville. Beckham scored in the semi-final and the final, and the following season made his full United debut aged 17 in that League Cup tie against Brighton & Hove Albion. He got 17 minutes, and a good old-fashioned bollocking from Ferguson afterwards for good measure.

Ferguson knew Beckham had an exceptional talent, but he still had concerns over his physical readiness for the senior side. He called him a 'late developer' and it wasn't until the 1995/96 season that the United manager trusted him with a regular place in his team. The departure of Andrei Kanchelskis forced his hand, but Beckham took his opportunity with a tenacity and hunger that proved to Ferguson he was ready. He started 33 games and scored eight times as United won the Double, taking inspiration from the man he now counted as a teammate and a role model – Eric Cantona.

For the fans, Beckham was a different proposition to Giggs and Lee Sharpe, the original pop star footballers of the Ferguson era. His game was not built on beating players, and he was not blessed with a searing pace that lifted fans from their seats. Beckham didn't glide around the pitch like a cocker spaniel, but he did work like a dog. And he struck a football more cleanly and with better technique than perhaps any player who'd put on the famous red shirt except, of course, Bobby Charlton. His passing and crossing were the stuff of coaching manuals, and as he'd prove time and again in his United career, there were few better at striking the dead ball.

If the 1995/96 season marked the launch of Beckham the footballer, then the next saw the dawn of Beckham the celebrity. His goal from the halfway line at Selhurst Park was the game changer, one sweet strike of his right boot putting his name on the lips of every football fan in the country. Then came his England debut and the news he was dating the good-looking one from the biggest girl band in British music history. 'Posh and Becks' were born and with them a corporate empire that would ultimately launch fragrances, clothing lines and plenty more besides. It was a dramatic rise to fame, and you got the feeling Beckham was relishing every minute of it.

He was also maturing as a player, and as an athlete. In the 1996/97 season he'd proved his worth to Ferguson and United, and completely left behind the notion that his footballing body was some way behind his footballing brain. The scrawny ball player had added bulk to his physique and his endurance levels were on a par with anybody at Old Trafford. He may have been a slow starter, but Beckham had now well and truly arrived.

But things were about to get complicated. For the first time in Beckham's career the script would deviate from the Roy of the Rovers fare he'd lived since he was ten years old and he'd be dealt some serious adversity. And like Cantona before him, he'd need the support of his manager to get him through it.

It all started when Beckham was dropped for England's opening game at the 1998 World Cup. Hoddle told him he didn't think he was focused enough, and it turned out his decision to spend time with Victoria while the rest of the squad were on the golf course had been his downfall. Beckham was hurt and frustrated, and this was not the treatment he was used to at Old Trafford. But he got his chance in England's final group game against Colombia and duly scored his first international goal – a superb free-kick curled over the wall from 30 yards. With that strike he was elevated from 'Posh Spice's boyfriend' to the fearless young midfielder who could help England win the World Cup.

There was no way Hoddle could leave him out now. Beckham was duly picked to start against Argentina in the last 16 and arrived in St Etienne in high spirits. Life got sweeter still when he got a call from Victoria to tell him she was pregnant with their first child. Normal Beckham service had resumed and the lad from Leytonstone was Roy of the Rovers again. What lay ahead was the perfect opportunity to announce his talent to a huge global audience, but it ended up being the worst night of his career.

England fell behind to a Gabriel Batistuta penalty early on, but responded in kind through Alan Shearer just a few minutes later. Then came the moment that made Michael Owen's career. The 18-year-old collected Beckham's pass just inside the Argentina half and accelerated away from his marker. With one man to beat he drove to his right in a white blur and found the composure to send a shot back across the goalkeeper and into the opposite top corner. Hoddle's team had come from 1-0 down to lead 2-1 and with Owen and Beckham in full flight looked like a side ready to ignite.

But Argentina's experience ensured they weren't put to the sword. In first-half injury time they manufactured a clinical equaliser, with Javier Zanetti collecting a disguised pass from a free-kick and shooting past David Seaman to make it 2-2. It was a harsh blow for England, who'd been the better side and arguably deserved to go into the break with the advantage, but worse was to follow.

Just two minutes into the second half Beckham was barged over by Argentina's captain Diego Simeone. It was a crude foul and Simeone compounded Beckham's annoyance with a patronising gesture to ruffle his hair. As he lay on the ground England's No. 7 reacted with a petulant flick of his left boot, which connected with the back of Simeone's leg and caused him to stumble backwards. The incident took place in full view of Danish referee Kim Nielsen who ultimately had little choice. He booked Simeone and gave Beckham a straight red card, in one gesture transporting the 23-year-old from national hero to national hate figure.

'The look in my eyes tells you everything,' said Beckham describing a press photo of the incident in his book *My Side*. 'I was in a different world. Simeone had laid his trap and I'd jumped straight into it. Whatever else happens to me, those 60 seconds will always be with me.'

England held on without him and for a euphoric 30 seconds we thought they'd won it at the death. Sol Campbell headed home from a corner, but the goal was disallowed what seemed like an age later for a foul by Shearer on the goalkeeper. Had it stood, the sole price for Beckham's petulance would have been his own disappointment. He'd have missed a quarter-final and the red card would be chalked up to experience. He might even have returned and helped England win the whole thing – or at least featured in a predictable defeat in the semis.

But England went on to lose the game on penalties and Hoddle, in the ultimate act of manager betrayal, publicly blamed Beckham for the disappointment. It was all the excuse the media needed to vilify Beckham like few footballers had been vilified before him. 'Ten heroic lions, one stupid boy,' read the headline in the *Daily Mirror*. 'Sad fans look Beck in anger,' led the *Sun*. 'Beckham: the most hated man in England,' claimed an account in an American daily. Every newspaper, radio station and television show in the country was delivering the same message – Beckham's 'moment of madness' had cost England their shot at World Cup glory.

The ferocity of the anti-Beckham backlash was stronger than even that directed at Eric Cantona, in the wake of his kung-fu kick at Selhurst Park. The *Mirror* printed a dartboard with a picture of Beckham's face on it, a death threat was hung on the gates at Upton Park and an effigy of him in an England shirt was strung up outside a London pub. England fans were talking to camera and saying he should never play for his country again. It was primitive justice, but the mass media were fully engaging the vigilante element at every opportunity. Beckham baiting was clearly good for business.

In the immediate aftermath of France 1998 Beckham found sanctuary in New York, where he took in a Spice Girls concert at Madison Square Garden and was introduced to Madonna within a surreal couple of hours of touching down at JFK. Perhaps it was just the distraction he needed, and being shown a scan picture of his new baby helped put things in perspective. It was in New York that he spoke to Ferguson for the first time about the events in St Etienne. The United manager told him to get back to Manchester, where he'd have the love and support of everybody around him. 'Don't worry about what anyone says,' he said. 'You can have your say back to the rest of them after the season begins.'

They were words of support and encouragement that should have come from Hoddle, but the England manager clearly didn't have Ferguson's nurturing instincts – and as a United fan I held Hoddle responsible for everything Beckham was subjected to. When Hoddle calmed down he said there should be 'no scapegoats' for England's exit, and told the public to respect 'that young David has done a fantastic job for England in the past'. But by that time he had already made clear his belief England would have won the game with 11 players on the field, and hence delivered Beckham as his sacrificial offering to the British media. The damage had already been done, and it was left to Ferguson to pick up the pieces.

The United manager had been through a similar experience with Cantona, but the animosity towards Beckham was stronger and more widespread. And while Cantona was a 28-year-old veteran of controversy and adversity when he jumped into the crowd at Selhurst Park, Beckham was a 23-year-old who'd barely put a foot wrong until he flicked his left one at Simeone. He'd known only success and acclaim, and adjusting to his reception back home was going to take some serious mental fortitude.

When he got off the plane in London Beckham was given a full police escort. His parents were advised to move to Manchester for their own safety and David's dad drove him to and from pre-season training every day. The press camped in large numbers outside Beckham's house and he could sense the animosity towards him every time he made an appearance in public. Things reached a head when he heard a loud bang in the middle of the night and opened his window to see a man standing with crossed arms, staring at him. Beckham stared back and eventually the man disappeared. It left him seriously shaken up.

But through all the intimidation and the abuse, Ferguson stood by his man. The pair wouldn't always see eye to eye during Beckham's time at Old Trafford, but he was left with an eternal debt of gratitude to the man who picked him off the floor and gave him the strength to produce a quite stunning season of redemption on the pitch. 'The gaffer's loyalty to his players mean they have cast iron respect for him as a man and absolute faith in him as a manager,' Beckham wrote in *My Side*. 'One of the reasons I went to United in the first place was his attitude to young hopefuls: the boss made you feel like you were joining a family, not just a football club. And through thick and thin, beyond any disagreement or confrontation between us, it always felt like that at Old Trafford. The gaffer is the reason why. Knowing he was behind me really helped me get through that summer in 1998, and the early part of the season that followed.'

You could only admire Ferguson's loyalty to Beckham, but this was by no means an altruistic act on the part of the United manager. He needed Beckham as much as Beckham needed United, and his fatherly instincts always seemed to be at their strongest with the players he valued most. Ferguson is a man capable of great sensitivity and compassion, but in his footballing life there has often been a motivating factor. And that is the success of his team.

Beckham returned to action for United in the Charity Shield against Arsenal. United were on the wrong side of a 3-0 defeat to the team who had outclassed them the previous season, and Beckham's every touch was booed by the Arsenal fans. It wasn't the ideal tonic to a summer of abject misery, but at least Beckham's performance was respectable. A comfortable home win in a Champions League qualifier against LKS Lodz followed, and Beckham was greeted by a rousing affirmation from United fans at Old Trafford.

When he returned three days later for the Premier League opener against Leicester City, it was time for his scriptwriter of old to get back in the chair. United were 2-1 down and the game was into injury time. When they won a free-kick 25 yards out to the left of the goal there was only one man who was going to take it. It was Beckham territory, an almost identical position from which he'd scored for England against Colombia, and you just knew what was going to happen next. He flicked a strand of hair from his face, stepped up and curled a shot over the wall and into the net. 'Love him or hate him, you can't keep a great footballer down,' came the commentary.

Beckham's celebration was sheer release. He spun himself round with arms outstretched and allowed the moment to wash over him like a cure. His United teammates mobbed him from all angles and the 55,000 packed inside Old Trafford leapt about in pure, unadulterated joy. It was precisely what everyone at United knew needed to happen, and the fact it played out on the opening day of the season gave Beckham a fresh impetus to propel the team to unprecedented success.

If not for the man management and nurturing of Ferguson, he might never have put on a red shirt again after that night in St Etienne. And as fans of United, and of Beckham, we owed a huge debt of gratitude to the great man for that. Ferguson had outflanked the thousands who wanted Beckham to run away in shame, and instead delivered them a footballer who was more motivated and focused to succeed than ever before.

CHAPTER 11
ROAD TO THE PROMISED LAND

After watching Arsenal outclass and outlast his team in the run-in to the 1997/98 season, Alex Ferguson pleaded with the United board to take the financial shackles off. He desperately needed new players and the suits heeded his call with £14 million for the collection. He brought in Ajax's Dutch international defender Jaap Stam for £10.6 million and winger Jesper Blomqvist for £4.4 million from Parma – the Swede having made a lasting impression on Ferguson in the colours of Gothenburg some years earlier.

Effectively that was the £14 million gone, but Ferguson was desperate to make one more signing and he was clearly in convincing mood. Having failed to land Patrick Kluivert and Gabriel Batistuta, he turned his attentions to Aston Villa's Dwight Yorke – in no doubt the striker could make the difference to United's title challenge and their ambitions in Europe. A fee of £12.5 million was agreed and Yorke made the move in mid-August, two days before transfer deadline day. To balance the books, United would put Yorke's fee into the accounts for the following season.

The acquisition of Stam would compensate for Gary Pallister's £2.5 million return home to Middlesbrough. Pallister was 33 and the fee represented excellent value to United, but Ferguson was still sad to see him go. His partnership with Steve Bruce had played a key role in bringing the good times back to Old Trafford, and he'd been a fine servant of the club for nine years.

His replacement Stam looked a long way from the world's most expensive defender on his full debut in the Charity Shield. Arsenal's Nicolas Anelka turned on his afterburners and the muscle-bound £10 million man was culpable in United's 3-0 loss. 'Where the faithful had expected a tower of strength, they discovered he was rather too comparable to the one at Pisa,' wrote Nick Townsend in the *Independent*. 'Alex in blunderland' came the headline from another newspaper, mocking Ferguson's decision to sign him. The general consensus was that Stam was too slow, and too lumbering a defender to cope with the speed of play in the Premier League. He'd be found out and United with him.

Dad and I watched the majority of the match in silence, pained expressions across both of our faces – huffing every time Stam was outmanned and shaking our heads like the helpless parents of an unruly toddler. But when the final whistle blew it was I who played the role of a three-year-old. 'Well that's the title gone then, may as well hand it to Arsenal and get it over with,' I pouted. 'What on earth was Fergie thinking signing a defender who can't even run? There's no point being built like a gladiator if you can't catch anybody to kill in the first place.'

But Ferguson never once doubted his convictions. 'I knew that was a crazy judgement, having seen enough of the Dutchman to identify him as the highest class,' he wrote in *Managing My Life*. 'Jaap is quick, decisive, formidably strong physically and has the technique to play the ball effectively out of defence. He is also blessed with a calm, well-balanced temperament… At £10 million he was a bargain.'

The widespread ridiculing of United's new acquisition made sure the fans took to him even more strongly than they might otherwise have done. We were already providing sanctuary to David Beckham, so why not extend the support to Stam. He was a colossus of a man who wouldn't have looked out of place in an action movie alongside Jean Claude van Damme and Arnold Schwarzenegger. He was football's version of 'The Terminator' and opposing forwards must have absolutely hated playing against him. Moreover, he ushered in one of the enduringly brilliant chants of the Ferguson era: 'Jip Jaap Stam's a big Dutch man, get past him if you f**king can. Try a little trick and he'll make you look a prick. Jip, Jaap, Jaap Stam.'

'From the start they made me one of them,' Stam said of the United fans at the end of the season. 'They didn't leave me in the corner to fight my way in. You have to get used to any new club, but especially a big one like United. I settled in Manchester quickly and I enjoyed the lifestyle. I wanted to come to a stronger league and a bigger club, but everybody expected too much too early. The biggest adjustment was to the speed of the game, it was much higher than I was used to.'

As for Blomqvist, it was the second time United had come knocking. In 1994 the young winger had roasted David May in the Champions League group stages, scoring and setting up a penalty in a 3-1 win for Gothenburg. He furthered his reputation a year later with a goal that mimicked Pele's outrageous dummy in the semi-finals of the 1970 World Cup – the only difference being Blomqvist managed to dupe the goalkeeper and score. Pele famously missed the target. United had made an offer in 1996, but Blomqvist chose AC Milan instead. This time Ferguson got his man.

Ferguson had been looking for natural cover on the left flank since Lee Sharpe left in 1996. Beckham and Karel Poborsky were right-footed in the extreme, and while Jordi Cruyff provided a temporary solution, a knee injury had limited Holland's famous son to just four starts in the 1997/98 campaign and he would ultimately fade into the background. Blomqvist was still young at 24, and his Champions League experience and left-footedness made him ideal cover for Giggs. The winger would play just 25 times for United, but one of those games would be the most important of the Ferguson era.

United's new complement was completed by Yorke, who became United's most expensive signing just a few weeks after Stam had briefly claimed the record. The deal had been almost a year in the making and complicated by claims from Aston Villa chairman Doug Ellis that United had been 'tapping up' the Trinidad and Tobago international while he was still under contract. Yorke had been spotted by Graham Taylor on a tour to the Caribbean in 1989, and Villa had spent nine years developing him into a world-class forward. They had their own title ambitions and saw Yorke as integral to realising them, but when he told them he wanted to go to United, Ellis ultimately conceded that the money was too good to turn down.

Villa manager John Gregory was not best pleased. He'd said he would only countenance the deal if Andy Cole moved in the opposite direction, but he found himself one game into the new season without either man at his disposal. 'Dwight Yorke came to me two weeks ago to say he wanted to play for Manchester United and not Aston Villa,' said Gregory. '… What he said hurt. It really got me. I had hoped he'd changed his mind. Yet in the last few days he made it very clear he wanted to leave.'

Yorke was a very different player from Batistuta and Kluivert, the two strikers Ferguson had failed to sign before he turned his attentions elsewhere. While they were blockbuster, Roy-of-the-Rovers forwards in the old-fashioned mould, Yorke represented a more subtle threat. He was a player of guile and invention, who frequently dropped off the front to operate in deeper areas. Yorke was quick, skilful and surprisingly strong on the ball, and probably the most laid-back personality you could hope to come upon in the world of professional sport. He practically had a smile glued on his face.

He reminded me of the great entertainer Sammy Davis Junior. There was an infectious enthusiasm to him, and you got the feeling he was revelling in every single moment of his cherished existence. Some players let the weight of expectancy pull them down, but Yorke's huge transfer fee did the opposite. It simply enhanced his appreciation of a life that allowed him to make money, a lot of money, from kicking a ball around and enjoying himself. If Cantona brought inspiration to Ferguson, and Keane a fierce will to win, then Yorke offered a happy-go-lucky personality that served to relax those around him – not least Andy Cole.

Yorke's arrival meant United now had four frontline strikers fighting for places, and for a while it looked like Ole Gunnar Solskjaer would make way to seek out regular football elsewhere. Tottenham, Everton and Newcastle were all interested, and some reports suggested United had accepted an offer of £5 million from Spurs. But Ferguson managed to convince him to stay and fight for his place. Nine months later, when Solskjaer put the ball in the net in the Camp Nou, Ferguson would be eternally thankful the little Norwegian came along for the ride.

United got their league campaign off to a stuttering start. The 2-2 draw against Leicester was made bearable by the late heroics of Beckham, but there were few positives to draw at Upton Park a week later. Yorke flattered to deceive on his debut, and Beckham was absolutely pilloried by the West Ham fans. It was at Upton Park that death threats had been hung on the gates in the wake of his 'moment of madness' in St Etienne, and the fervour of the abuse Beckham took from the moment he stepped off the bus in East London left him wondering if he could make it through the season.

But then things started to click. United beat Coventry and Charlton comfortably in the league and then played their part in a scintillating 3-3 draw with Barcelona at Old Trafford in their opening game of the Champions League group stages. Beckham was the catalyst, picking out Giggs to head home the first, sending over the cross that led to the second, and then curling yet another of those free-kicks into the top corner for United's third. If anybody needed convincing he could come back from the traumas of the summer, this was the performance that silenced his doubters. Beckham took on the Spanish champions of Rivaldo, Figo and Luis Enrique like a man possessed.

'He's quality and I knew that before the game, and if you have quality like he has then that is always going to be a big advantage,' said Barcelona goalkeeper Ruud Hesp after the game. 'I knew where he was going to shoot for his free-kick, but he shoots so hard and so well that it is very hard to stop the ball. The first goal for Giggs came from his [Beckham's] foot and the second goal came from his good ball into Yorke. He had an influence in all three goals so, yes, that was some performance.'

United had been drawn in an ominous-looking group with Barca, Bayern Munich and Swedish champions Brondby, so a point at home wasn't ideal. But a 2-2 draw in Munich was followed by two crushing victories against the Swedes, by an aggregate score of 11-2, and United were well placed as they prepared to face Barcelona in the Camp Nou on 25 November 1998. Five years earlier Ferguson's team had been ravaged 4-0 in the same stadium, and their European ambitions dealt a crushing reality check. But this time it would be different.

It was the night that set the tone for United's Champions League adventures to come, with Yorke and Cole highlighting the devastating potential of a partnership that would deliver 53 goals in all competitions. Yorke scored twice to take his tally to five goals in five European appearances, and he and Cole combined for one of the great United team goals. Beckham was once again effervescent alongside Paul Scholes, Roy Keane and Giggs in midfield, and it was his pinpoint cross that invited Yorke to dive and head home United's third.

The match finished 3-3, again, with Rivaldo summoning an outrageous overhead kick to earn Barca a point. It was a display that had critics suggesting United had finally found the formula for success in Europe, but worryingly they were still not assured of a place in the quarter-finals.

The group stages came to a head in early December, with frontrunners Bayern Munich the visitors to Old Trafford. United were held to a disappointing 1-1 draw, but results elsewhere went their way and Ferguson's team advanced as one of two best runners-up to face Inter Milan. 'At the start of the group it looked a really difficult task for us and we have achieved a lot to come through as we have,' Ferguson said afterwards. 'We have scored 20 goals and you can't dispute that, that is good form. Even tonight we looked like scoring goals and we have shown we have got the ability to do well.'

By the time the quarter-finals came around the following March, Ferguson had a new man alongside him in the dugout. After seven years as his assistant, and two before that helping to harvest the finest crop of young players United had produced for 30 years, Brian Kidd decided the time was right to move on. Struggling Blackburn Rovers wanted him to replace the sacked Roy Hodgson as manager, and Kidd decided it was now or never for his own managerial ambitions. He was 49 years old and ready to make the step up to number one.

The two had a mutual respect, but Ferguson wasn't convinced Kidd was cut out for management. He questioned his ability to make unpopular decisions, and admitted he had 'serious reservations' about his friend ever taking over at Old Trafford. He saw Kidd as a fine coach, who thrived working at close quarters with players in the inner sanctum at United, but doubted whether his personality was suited to more distanced relationships and the pressures that came with the main job. He was ultimately proved right. Rovers were relegated, and Kidd was sacked early the next season. He's worked as an assistant ever since.

Ferguson clearly appreciated the ruthless streak that had furthered his own ambitions. People talk of him as a loyal manager, a manager who's always ready to lend his ear to a player in need – and there's plenty of anecdotal evidence to back that up. But he's never been afraid to make controversial, unpopular decisions, or tell his players what he thinks of them. He's as likely to deliver a kind word of advice as he is a monumental bollocking, and if he doesn't think you're right for the game he'll drop you – no matter what your name is or how much you're being paid.

The way I saw it, Ferguson was right about Kidd – even if he chose to handle the whole affair like Simon Cowell passing verdict on an unconvincing *X Factor* audition. I've never met a United fan who thought Kidd was equipped for the job at Old Trafford, and his career trajectory since leaving United proved all of us right. Ferguson had been asked the question countless times, and eventually he decided to go with a brutally honest answer. It hurt his relationship with Kidd, but deep down they both knew he was right. Compassion is all well and good, but no one measures managers on the happiness of their past players or the fan consensus of their decisions. They measure them on trophies.

The man who replaced Kidd was a relative unknown called Steve McClaren. Jim Smith's number at Derby County had been identified as the best young coach in the country, and Ferguson pushed hard to get him. The deal was finalised shortly after United beat Derby 1-0 on a Wednesday night at Old Trafford, and three days later McClaren was alongside Ferguson as United took on Ron Atkinson's Nottingham Forest at the City Ground.

The players served up quite an introduction for their new assistant manager. United won 8-1, with Solskjaer coming on as a substitute to score four times in the last ten minutes. Cole and Yorke helped themselves to two goals apiece and it could have been double figures if not for some fine saves from Forest's keeper Dave Beasant. The romp meant United took their goals tally to 92 for the season, and it was only February. It was a rampant performance, the biggest away victory since the inception of the Premier League, and it meant United maintained their 100 per cent record at the start of 1999.

McClaren was suitably impressed. 'Not bad, lads, is it like this every week?' he asked in the dressing room afterwards. The appreciation soon became mutual. McClaren's approach on the training ground, his eye for detail and his openness to new ideas, quickly won the players over.

As for Solskjaer, he had already given United more value than the £5 million they could have taken from Tottenham. The 'baby-faced assassin' was on his way to 18 goals for the season, and two of those would be dramatic late winners in remarkable come-from-behind 2-1 victories. The first came against Liverpool at Old Trafford, in an FA Cup fourth round tie that provided a taste of things to come.

United had been chasing a Michael Owen goal since the third minute, and the visitors were a matter of seconds away from inflicting their first FA Cup defeat against United for 78 years when Yorke stabbed home a late, late equaliser. As if that wasn't sweet enough, Solskjaer came off the bench to drive home a sensational winner in injury time. 'The one thing we didn't want was a replay,' said Ferguson. 'But we also showed by our substitutions that you have to take risks to win matches like this. I felt we deserved what we got because we were prepared to take those risks.'

For the fans it was another thrilling episode in an already epic season. We'd seen two 3-3 draws with Barcelona, 6-2 wins against Brondby and Leicester, an 8-1 hammering of Nottingham Forest and an incredible comeback win against our greatest rivals. 'It was a season in which wonderful games arrived as if by conveyor belt. Sophoclean drama was served up almost weekly,' wrote Jim White in *Manchester United: The Biography.*

Dad and I were beginning to sense this could be United's year to make a move in Europe. We were monitoring Champions League final packages to Barcelona and weighing up whether to commit as early as the quarter-finals. But recent history told us to wait. Ferguson's teams had failed on their last four attempts and with Inter Milan up next we decided to err on the side of caution. But the phone numbers were written down and we were ready to go if they could get past the Italians.

At their free-flowing best, United were a quite irresistible attacking force. Beckham, Scholes, Keane, Giggs, and to a lesser extent Butt and Blomqvist, were all comfortable playing an expansive midfield game, and all six showed a willingness to get forward in support of the strikers. Each brought a different attribute that added to United's potency. Beckham and Scholes shared superb technique and the ability to unlock a defence with a raking pass. Giggs and Blomqvist offered guile and artistry on the flanks. Butt and Keane brought a combative intensity that gave United their momentum.

In defence, the Neville brothers and Denis Irwin offered assuredness and reliability at full-back. Neville dovetailed superbly with Beckham and was willing and able to get forward in support of his good friend whenever the opportunity arose. Stam was the rock Ferguson always knew he would be, while the combination of Ronny Johnsen and Henning Berg provided more than competent support alongside him.

As for the forward line, few could have predicted the chemistry between Yorke and Cole. The pair formed an instant kinship and played with almost instinctive sense for where the other was. And when Ferguson needed fresh impetus he had Solskjaer and Teddy Sheringham in the wings, intelligent players with vision and invaluable composure in front of goal.

But it wasn't all sweetness and light within the United squad. Cole and Sheringham didn't speak to each other, and they still haven't since. Cole traces the feud back to his England debut against Uruguay in 1995, when he replaced Sheringham as a substitute midway through the second half. He was expecting words of encouragement from the more experienced man, but he claims Sheringham snubbed him completely and he's never forgiven him for it. 'I wouldn't ever cast aspersions on Sheringham's talent as a top-rate footballer for his clubs and country. I've just loathed him personally for 15 years,' Cole said in 2010.

Cole's feelings didn't stop the pair providing United with plenty of goals during their time together at Old Trafford. In the 4,581 minutes they spent on the pitch together they scored a combined 54 goals for United, according to a statistical breakdown in the *Independent*. That's better than a goal a game, and it speaks volumes for the professionalism of the two players concerned. Having said that, there were surely occasions when Sheringham had the ball, Cole was in a great position and he couldn't bring himself to call for it. Perhaps they should have had an on-field intermediary.

The hateful Cole-Sheringham partnership was a fruitful one, but it was alongside the man Ferguson called his 'soulmate' that Cole truly excelled. He was the ultimate confidence player and Yorke's presence coaxed the best out of him. Cole had already formed one impressive partnership, with the genial Peter Beardsley at Newcastle, but his bond with Yorke would yield three successive titles and a Treble. And in the 1998/99 season it would prove not only the most potent of Ferguson's reign, but arguably the most feared in the whole of Europe.

Watching the pair in action was a joyous, life-affirming thing to behold for a United fan. At times they frolicked like inseparable five-year-olds chasing girls in a playground, never further than a short distance apart and always reacting to what the other was doing. They did things quickly and simply, and all too often the most experienced of defences were outmanned by their sheer exuberance. They were like brothers on and off the field, and they clearly revelled in each other's company for as long as it lasted. Most of all, they played with a sense of joy that sent a message to every club on the continent. Here was a team so good, they could afford to enjoy it.

When Yorke retired from the game in 2009, at the age of 37, Cole paid gushing tribute to the footballing romance that defines both of their careers. 'When we started playing together, it was like meeting a special woman and falling in love,' he said. 'Everything felt right. Whatever he did, I did the opposite. We never had a cross word. If I was upset with him, or he with me, we'd look at each other and say

"OK". Dwight's arrival changed my whole United career and our part-nership got stronger.'

It was Yorke to the fore once more when United returned to European action in March against Inter Milan at Old Trafford. United were top of the league and unbeaten since the turn of the year, and Ferguson was relieved that Brazilian striker Ronaldo would not be fit for the first leg. The UEFA Cup winners still had a wealth of talent at their disposal, however, including Roberto Baggio, Ivan Zamorano, Youri Djorkaeff and Javier Zanetti – not to mention Beckham's World Cup nemesis Diego Simeone. Ferguson was fearful of their threat and keen to take a cushion into what he knew would be an intimidating second leg at the San Siro in Milan.

United took the initiative early. Yorke won a header on the edge of the Inter box and Beckham clipped a superb first-time cross back into his path. The striker was unmarked on the six-yard box and he steered a diving header past Gianluca Pagliuca to put the home side ahead, in what was an almost carbon copy of the goal he'd scored in Barcelona. The same combination made it 2-0 at the end of the first half, Yorke rising at the near post to meet a trademark dipping cross from Beckham and heading home with ease.

Old Trafford was rocking and Beckham was having one of those nights. He was everywhere and picking out his teammates at will. All the media build-up had been about the resumption of hostilities with Simeone, but having shaken hands with the Argentine before the game, Beckham got a ferocious tackle in early and proceeded to play him off the park. There was a newfound maturity to his game now, and every ounce of his exuberance was being channelled with maximum efficiency. The lessons of St Etienne had been learned and with the support of Ferguson and everybody concerned with United, Beckham, it seemed, had been rehabilitated.

United should have added to their lead in the second half, but Giggs and Cole both missed glorious chances. At the opposite end Schmeichel denied Inter an away goal with a characteristically domi-nant performance. Most memorable was a breathtaking diving save from Zamorano's header that had United fans and the media alike drawing comparison to Gordon Banks' famous stop from Pele at the 1970 World Cup. All things considered 2-0 was a fine result. Ferguson said his team were an away goal from the semi-finals, and he fully expected them to get it.

But his confidence wasn't shared in our living room – as yet another nervous night ended contemplating the next one. By now there was too much heartache at risk to get carried away. United's European failures under Ferguson urged caution, and my instincts called for self-preservation. Dad and I both talked up a pending defeat, but we were both lying and we both knew it. They were lies born of fear, and in 1999 the overwhelming fear was that crushing disappointment was surely inevitable. Sooner or later, the world would come crashing down around United – and the more prepared we were for it, the easier the recovery.

Before the trip to the San Siro United had a tricky sixth-round FA Cup tie against Chelsea, and league meetings with Liverpool and Newcastle to negotiate. The fixtures were coming thick and fast and, in an effort to maintain the freshness of his key players, Ferguson saw fit to shuffle his pack.

He rested Yorke and Cole for the Cup game at Old Trafford, but ironically the decision proved counter-productive. United missed a hatful of chances in a 0-0 draw and Scholes got himself sent off late on. Ferguson and his team now had an extra game to play and a suspension for Scholes to deal with – but at least the game against Liverpool was postponed to make way for the replay. Unsurprisingly Cole and Yorke were returned to the line-up and Yorke duly scored goals 25 and 26 for the season as United ran out 2-0 winners at Stamford Bridge. The second was a beauty, Yorke taking the ball in his stride and casually chipping Ed de Goey from 20 yards with the outside of his boot.

Yorke's first was memorable for other reasons. Having volleyed home just three minutes into the game, he led his teammates in the 'cradle' celebration coined by Brazilian striker Bebeto. It was to mark the birth of Beckham's first child Brooklyn, but it elicited a predictably volatile response from the Chelsea faithful – a good number of whom were still harbouring some concentrated Beckham hatred from the 1998 World Cup.

Yorke had reinstated United's much-vaunted attacking thrust, but there was also much to cheer in their defensive performance of Ferguson's team. The result brought their seventh clean sheet in ten matches. Schmeichel was in the form of his career and the central pair in front of him managed to play like the settled duo they never really were. Whether it was Johnsen and Stam, Stam and Berg, or even Johnsen and Berg, it didn't seem to matter. United had leaked too many goals in the first half of the season, but they were now playing with an Italian efficiency that bode well for their hopes on all three fronts.

The stars were aligning, and even the most pragmatic of United fans couldn't help but contemplate the possibilities. A fellow Red told me recently he felt as though the players were unusually connected to the fans in the 1998/99 season, and most of us can appreciate what he means. It was as if they knew exactly what we wanted, and for those nine months were able to deliver it in the most entertaining way possible – like a rock band in the prime of their career, working a crowd effortlessly through the set list of the season. And while United had never been short on front men and lead guitarists, they now had a rhythm section to compare to the best in Europe – and a manager intent on conquering the world.

And so to Milan they went, armed with a 2-0 lead and with the growing consensus that this was surely United's year to finally win a second European Cup – 31 years after Sir Matt Busby and his team had become the first English team to lift the trophy. Ten thousand United fans travelled to Milan and arrived to the news that two-times World Player of the Year Ronaldo would be making a shock return to the Inter starting line-up.

Fortunately for United, the Brazilian was as lacklustre as he'd been in the 1998 World Cup final, and he was substituted early in the second half with the score still at 0-0 and United fans praying he'd stayed on the pitch. All too predictably the Italians were celebrating just four minutes later, when his replacement, Nicola Ventola, capitalised on a mistake by Keane to side-foot past Schmeichel and put the game on a knife-edge. Inter suddenly had the momentum and for an unbearably tense 25 minutes we watched on convinced they'd score a second and take the game to extra-time.

Time refused to tick on. As red shirts scurried frantically to protect their besieged goal, you felt certain of an impending doom to crush the Treble dream. It was desperate stuff, or at least it felt like it from an armchair, drinking bottles of cheap lager like prohibition was coming tomorrow. With a defeat here would go our confidence, and with that our chances of the league title and the FA Cup. How about that for a gift to baying United haters who stalked every pub and workspace in the country? It couldn't happen, could it? Surely not…

Not this time. United withstood the deluge and with two minutes left scored the goal that made sure of their progress. Cole cushioned a header into the path of Scholes, who passed the ball into the Inter net as if he was scoring in a six-a-side at training. It was a delightfully simple goal and with it came a place in the semi-finals and a meeting with Juventus. 'I'm very, very proud of them,' said an ecstatic Ferguson afterwards. 'They were all outstanding. They've deserved the result. There have been times in the past when we haven't got the luck.'

Whispers of an unprecedented Treble were now audible in every social situation you could imagine, and it was starting to feel like the eyes of the world were on Ferguson's team and what they would do next. Like most United fans, I was finding it harder and harder to get on with my everyday life. By now I was working as a post boy at a record company in London, but all too often my rounds were interrupted by lengthy United discussion with the football-loving executives who roamed the corridors. For a while it felt like the only thing anyone was talking about was the Treble, and with that came a nervous excitement that no amount of beer could dissipate.

United went four points clear of Arsenal at the top of the Premier-ship with a 3-1 win against Everton, and April arrived with semi-finals in both the Champions League and FA Cup to look forward to. It was the heady, exhilarating stuff of fan fantasy, but with the enormous expectancy came the frightening possibility they could yet finish the season empty-handed. Arsenal would provide the opposition in the league and the FA Cup, and if their efforts under Arsène Wenger the previous season were anything to go by, the Londoners were more than capable of undermining the United challenge on both fronts.

Standing in the way of United's progress to a first Champions League final in 31 years were Juventus, who'd been runners-up for the past two seasons. With the likes of Zinedine Zidane, Edgar Davids and Didier Deschamps at their disposal, the Italian giants were positively brimming with experience in the further reaches of European football's premier competition – Zidane and Deschamps were World Cup-winners to boot. But United would lean on the 3-2 victory in the group stages the previous season for inspiration, and the bookies agreed they were favourites.

But Ferguson's team looked a naive bet in the first half of the first leg at Old Trafford. Juve swarmed all over them in midfield and Antonio Conte's goal took them into the break with a deserved lead. You couldn't help feel as though the Treble talk added an extra pressure that was far from conducive to the kind of expressive, attacking football they needed to ignite the home support. But in games of this quality a fan has to accept their team will suffer a dip, and my fears were tempered by the fact Juve didn't score a second in the first half – and were unlikely to enjoy the same dominance in the second.

Ferguson made some tactical adjustments at the break, and United gradually got a foothold in the tie. It was time for another of 1999's late, late goals, and this time it was Giggs who'd provide it. With the game into injury time he pounced at the far post to leather a half-volley into the roof of the net and draw United level. It brought huge relief, but didn't change the fact that a 0-0 draw – that most Italian of football dishes – would be enough for Juve in the return match.

For the neutrals the tie could not have been more perfectly poised. United would have to take the attack to the Italians and that meant the potential for plenty of goals. But for nervous United fans contemplating a trip to the final, the 1-1 draw posed something of a quandary. Did we really believe they could get a score draw or beat Juve in Turin? Dad still wasn't convinced. He'd called a tour operator in Manchester who still had final packages to sell, but he was reluctant to hand over the cash until we'd seen at least the first half of the second leg. It was a dangerous strategy, and PJ wasn't prepared to wait. He bought flights and tickets and had absolute faith he'd be watching United take on Bayern Munich or Dynamo Kyiv at the Camp Nou that May.

It was a bold move, but bold moves were very much de rigueur when it came to Manchester United in 1999.

CHAPTER 12
CHEST WIGS AND BROKEN DREAMS

It was one of the defining moments in a season that boasted more than most. A bare-chested Ryan Giggs swinging his shirt around his head in wild celebration as he sprinted up the touchline, deep into extra-time of a tumultuous, impossibly epic FA Cup semi-final replay against Arsenal at Villa Park.

Giggs collected a misplaced pass from Patrick Vieira and carried the ball past four red shirts, slaloming in and out of tackles, before driving a ferocious shot into the roof of the net from a tight angle. 'He's ripped Arsenal to ribbons,' came the commentary. His sensational goal came with ten minutes of extra-time remaining, and gave Ferguson's United yet another dramatic late, great triumph for the ages. He called it 'one of the best goals ever scored in major football'. And I wholeheartedly agree.

Giggs' mesmeric effort was a fitting crescendo to a semi-final that lasted four hours and saw the top two sides in English football go at it like heavyweight boxers who refused to hit the canvas. The first leg finished 0-0, and with Ferguson furious that a Roy Keane goal in the first half was disallowed for offside. Arsenal had Nelson Vivas sent off early in extra-time and there was plenty of fractiousness between two teams who were both unbeaten since the turn of the year, and both chasing the domestic Double. Neither side wanted a replay, but

Arsenal probably emerged happiest with the result – especially as they would welcome back French World Cup-winner Emmanuel Petit for the sequel, three days later.

For the replay, Ferguson shuffled his pack and decided to keep Giggs and Dwight Yorke on the bench. Teddy Sheringham and Ole Gunnar Solskjaer started up front and United went ahead midway through the first half when David Beckham beat David Seaman with a superb curling effort from 25 yards. United were in cruise control, but Dennis Bergkamp produced an equaliser on 69 minutes and things went from bad to worse when Keane was sent off for a second bookable offence soon after.

In the dying seconds it looked like the Treble dream was dead in the water. Ray Parlour attacked Phil Neville inside the box and Neville's tired legs brought him down to give Arsenal a stonewall penalty, and a glorious chance to win the game. In the context of the season it was a monumental moment for both teams. If Arsenal scored you felt they would not only go on to win the FA Cup, but also carry the belief into their league campaign and make it back-to-back Doubles under Arsène Wenger. United would take the disappointment into what was already a tough-looking European tie in Turin, and could conceivably finish the season empty-handed.

I was at home, on the sofa, on my own. And I couldn't bear to watch it. I stood up and walked to the kitchen, but my flat was so small I couldn't escape the commentary. It was Bergkamp against Peter Schmeichel, Holland against Denmark, and an unbearable moment of sporting theatre for fans of both teams. Phil Neville had his head in his hands, and you feared his mistake might not only define the match, but the season, and maybe his entire career. But Schmeichel guessed right, diving to his left to push away Bergkamp's spot-kick to delirious reaction from his teammates and the United fans alike. Once again the big Dane had kept his team alive and somehow United survived to extra-time. For that, Neville owes him an eternal debt of gratitude.

Extra-time brought another chance for Bergkamp to win it, but once again Schmeichel's imposing frame came between him and hero-ism. And he summoned another superb reaction stop when a corner deflected off Ronny Johnsen and fizzed towards goal. Then came Giggs' moment. Vieira's rare mistake let him in, but nobody could have expected the culmination of a run that started with the Welshman 60 yards from goal and with a handful of experienced international players between him and his destination. It was, as Andy Gray rightly put it, 'a goal fit to win any football match'.

Giggs beat Lee Dixon (twice), Martin Keown, Tony Adams and Vieira – a foursome that included half of the most famous back four in recent English football history and a World Cup winner. That he still had the composure to shoot past England's international goalkeeper made for a truly remarkable goal that turned out to be the last ever scored in an FA Cup semi-final replay. Wenger said 'the two teams are very close to each other and in the end the luckiest won,' but there was no luck involved where Giggs' goal was concerned – just a cocker spaniel chasing the silver paper like he'd been doing since the first time Ferguson marvelled at his talent.

It was Giggs at his fluent, instinctive best – running at a defence with balance and speed, with the ball an obliging companion to his every feint and change of direction. It was a throwback to the exuberance of his fledgling years at United, and it left Ferguson yearning for the raw, natural talent that had once left him speechless on the training ground. 'His inner struggle to become the complete player had frequently inhibited the expression of the amazing talent that broke Arsenal on 14 April,' he wrote in *Managing My Life*. 'The real Ryan Giggs should step forward more often.'

United fans poured onto the pitch at the final whistle. Beckham was carried aloft on their shoulders and Giggs had that curly black mop of hair ruffled so vigorously, and by so many hands, that it's a wonder there's still any of it left. When the players finally reached the dressing room they celebrated with champagne and were left to contemplate the role they'd played in making football history. 'Something special had just happened,' wrote Beckham in *My Side*. 'It was about as good a game of football as I'd ever played in.'

Meanwhile, I was slouched back in the sofa in a delirious haze – like someone who'd just survived a game of Russian roulette. My voice was hoarse, my emotions frayed and my heart racing like a bare-chested Giggs down the touchline. It was almost too much to bear, but the raw thrill of a dramatic victory stayed with me for days. No matter how many times I watch it back, I still expect Bergkamp to score the penalty, and I still can't explain how Giggs ran half the length of the field through the best defence in the country. There was something otherworldly at work that night, and destiny clearly had a plan for United in 1999.

It was back to league action that Saturday against Sheffield Wednesday at Old Trafford. Ferguson took the luxury of resting Giggs, Schmeichel, Johnsen and Cole, and started with Beckham and Yorke on the bench. This time he wouldn't regret the decision. United strolled home 3-0 and Ferguson was even able to withdraw Keane and Jaap Stam just after the hour mark. It was the ideal preparation for the trip to Turin.

Ferguson had been telling reporters he had 'a feeling in his bones' that this was United's year. The dramatic win against Liverpool and the incredible semi-final against Arsenal had enhanced the belief that United were inexorably bound for glory in 1999, but they would need to surpass both of those victories to keep hopes alive in the Champions League. Juventus were a European superpower, who had reached the final for the past three seasons and boasted a raft of the most experienced players in world football. They were also an away goal to the good.

If United were to summon another miracle at the Stadio Delle Alpi, they'd have to do it without the marauding chest-wigged hero Giggs – who was ruled out through injury and would play no part in the game. 'I've got to analyse in my own mind what I think Juventus will do and that will have a bearing on how I pick my team,' Ferguson said. He went with Keane, Beckham, Nicky Butt and Jesper Blomqvist in midfield, and naturally had Yorke and Cole resume their roles in Europe's most potent strike force. Scholes, Sheringham and Solskjaer would be among the substitutes.

The tension in our living room was unbearable. Dad had held back on buying the package for the final, but he had the number written on speed dial and the phone ready to draw in his back pocket. 'This way, if they go out we won't have to suffer the humiliation of trying to track down Juventus fans living in London to sell them the flights and tickets,' he said. 'And if United get the result and the packages are sold out when I make the phone call, at least we'll have their success to keep us going.' Meanwhile PJ the gambler was in Turin, preparing to watch United take our fate, and his money, in their hands.

United got off to the worst possible start. Filippo Inzaghi, one of the most prolific goal-poachers European football has ever known, tapped in from an inch after just six minutes to put the home side ahead. The striker looked to have ended the game as a contest four minutes later, when his shot deflected off the meaty thigh of Stam and looped over Schmeichel in the United goal. Juventus were leading 3-1 on aggregate with an away goal, and were threatening a rout. 'Manchester United need a minor miracle now,' said Clive Tyldesley on the commentary. Meanwhile, there was silence in the Tidey living room. PJ must have been having Italian kittens.

United were no strangers to comeback heroics under Ferguson. In 1999 they'd already added the Solskjaer winner against Liverpool and the Giggs goal against Arsenal to the archives. But if they could pull this one off it would overshadow all of those by a country mile. It would be the greatest comeback in the club's history. And so it began. With 24 minutes on the clock United won a corner on the left. Beckham scampered over to take it. Keane powered into the Juventus box, and timed his leap to perfection to get in front of the goalkeeper and glance a superb header into the far corner. Up from his chair came Dad, punching the air Bryan Robson style and swearing a ferocious celebration from between his gritted teeth. I showed no such control, completing a lap of the downstairs like a wild toddler and waving my arms around in delight. I came back with a couple of beers and the adrenaline flowing manically through my veins.

United were back in business, and who else but their barnstorming captain to send a message of intent to the Italians that the game was far from over. Keane had grabbed the game by the scruff of the neck and set the tone for his teammates to follow. The fear was gone, and the game was there for the taking.

But United's captain was in for a mixed night. Minutes later he tripped Zinedine Zidane, and when referee Urs Meier showed the Irishman a yellow card it meant he would miss the final. It was Paul Gascoigne at Italia 90 all over again, but this time there would be no tears, and no histrionics. Keane brushed himself down and resumed hero duties as if it was the most natural thing in the world. If anything it galvanised him. 'I didn't think I could have a higher opinion of any footballer than I did of Roy but he rose even further in my estimation against Juventus,' said Ferguson afterwards. 'Roy seemed to redouble his efforts. It was the most emphatic display of selflessness I've seen on a football field, inspiring all around him.'

United almost immediately found an equaliser. Gary Neville sent a long ball forward and Beckham did well to nod it back into the path of Cole. The striker took a touch to control it, then, with the ball still bobbling in front of him, half-volleyed a cross towards Yorke inside the Juve box. Yorke had pulled away from his marker and found space to send a diving header back across goal and into the opposite corner. It was goal number 27 for the season for Yorke, and yet another endorsement for the most prolific partnership in the Premiership. 'United have seen Juventus' away goal, and they have raised it,' said Tyldesley on the ITV commentary. Barcelona was back on. Still Dad waited to make the call.

The situation remained precarious. Stam had already made a clearance off the line and Inzaghi had a goal disallowed for offside early in the second half. At the opposite end Yorke and Irwin both hit the inside of the post with drives from the edge of the box. It must have made for thrilling viewing for the neutrals, but it was unbearable drama for the fans of United and Juventus.

In the final ten minutes the game was so open you felt certain one of the sides would score. Juve threw on Uruguayan striker Daniel Fonseca up front and sacrificed a defender, and suddenly there were big open spaces all over the pitch. By this time Ferguson had replaced Blomqvist with Scholes, a decision he would deeply regret after Scholes picked up a booking for a two-footed tackle and became the second influential United midfielder ruled out of the final.

Finally the *coup de grâce* arrived. Schmeichel boomed a huge kick down the throats of the Juve central defenders and they failed to deal with it. The ball cannoned back into the path of Yorke and he somehow dissected the pair of them to put himself clean through on goal. Juve goalkeeper Angelo Peruzzi rushed out and brought Yorke down, but before the referee could award a penalty Cole darted in to slide the ball into an empty net and send the 4,000 travelling United fans, and the two men in our front room, into wild celebration. 'Full speed ahead Barcelona,' came the commentary, and with it Dad pulled the phone from his back pocket and called the travel company. 'Have you got any packages for the final left?' he asked. A long pause, then finally… 'Really, yes definitely, absolutely. Do you take credit cards over the phone?'

The reports the following day lauded United for producing one of the great European performances in English football history. 'Red heroes', 'Eur the tops', 'Unfergettable' and 'Fergie you're the tops', were among the headlines. Frank Malley of the Press Association summed up the mood when he wrote, 'It was brilliant and breathtaking. It was dramatic and devastating. At times the tension was like torture. But in the end, the triumph was truly memorable and thoroughly deserved, and no superlative seemed sufficient.'

For Ferguson, United's first win on Italian soil was the culmination of everything he'd been striving for. For too long United fans had waited for a team to emulate Sir Matt Busby's class of 1968, and they were now in touching distance of the prize Ferguson coveted above all others. 'It is a very proud moment for me. This is the level we want to play at,' he said. 'My players were absolutely fantastic, absolutely magnificent. I thought the first 45 minutes was the best in my career as a manager. It was absolutely terrific. We gave them a start. But I am proud of the way they recovered and kept their composure, and I think they deserve to be there.'

But the celebrations were tinged with sadness for the fates of Keane and Scholes – victims of what I've always considered to be the cruellest rule in football. For a straight red you can understand it, but when a player strives his entire career to play in a major final it seems draconian that a couple of flippant yellow cards can deny him the opportunity. 'It's a tragedy,' said Ferguson. 'I don't know whether we can appeal. But it's absolutely tragic for them to miss the final, I feel for them.'

Typically, Keane refused to dwell on his plight. He admitted the yellow card was justified and having delivered arguably the performance of his life he consolidated Ferguson's belief there was not a more selfless player in the game. 'It's one of those things,' Keane said. 'It was a bit of a bad first touch from me but it doesn't really matter. The important thing is that the club got to the final. I knew before the match what the score was but I think I deserved it. We made it hard for ourselves, but even at 2-0 down I thought we would do it.'

United had a game in hand, but they also had to go to Anfield to play the rearranged fixture against Liverpool. It proved yet another exhilarating, highly controversial clash between the masters of English football past and present, and it ended with Ferguson furious at referee David Elleray for two decisions that cost his team victory.

Ferguson had a point. With half an hour left and United 2-0 up through goals from Yorke and Irwin, Elleray awarded Liverpool a soft penalty. Minutes later Irwin was sent off for kicking the ball away down the touchline, and United's misery was compounded when none other than Paul Ince stole in to grab a dramatic equaliser with two minutes to go. The once beloved Guv'nor of Old Trafford proceeded to embark in a furious celebration that we haven't forgiven him for since. It's bad enough to sign for Liverpool, let alone revel in a goal against the club that made your name.

Ince's goal could conceivably have cost United the title. Arsenal had beaten Tottenham to take a three-point lead at the top of the table and once again Wenger's team were demonstrating their stomach for the battle down the stretch. Ferguson vented his frustration at Elleray after the game. 'I think the referee has handed it to them and it does not do our game much good when you see things like that,' he said.

United still had a game in hand and, thanks to Yorke's winner at Middlesbrough, they drew level with Arsenal at the top with two matches remaining. It couldn't have been closer. Both teams had 76 points from 36 matches and an identical goal difference. Arsenal had Leeds away and Aston Villa at home, while United would go to Blackburn before taking on Tottenham at Old Trafford on the final day of the season.

Arsenal were up first, and this time they faltered, going down 1-0 at Elland Road, and when United took a point from a 0-0 draw against Blackburn, relegating Brian Kidd's team in the process, it meant a victory against Tottenham would win them the title. United's impossibly epic season had come down to three matches in the space of ten days. Three wins would bring them the Treble. Three defeats would almost certainly leave them empty-handed. Talk about 'squeaky bum time' – the fear was now so strong I tried everything possible to stop myself from thinking about it.

But no amount of partying, tidying my room or planning the rest of my life could take those three trophies from the front of my mind. Conversation about anything but United was a waste of time, and the nerves grew more acute by the day. We could see the prizes, but there was still an epic journey to complete before we'd get anywhere near touching them. And with great expectancy comes the potential for epic disappointment. Triumph or disaster, there was no middle ground at the end of the 1998/99 season.

Tottenham came to Old Trafford with nothing to play for, but when Les Ferdinand lobbed Schmeichel to put them ahead on 24 minutes, United fans sensed yet another unbearably tense shift at the altar. For the rest of the first half United poured forward and laid siege to the Spurs goal, until finally Beckham found a way through. Collecting the ball on the right edge of the penalty area he steered a wicked curling shot into the opposite corner to take United into the break level at 1-1. Just three minutes after the restart they went ahead when Cole showed superb technique to control a high ball and chip the onrushing Ian Walker.

United fans wanted a third, desperately. But it wouldn't come. And for the last 20 minutes we watched on in agony as Tottenham created the occasional chance and United nervously defended their lead. Finally, what seemed like decades later, the referee blew his whistle and Ferguson was heard by half of Old Trafford screaming with joy on the touchline. Beckham and Scholes dropped to their knees in the centre circle, and 55,000 inside Old Trafford set about getting the party started with a rendition of Queen's 'We are the Champions'. It was United's fifth title under Ferguson; their 12th in total, and the first part of the Treble was in the bag.

The second part came all too easily against Newcastle at Wembley, where Sheringham produced an imperious display after replacing the injured Keane early on. He scored the first and set up the second for Scholes, as United ran out comfortable winners. Ferguson was able to rest Stam, Blomqvist and Yorke on the bench, and he could barely have wished for a more routine victory with the Champions League final just four days away. It brought United's third Double in five years and served as the ideal fillip ahead of the biggest game the club had played for 31 years.

Full speed ahead Barcelona.

CHAPTER 13
24 HOURS IN BARCELONA

It was barely six o'clock in the morning and Dad needed some convincing. 'It's the European Cup final, normal social rules don't apply,' I told him. And with that he walked up to the bar of an empty chain pub in Stansted Airport and ordered two pints of Stella for breakfast – a winning start to any day, let alone for two people about to watch their beloved football team reach the culmination of the most remarkable season in British football history.

Soon enough the tables around us filled with United fans, the beer flowed, and talk turned to the relative merits of the 1968 European Cup winners and Ferguson's class of 1999. Most agreed the current crop were a better side player for player, but only if they did the business in Barcelona could they be considered truly worthy of Sir Matt Busby's legendary vintage of Charlton, Best and Law. Would they do it? 'It's 1999, of course they f**king will,' said one already well-lubricated fan to the rest. You couldn't help but agree with him.

Everybody was going to the game, but nobody had tickets yet. We were initially told they'd be posted out two weeks before the trip; then they'd be at Stansted for check-in; then they'd be at Girona Airport when we landed. Nobody seemed overly concerned, so we saw no reason to suspect anything was out of the ordinary. The company involved had been working as agents for United's travels abroad for years, and earned a reputation as being trustworthy and reliable, if a little disorganised. It was a major operation for them and there were bound to be some last-minute adjustments.

So we boarded the plane a couple of pints to the good and spent the flight discussing Ferguson's selection. United would be without the suspended Paul Scholes and Roy Keane, and that meant much rested on the shoulders of David Beckham, who was set to be handed a role in central midfield alongside Nicky Butt. Beckham had been used almost exclusively on the right since breaking into Ferguson's team, so thrusting him into the boiler room for a game of this nature represented something of a gamble.

But Ferguson didn't have much choice. He'd toyed with playing Ryan Giggs centrally, but Beckham offered a superior range of passing and more physicality to the role, while Giggs' pace would be far more useful out wide. Beckham relished the opportunity. He saw himself eventually moving inside and playing in the middle anyway, so an opportunity to prove his credentials in the biggest club game in Europe was quite an honour. He was grateful to Ferguson for giving him the opportunity, and even more grateful for the accolades he received from his manager after the game.

Three bottles of lager later we landed in Girona. The airport was heaving with United fans and armed Spanish police, and there was unease in the air. We were moved quickly through customs and then herded into the coach park where a representative of the travel company was due to meet us to distribute tickets. When we got there the spaces marked for our coaches were empty. There was nobody to be seen. And after an hour of waiting under the hot midday sun, we were all beginning to suspect foul play. A call to the tour operator's offices in Manchester got no reply. Another fan managed to talk to a friend who walked by and said the windows had been boarded up. 'They've f**king done a runner,' he said.

Dad immediately suggested we should get on the next plane back to London, but it wasn't an option. The police told us that we were causing a problem by lingering at the airport, ordered us to board some replacement coaches and sent us on to Barcelona, knowing full well none of us had tickets. The air conditioning was broken and the hour and a half journey to Barcelona was uncomfortable in every sense. Grown men sat with their heads in their hands, Dads were having to tell their young children they were not going to the game, and all that was left to do was to try and find information on a good bar in which to watch it.

When we finally arrived we were met by hundreds more United fans who'd booked with the same company. As many as 2,000 people in total had been victims of the scam and United fans were strewn across the coach park in varying states of anger and disbelief.

It was oppressively hot and there was little else to do but to find shade, then head to a bar in which we could drown our sorrows. Dad and I slipped away from the maddening crowd and began plotting a back route towards the stadium. I was desperately disappointed, but I didn't want the old man to know it, so I tried my best to emphasise the positives. 'In years to come people will ask us where we were when United won the Treble,' I said. 'We'll be able to say we were there, right there in the city in which they did it.' He shrugged his shoulders and kept on walking, forcing a smile but knowing full well I was talking rubbish. We were well overdue a 1999 moment.

Then from out of a side street darted a young Spaniard in a Barcelona shirt, looking furtive and nervously scanning the area. We were the only people within 100 yards when he appeared and the only people to hear him say, 'You guys… tickets to the match?' before ducking back down the alleyway. Dad was sceptical, but I decided to go and talk to him. He explained that Barcelona had released 2,000 tickets to local students and while he really wanted to go to the game, he was also in desperate need for some extra cash. 'One hundred and twenty euros each,' he said. 'Must be now, must be right now.'

It was a lot of money, and there was a lot of risk involved. There was no way of knowing whether the tickets were genuine or even that the transaction itself would run smoothly when we made the exchange. But we were desperate and decided to go for it. The next problem was getting the cash out. Dad tried both his cards and for some reason could only withdraw 100 euros. We still had to find another 140 euros, and all hopes rested on my bank balance. I wasn't confident. But somehow, after sprinting around the outskirts of Barcelona like a man possessed and visiting three different cashpoints, I managed to get it together. Thank god for overdrafts.

We did the business and the two tickets were ours. There was still a major doubt whether they'd get us in the stadium, but there was no point worrying about that now. As we turned a corner we were treated to the welcome sight of a terrace bar absolutely heaving with the red and white masses in full voice. 'Jip Jaap Stam's a big Dutch man, get past him if you f**king can…' came the chant. And there we were, right in the middle of the biggest party in Barcelona that afternoon, and with fully six hours to go until kick-off.

It was a riotous afternoon fit for the occasion. We ate steaks, drank San Miguel and sang our hearts out. United fans of all ages, from all parts of the world, joined together and 'partied like it was 1999' – swapping stories and buying each other drinks as the sun began to set on what had already been a highly eventful day. And fortunately for the owner of the bar, Dad's credit card was working again when the time came to pay the bill and head to the stadium.

The next hour set the tone for the game ahead – it was unbearably tense and largely frustrating. Spanish police on horseback escorted us to the ground at a painfully slow pace, and when the time finally came to enter the turnstiles we could hear people being turned away with illegal tickets. They were scanning every ticket stub going into the ground and Dad and I were terrified we'd be found out and then struggle to get back through the crowds to find a bar – completing what would have been a disastrously expensive misadventure. But the Spanish student had been good to his word. Our tickets were genuine and we were admitted to the stadium.

We climbed the endless concrete stairs to the very top tier of the Camp Nou, swaying with the rest of them, and emerged to find ourselves amid a happy mixture of United fans and Spanish locals. The Bayern fans were away to our left and already packed in ready for the game, and the atmosphere was everything you'd imagine. It was a balmy, still night, and the pitch below looked immaculate – glistening invitingly under the floodlights. The players were out warming up and the announcer was running through the two line-ups.

Things were going a little too smoothly. But as we handed our tickets to the steward at the top of the stairs he did a quick double take. 'Your ticket is right up there,' he said to me. 'But this one is all the way down there,' he said to my Dad. 'Your seats are not together, maybe you can swap?'

He was right. We had consecutive numbers, but the letters beside them were different. In the confusion we hadn't even noticed, and were now left contemplating watching the game about 100 yards away from each other. In these situations the officious rarely back down, but this was Barcelona in 1999 – anything was possible. Dad put a hand on the steward's shoulder. I couldn't hear what he said but he turned to me with a smile on his face. 'He's going to let one of us sit in the aisle next to the seat down there,' Dad said. 'He'll just pretend he didn't notice.' It was a well-deserved break.

United were to start, as expected, with Beckham and Butt in the middle of the park. Jesper Blomqvist would be on the left, with Giggs asked to switch wings and take up Beckham's usual role on the right. Elsewhere the team pretty much picked itself. Peter Schmeichel was in goal, with a back four of Denis Irwin, Jaap Stam, Ronny Johnsen and Gary Neville. After the season they'd had together, scoring a combined 53 goals, there was never any doubt that Dwight Yorke and Andy Cole would be chosen to start up front.

It was a particularly poignant night for Schmeichel. The great Dane would be making his 398th and last appearance for United in Barcelona, having announced his retirement the previous November. 'I am not trying to think about it as my last match,' he said. 'I am just going about it as normal and concentrating on how I'm going to play. We've been trying for years to get to this point and the way it is, is just a coincidence. I think it was inevitable we were going to reach the European Cup final one way or the other, and I am just pleased it has happened in my time here.'

Schmeichel deserved a glorious swansong, but his first meaningful act of the night was to pick the ball out of the United net. There were just six minutes on the clock when Mario Basler's tame free-kick put the Germans ahead. Markus Babel peeled off the edge of the wall to clear a path for his shot and Basler obliged with a low drive into the bottom corner. It was as soft a goal as United had conceded all season and left Ferguson's team of 1999 once again needing to come from behind.

Up in the gods of Camp Nou the game was drifting by like a blur. United were enjoying some good possession, but there was no sign of the expressive, dynamic attacking play we'd become used to that season. Beckham and Butt were feverishly working away, but that couldn't disguise the lack of creativity in the key areas of the pitch. Meanwhile Blomqvist was anonymous on the left and Giggs achieved little cutting in from the right every time he got possession. United failed to create a single clear-cut chance in the first 45 minutes and they were in danger of letting the match pass by without making a memorable attacking contribution.

From the stands, it was starting to feel like the anti-climax every United supporter had dreaded. Dad and I tried to stay positive, but there was little cause for optimism in the first 45 minutes. This was not the United who'd thrilled us all season, and won friends and fans all over the world with their endless spirit and drive. It felt like a game too far, a stage too demanding for a team who'd spilled blood and guts in the name of the impossible Treble. If Bayern scored again you felt sure it was over. United hadn't looked like scoring at all, let alone scoring twice – and weight of expectancy appeared to be draining legs and minds on the club's biggest night for 31 years.

I was particularly frustrated with the Blomqvist/Giggs situation. The hard-working Swede was efficient, but short on inspiration. And why waste the potential match-winning guile of Giggs on the opposite side of the pitch to the one he'd mastered as a teenager? All around us, United fans were calling for Sheringham. There was a sense his experience and composure was exactly what United needed, and when Ferguson heeded our call after 67 minutes, Teddy was greeted to a huge roar and a sense of hope returned. Sheringham replace Blomqvist and Beckham and Giggs were sent out to the flanks on which they'd built their careers. United responded by creating chances for Stam and Butt, but both failed to trouble Oliver Kahn in the Bayern goal. Was it too little, too late from Ferguson? Had he got it all wrong by going with Beckham in the middle? Why had he wasted Giggs on the right? The doubts were start-ing to creep in among the fans. Tensions were running high.

Then came the moment it looked like the Germans had won it. Basler released Mehmet Scholl and he found himself bearing down on Schmeichel with 11 minutes to play and Champions League glory in his sights. His chip was perfectly weighted, but it bounced up and caught the inside of the post, before landing softly back into Schmeichel's bear-like hands. Had it gone in United would almost certainly have lost, and the media would have rounded on Ferguson and blamed his tactics for the defeat. A good number of the fans would have joined in too, and Dad and I would have been among them. It was a fickle place to be, and the tactical shortcomings of United in Barcelona were looking like they'd killed the Treble.

With ten minutes left Ferguson played his last attacking card. He brought on Ole Gunnar Solskjaer for Cole and the Norwegian striker almost made an immediate impact when he headed straight at Kahn. The game was now stretched and being played at a frenetic pace. Schmeichel made a superb save to deny Scholl at one end and then Yorke mis-kicked with the goal at his mercy at the other. But time was running out on United. And for all their tireless running, nobody in a red shirt seemed capable of summoning the inspiration we needed.

With the scoreboard clock showing 89 minutes I was almost ready to give up and leave. But then Beckham scurried over the corner flag directly beneath us and prepared to take a corner. He didn't have much room, and barely any time, but he still managed a decent delivery that was almost met by Schmeichel – who'd come all the way forward for one last hurrah. Yorke flapped at it at the far post; then a Bayern defender sliced a clearance to Giggs on the edge of the box. Giggs scuffed his shot, but Sheringham was in the right place to sweep it home from six yards and send the United fans into wild, emotional celebration in every corner of the stadium.

'Name on the trophy!' said ITV commentator Clive Tyldesley who'd been stressing a sense of destiny at every stage of United's European campaign. And in the top tier of the Camp Nou strangers were hugging and kissing each other like it was the most natural thing in the world. Dad reached for his top pocket and pulled out a cigar he'd saved for the match, but he didn't have time to light it. Down below Beckham was taking another corner. He swung it over and this time Sheringham flicked it on at the near post. The ball fizzed past the Bayern defenders like a meteor, but Solskjaer appeared to see it in slow motion. He adjusted his body and stuck out a leg to volley the ball into the roof of the net, winning United the European Cup and the Treble in one sweet poke of the toe. 'Manchester United have reached the Promised Land,' pronounced Tyldesley.

Solskjaer slid on his knees to the corner flag, Schmeichel did a cartwheel and two thirds of the stadium erupted for the second time in two minutes. The other third sat in stunned silence. Bayern's players had been within seconds of glory, but now they were broken men. With ten minutes to go Ottmar Hitzfeld had taken off his captain Lothar Matthäus, and he surely regretted it now. The Germans trudged vacantly back to the centre circle, looking like the startled victims of a devastating explosion, and Stefan Effenberg humped one last, tired ball towards the United box. Nobody thought for a second they could summon an equaliser. Butt smashed the ball back with interest and referee Pierluigi Collina peeped three times to complete one of the most extraordinary climaxes you could wish to imagine.

'History is made and nobody will ever win a European Cup final more dramatically than this,' said Tyldesley. '… Memories are made of this. Forever and a day United fans will ask, "Where did you watch the 1999 European Cup final?… Where did you watch Ollie Solskjaer win it with virtually the last kick of the final?" And 50,000 or so will be able to say, "I was there".'

Down below us the celebrations were in full flow. United's Treble winners were hopping about like wildly excited children, squealing in hysterical delight and throwing their arms around anyone within reach. Even the unused substitutes were in on the act – David May, Wes Brown and Phil Neville mobbing Schmeichel in quick succession and engulfing the retiring great in a blanket of red. Beckham had been in perpetual motion for 93 minutes, but he still found the energy to run towards the United fans and punch the air in delight.

Up in the stands United fans were delirious. The songs were flowing and we'd been on our feet since the moment Sheringham swept home the equaliser. People were shaking hands and a good number had tears in their eyes. And for the stunned and heartbroken Bayern fans sat in respectful silence across from us, there was already a chant to remind them of the most painful defeat you could wish upon a football supporter. The baby-faced assassin had larruped Liverpool, and now he'd buried Bayern. 'Who put the ball in the Germans' net?' we sang. 'Ole Gunnar Solskjaer.'

'My players never give in. You always expect them to be doing something. But this time I thought they were beaten,' said a euphoric Ferguson after the game. 'The team spirit is just unbelievable. Everyone works together and everyone is in this together... They are incredible human beings. You can talk about tactics all you like, but spirit is unbeatable at times.'

It was left to Schmeichel and Ferguson to lift the over-sized Champions League trophy, stood upon a hastily erected stage that threatened to give way under the riotous celebrations of the United players and staff. When they finally retreated to the dressing room United's kit man, Albert Morgan, was thrown into the Jacuzzi. Champagne was everywhere and the tensions of an impossibly epic 63-game season flowed out in a carnival atmosphere. When the players finally got dressed the party moved to the Ballroom of the Arts, a luxury Barcelona hotel, where they were joined by their wives and families to drink the night away.

For United fans heading back to the UK that night the surroundings were not quite so grand. We packed into coaches and spent the early hours camped in Girona Airport waiting for somebody to tell us when a plane might be available to take us home. We were emotionally and physically drained and by 3 a.m. there was barely a sound to be heard from anybody in a red shirt. But it had all been worth it. Eventually, at 7 a.m. the following morning, we boarded a flight and slept like contented babies all the way back to Stansted.

'Forever and a day United fans will ask, "Where did you watch the 1999 European Cup final?... Where did you watch Ollie Solskjaer win it with virtually the last kick of the final?"'

We were there Clive. We were there.

CHAPTER 14
ARISE SIR ALEX

United's remarkable comeback in Barcelona was a triumph for their never-say-die spirit, the product of a cultural revolution Ferguson had been leading since the day he walked into Old Trafford in 1986. On their day his team could attack with the best of them, fashion devastating passages of play and score goals at will. But unlike the United sides that came before him, Ferguson had instilled a steely nerve and the ability to win matches when the inspiration dried up. Against Bayern they fell flat for 90 minutes on the biggest night of their season, but still they toiled and still they believed it could happen. It said everything about their fantastical campaign that when Teddy Sheringham scored the equaliser there was an inevitability to it that was not lost on anyone.

'Can Manchester United score... they always score,' came the commentary as David Beckham swung over the corner that led to the goal. And a nation watched on expecting the same. Moments of individual brilliance and players of genius were all well and good, but to win a Treble you needed more than talent. You needed a collective stubbornness in the face of adversity, and an outright refusal to accept defeat as a possibility. You needed a team who, for want of a less corny headline, never stopped believing.

There was something to aspire to in that. You could hate United and what they stood for – the corporate megastore, the cocky midfielder who lost England the World Cup and the manager who played mind games – but you couldn't help but admire that kind of pluck and persistence. They'd done to the Germans what the Germans had so often done to England on the international stage, and that was reason enough for most of the country to stand up in recognition. Not since 1984 had an English team won the European Cup. Ferguson's United had done much to restore the continental pride that was lost during the five-year ban on English clubs following the Heysel disaster, and you didn't have to be a Red to revel in it.

The European success, and the unprecedented Treble, called for recognition. And when the Queen's honours list was announced less than a month after the Champions League final it was no surprise to see the 57-year-old Ferguson awarded a knighthood to add to his OBE. 'I see this not just as an honour for me, but for the people who have supported me through my life and made me what I am,' he said. 'I am delighted and honoured.'

Ferguson had matched Sir Matt Busby's feat in lifting the European Cup and now he'd matched his knighthood. Thirty-one years after Busby's team triumphed at Wembley, United were kings of Europe again and Ferguson had made quite a journey from the working-class Clydeside district he'd grown up in.

It was coming up to 13 years he'd been at United, during which he'd brought the club 12 major trophies – including two Doubles and a Treble – and treated the fans to some of the most breathtaking football they'd ever seen. Ferguson had taken a hungover giant, shaken it from its foggy slumber and set a march on English football that had defined the decade. If there was a perch, then Liverpool were long since off it and United had built a five-storey house on top of it. The balance of power had emphatically shifted and one man was largely responsible.

Ferguson had achieved it all by marrying attractive, expressive, attacking football with a ferocious competitiveness and an uncompromising mentality. His players cherished his loyalty and feared his wrath, and they worked like dogs to please him. He'd turned Old Trafford from a social club of drinkers to a trophy-winning factory where players stayed after training and fed on each other's unswerving commitment to the cause.

His man management spoke for itself. Howard Wilkinson couldn't handle the impassioned Eric Cantona at Leeds, but Ferguson harnessed his gifts and made him a king. And when he ventured into infamy at Selhurst Park in 1995, it was Cantona's ever-loyal manager who stayed by his side and ultimately coaxed him back into a red shirt, to the eternal gratitude of every United fan in the country. Never once did he say a bad word about Cantona in the press, never once did he doubt him. If anything he played on the Cantona controversy to galvanise the club and embrace a 'them against us' mentality that only strengthened the will of his players, and the devotion of the fans.

He'd performed a similar rehabilitation with Beckham after his red card in St Etienne, and less than a year after that fateful night at the World Cup his midfielder stood on the pitch in Barcelona getting his photograph taken with the European Cup. Ferguson and United had cocooned him in those difficult days and restored his broken confidence to stunning effect. Beckham's 1998/99 campaign was his most influential yet, and he fully admitted it wouldn't have been possible without Ferguson's fatherly influence.

The same could be said of Beckham's contemporaries, the classes of 1992 and 1993. Ryan Giggs, Nicky Butt, Paul Scholes and the Neville brothers had been fortunate enough to emerge in the Ferguson-era United where work ethic was paramount and giants like Steve Bruce, Peter Schmeichel and Cantona roamed the training ground. But most of all they had been lucky enough to take their first steps in senior football under a manager who trusted them.

Ferguson could be ruthless and reactionary, but he was also one of the great nurturers of young talent. He protected his Fledglings from the media and played his part in grounding them. Theirs was a triumph not just of ability, but a maturity that Ferguson helped bestow on them. And it paid off. The team that won the 1999 Champions League final included Giggs, Butt, Beckham and Gary Neville, and had Phil Neville and Wes Brown on the bench. If not for his suspension, Scholes would have taken that quota to seven.

The fact that all of those players were still relatively young could only bode well for the future. Barring injury they'd all peak in their late 20s and early 30s and Ferguson would have at his behest a team of one-club men who were red to the core and knew better than most how to win things. If success breeds success, then United were surely on the verge of a decade in which they'd be even more dominant than the last.

Ferguson collected his knighthood from the Queen on 14 July 1999, the culmination of 13 years at United – a reign that defined my association with the club I loved, and had charted my fandom from an obsessive boy to an obsessive man. Those years had taught me the virtues of fierce conviction, determination and loyalty – but also that genius is unfailingly flawed. Ferguson the football manager could be a ferocious, cold and clinical operator. That he did it all in the name of United was the reason we loved him, but there wasn't a United fan in the country who didn't appreciate why a good number of rival fans wanted him burned at the stake.

The Treble success wouldn't help his popularity outside Old Trafford. The rival fans who saw him as the master manipulator of the media; a power player who leaned on referees and officials to bring his team favour, now had more ammunition than ever. Ferguson was no longer just the grumpy manager of the most successful football team in the country, he was a knight of the realm and moving in the kind of circles that brought influence everywhere he went. And if you had your reservations before the Treble, you positively hated him after the accolades that followed.

His detractors wanted nothing more than for Ferguson to fall on the sword that had knighted him, but Sir Alex had no intention of resting on his laurels.

CHAPTER 15
THE PROBLEM WITH SUCCESS

How do you follow the most successful season in British football history? That was the problem facing Ferguson and his squad ahead of what was always going to be 'the season after the season before'. What they'd achieved in the space of ten remarkable days in May 1999 – winning the Premier League title, the FA Cup and the Champions League – might not be matched in their lifetimes, let alone their next season. And for that reason, whatever came next was going to feel like an anticlimax.

United fans tried to stay grounded, but after gorging on the glorious excesses of 1999 it wasn't easy. We had the best manager in the world and a squad of players who'd won it all and, for the most part, remained in the prime of their careers. Only Peter Schmeichel would be missing from the class of 1998/99 and, while the big man was a mighty loss, we fully expected Ferguson to replace him with a world-class goalkeeper fit for the job. Everything pointed to more of the same, but could we really expect the stars to align as they had in 1999?

There were certainly more obstacles at the outset this time. United returned for the new season in defensive flux. Ronny Johnsen, Wes Brown and David May were ruled out for virtually the whole season, while new arrival Mark Bosnich looked ill equipped for the colossal task of taking over from the departed Schmeichel in goal.

Bosnich was a product of United's youth system, and having been impressed by his performances for Aston Villa, Ferguson was convinced he was ready to fill the sizeable gloves of the man he'd called the best goalkeeper in the world. The 27-year-old Australian was high on self-confidence but low on fitness, and when he injured a hamstring in United's third game of the season Ferguson acted swiftly to bring in Italian Massimo Taibi for £4.4 million from Venezia – not just as cover, but as a potential replacement. It wasn't his best move in the transfer market.

Taibi's United career is told as a cautionary tale by Ferguson of what can happen to good players when they arrive at Old Trafford. He gave away a soft goal on his debut against Liverpool, made a terrible mistake in a 3-3 draw at home to Southampton and was on the receiving end of a 5-0 battering from Chelsea at Stamford Bridge – prompting the press to call him 'the blind Venetian'. He'd made just four starts for United, conceding 11 goals, when he was sent on loan to Reggina in January 2000. Unsurprisingly he never came back and Bosnich was left to fight it out for the No. 1 shirt with veteran Raimond van der Gouw when he returned from injury.

United coped, but in truth Ferguson failed to find a worthy successor to Schmeichel until the arrival of Edwin van der Sar five years later. For that reason, many have argued Ferguson's teams failed on the European stage as a direct result of their goalkeeping shortcomings in the period between the Dane and the Dutchman. That said they still managed to win three Premier League titles and an FA Cup in the intervening years – a veritable gluttony of success for any other club bar Ferguson's United.

United also had problems in midfield. When Jesper Blomqvist suffered a serious knee injury on the club's pre-season tour to Australia and the Far East, it turned out he'd played his last competitive game for United in the Champions League final in Barcelona. The Swedish winger was just 25 years old, and Ferguson had expected him to grow in influence after playing his part in the Treble season, but it wasn't to be. Blomqvist eventually left for Everton in 2001, then moved to Charlton a year later, but his best years were already behind him.

Then there was the Roy Keane contract dispute. United's tub-thumping captain was among the most wanted players in Europe, and with just a year left on his current deal he was adamant he should be earning in the region of £50,000 a week. United's initial offer was around half that amount, and when they made a 'final offer' of £32,000 in July 1999, Keane flatly refused it. 'Deep down they must have known it wasn't something I could sign,' he said. 'Our dealings have to be realistic. I am not naive enough to settle for anything less than a reasonable valuation of my worth.'

Something would have to give. United had a wage structure in place that meant their most valuable players were on 'comparable terms', but Keane was demanding nearly twice what any other player at Old Trafford was earning. On the strength of the Treble, and with the midfielder's stock at an all-time high, he couldn't have picked a better time to have a run at the bank. United faced an ethical and financial dilemma. If they gave Keane the salary he wanted, others would unquestionably be knocking on the door and demanding the same. If they didn't, he'd leave the club and they'd face not only the wrath of the fans who adored him, but that of a manager who'd built a team around him. And he'd been lining up against United in some-one else's colours.

That thought was enough to get the majority of United fans on his side. Keane might have been an outspoken, cut-throat of a foot-baller, who barged his way head-first through a career of controversy, but all the while he was in red we had an advantage. And anybody in a job completely understood where he was coming from. Other players in the Premier League were getting paid considerably more for doing a lesser job, and he simply wasn't prepared to sit back and take it. Whether money or pride was the defining motivation is not clear, but you can't deny the man was a trailblazer for players' rights at Old Trafford. To be honest, I just wanted United to pay whatever he wanted. And I'm sure plenty of Reds felt exactly the same.

Ferguson played both sides of the argument. He called for United's chief executive Martin Edwards to break the bank for Keane, but at the same time suggested a salary cap for football's big earners. 'Wages have to be capped or the game will not be able to cope – something will break,' he said. 'Football has to start thinking about tomorrow rather than what it can do today. I know some clubs are on the brink and with each season the situation only worsens.'

History attests Ferguson had a point, and United's once great rivals Leeds are the case study for footballing financial meltdown. But money troubles haven't stopped fans demanding their club spend huge sums on transfer fees and wages to attract the best players.

As for Keane, United's captain had always been strong-willed and outspoken on the pitch, but now he was taking his fight to the boardroom. He knew United would need to spend £10 to £15 million or more to replace him, and that they'd not be able to attract his like without breaking their wage structure anyway, so he had all the bargaining power he needed. By constantly reiterating his desire to stay at United he had the fans firmly on his side. It was a power play that set the tone for contract negotiations to come at Old Trafford, and the United board were ultimately left with little choice.

Finally, in December 1999, United baulked and offered Keane a four-year deal worth £52,000 a week. Ferguson's powers of persuasion had clearly made the difference and the Irishman became the highest paid footballer in the country – ahead of Alan Shearer and Duncan Ferguson, who were both earning around £10,000 a week less. The fans were delighted, but they were given a harsh lesson in the economic realities of the deal when United announced at the end of the season they would hike ticket prices to cover the cost of keeping their talismanic midfielder at Old Trafford.

It was a cheap-shot PR move from United, designed to excuse their reluctance to give Keane more money, and I was appalled when I heard about it. How dare the suits play themselves off against the club's best player; and what on earth were they thinking upsetting the most volatile man at Old Trafford just a few months after getting him back onside? Ultimately both Keane and the United board had decided to play out their private business dealings in public, and it left a nasty taste in the mouth. But Keane was just an unhinged footballer with a chip on his shoulder; they were the biggest football club in the world. They should have known better.

Just a couple of months after the Keane contract saga came to an end, Ferguson faced a very different problem with another of his midfielders. This time it involved David Beckham, who'd married Victoria in a preposterously lavish ceremony the previous summer and by now had taken residence in the Hertfordshire mansion the press dubbed 'Beckingham Palace'. Posh and Becks were ubiquitous in the media, and the trappings of their combined fame unquestionably rankled with the United manager. To a no-nonsense steelworker's son from Govan, Beckham's increasingly public life was at odds with the demands of being a professional footballer. And Ferguson didn't like it.

Things came to a head in the week before United travelled to Leeds for what was a key match in the context of the title race. Beckham's son Brooklyn fell ill with gastroenteritis and after setting off on the Thursday morning to report for training, he decided to turn his car around and return home to be with his family. He left a message for United's assistant manager Steve McClaren, but never heard back, so assumed United knew what was going on and there was nothing to worry about.

But when he reported for training the next day Ferguson was furious. He'd seen pictures of Victoria out at a charity event the night before and treated Beckham to a public dressing down in front of the entire first-team squad. Beckham was ordered to go and train with the reserves, but he refused and instead went into the gym and worked out on his own. And when he finally confronted his manager to have it out, Ferguson told him in no uncertain terms not to report for the Leeds game. 'Your responsibilities are here at the club, not at home with your son,' is how Beckham remembers it. 'You were babysitting while your wife was out gallivanting.' Beckham bit back. 'Don't talk about my wife like that, how would you feel if I was disrespectful about your wife?' he said.

Ferguson says he lost his temper because Beckham refused to accept he'd done anything wrong. 'I don't go out of my way to prove to people who is the manager,' he wrote in *Managing My Life*. 'But from time to time somebody in my job is confronted with a situation which must be handled in a manner that signifies control.' United's manager was making a statement that no one player was bigger than the club, and to make it with Beckham – the most famous footballer in the country – made sure it was headline news all over the world.

Beckham was photographed sitting dejected in the stands at Elland Road, and the rumours were rife he was set to leave United in protest. There had already been talk that Victoria wanted him to move to London and join Arsenal, and now Barcelona was being tipped as a possible destination. But Beckham didn't want to go anywhere, and when he made his peace with Ferguson and agreed to base himself in Cheshire rather than Hertfordshire during the weekdays, both parties were relieved to put the whole affair to bed.

To the fans the public feud demonstrated how fiercely Ferguson would protect the code of discipline he'd ushered in at United. Most managers would have buckled and picked Beckham for the game against Leeds, but Ferguson would rather have lost at Elland Road than betrayed a weakness in dealing with what he felt was unacceptable behaviour. It was all about principles. By sticking to his guns when it could conceivably have cost his team three points, the league title and perhaps even Beckham altogether, Ferguson was sending a message of intent to his entire squad – step out of line, and you'll be out. It doesn't matter what your name is or how good you are.

It was hard to accept as a fan. Whatever the morality of a situation, all I wanted was to see the best possible United side take the field every time they played. And when you've paid good money to watch a football match, nobody wants to see one of their team's best players sitting in the stands as a result of a petty feud. And while I could see the bigger picture, that of Ferguson keeping his house in order, it was hard not to see him dropping Beckham as a power play in their increasingly strained relationship. The old-fashioned father figure was putting his precocious son in his place, and you couldn't help wonder if he'd have dealt the same justice to a player with a lower public profile like Gary Neville.

United seemed to court controversy at every turn in the 1999/2000 season, not least when they announced they would not be entering the FA Cup. Instead they would travel to Brazil to compete in the inaugural Club World Championship – an eight-team tournament that was scheduled to take place during the fourth round of FA Cup matches in January.

The goal that started it all. Stormin' Norman Whiteside celebrates scoring the winner in the 1985 FA Cup Final against Everton, with Gordon Strachan and Paul McGrath.

My all-time United hero. Captain marvel Bryan Robson holds aloft his winners' medal.

New dawn at Old Trafford. Alex Ferguson before his first home game in charge of United, on 22nd November 1986.

United chairman Martin Edwards makes sure his new manager is well versed in the club's history.

"Right you two, how's about less of the lager and more of the inspirational stuff on the football pitch?" Ferguson with Paul McGrath and Bryan Robson in 1987.

Mark Robins celebrates his winner in the 1990 FA Cup semi-final replay against Oldham. The striker would prove an unlikely saviour for Ferguson.

United line up before the 1991 European Cup Winners' Cup Final. Back (left to right) Paul Ince, Mike Phelan, Les Sealey, Gary Pallister, Brian McClair, Steve Bruce. Front (left to right) Lee Sharpe, Clayton Blackmore, Bryan Robson, Mark Hughes, Denis Irwin

Mark Hughes scored twice as United beat his former club Barcelona 2-1 on a memorable night in Rotterdam.

Ferguson holds aloft his first
European trophy as a United
manager.

The King is born. Eric Cantona in
action shortly after joining United
from Leeds.

Lee Sharpe and Eric Cantona celebrate Cantona's goal against City, in March 1993

Captains both. Steve Bruce and Bryan Robson lift the Premier League trophy at Old Trafford, in May 1993.

Alex Ferguson passes on his instructions, as United prepare for extra-time in the 1994 FA Cup semi-final against Oldham at Wembley.

Roy Keane joined United in 1993, bringing a snarling intensity to the midfield and an all-consuming commitment that inspired everybody around him.

The classic bath shot. Mark Hughes, Gary Pallister and Bryan Robson toast the 1993/94 Premiership title.

Nice one Eric. Cantona is mobbed by Paul Ince, Roy Keane and Ryan Giggs after scoring from the penalty spot in the 1994 FA Cup Final win against Chelsea. Victory sealed United the Double.

Eric Cantona, shortly before he journeyed into infamy for attacking a fan at Selhurst Park in January 1995.

The prodigal son returns. Cantona celebrates scoring against Liverpool at Old Trafford, on his first game back after an eight-month ban. He'd lead United to another Double in the 1995/96 season.

Ryan Giggs, seconds away from revealing his chest wig after scoring a remarkable solo winner against Arsenal in the 1999 FA Cup semi-final replay.

A star is born. David Beckham celebrates scoring from the halfway line against Wimbledon in August 1996.

Dwight Yorke and Andy Cole came together for 53 goals in the 1998/99 season, and wreaked havoc all over Europe.

Alex Ferguson celebrates with his team, after United produced a remarkable comeback in Barcelona to beat Bayern Munich 2-1 and complete the Treble. It was United's first European title since 1968.

Sir Alex Ferguson with his wife Cathy, after receiving his knighthood from the Queen at Buckingham Palace in 1999.

Arsenal's Martin Keown taunts Ruud van Nistelrooy, after the United striker missed a penalty at Old Trafford in September 2003. Ugly scenes followed.

Come in number seven. Cristiano Ronaldo signed in 2003 and proved himself a worthy successor to David Beckham in United's famous number seven shirt. Arsenal's Patrick Vieria gives chase at Old Trafford.

A new adversary. Ferguson and Jose Mourinho shared a mutual respect, but it was Mourinho who prevailed during his time as manager of Chelsea.

Nemanja Vidic and Rio Ferdinand pictured in 2006. They'd form one of the most effective defensive partnerships in United history.

Roonaldo. The partnership of Wayne Rooney and Cristiano Ronaldo offered up 60 goals in the 2007/08 season. On their day they were unplayable.

European champions once more. United celebrate with the Champions League trophy, after beating Chelsea on penalties in Moscow, in May 2008.

Just the two then. Sir Alex Ferguson poses with the 2007/08 Premier League and Champions League trophies.

Wayne Rooney scores a spectacular winner against City at Old Trafford, in February 2011.

The future's bright. Javier 'Chicharito' Hernandez wheels away after scoring against Chelsea in the Champions League quarter-final at Old Trafford, in April 2011.

United were pilloried from all angles for their decision, which would leave the competition without its reigning champions for the first time in its 127-year history. The *Daily Mirror* launched a 'Save the FA Cup' campaign and criticism rained in from all directions. To outsiders it looked like United were betraying their heritage, but Ferguson maintains the club were put under intense pressure by the government and ultimately had little choice in the matter. 'We did it to help England's [2006] World Cup bid,' Ferguson said. 'That was the political situation. I regretted it because we got nothing but stick and terrible criticism for not being in the FA Cup when really it wasn't our fault.'

Whatever the reasoning, United's decision only further exaggerated the club's standing as the evil empire of English football. And when I tried to justify the move to fans of other clubs, I found myself agreeing with them. Leaving the FA Cup would have been unthinkable to the United I'd taken to my heart in 1985, but there were now dastardly Orwellian forces at work – and they seemed so carried away with their own success, they'd forgotten what put them at the top of the pile in the first place. After all, last I checked you couldn't win a Double or a Treble without the FA Cup.

United's South American adventure was a strangely underwhelming affair. They failed to get past the initial group stage and England lost out to Germany in the bidding for the 2006 World Cup. But United clearly enjoyed some fringe benefits. Ferguson and his team had two weeks in the sun and returned to a fixture list freed up from the commitments of the FA Cup. He has since reflected that both factors played a part in United's romp to the Premier League title that season. It's a perspective that further inflamed those who accused the FA of giving them preferential treatment by allowing them to boycott the most famous competition in club football.

But to be fair they didn't need any favours to win the league. Amid the controversies of Keane, Beckham and the FA Cup withdrawal, United delivered yet another superb domestic campaign in the 1999/2000 season. They scored a record 97 Premier League goals and rounded off the season with 11 straight victories to finish 18 points ahead of Wenger's Arsenal. Once again the partnership of Dwight

Yorke and Andy Cole did much of the damage, combining for 46 goals in total, but this time Keane, Ole Gunnar Solskjaer and Paul Scholes all joined them in double figures.

At the back Ferguson brought in Mikael Silvestre from Inter Milan as cover for the injured trio May, Johnsen and Brown. The Frenchman would ultimately succeed Denis Irwin as United's first-choice left back, but for the time being he was used centrally and with mixed results. Silvestre was quick, athletic and good in the air, but he was also prone to mistakes and United fans remained sceptical during his first season at the club.

Ferguson's approach in the Champions League seemed to suggest he shared our concerns. Silvestre started just twice in Europe, with Henning Berg preferred as a partner for Stam as United set about defending their title. This time around the format was changed to incorporate a second group stage, and after United finished top of their league in both rounds they were drawn against the mighty Real Madrid in the quarter-finals. It was a tie that pitted the undisputed kings of the continent against the pretenders to their throne, and brought together two of the most glamorous and storied football clubs on the planet. Standing in the way of United and a third European crown were the seven-times champions with whom they'd shared some classic matches in the past.

It was time to reminisce about United's 4-3 aggregate win against Real in 1968, where Sir Matt Busby's brilliant team came from behind at the Bernabeu on their way to a first European triumph. And to re-imagine the legendary Madrid side of Alfredo di Stefano, Francisco Gento et al, who were made to fight by a plucky brood of Busby Babes in 1957. Now they'd meet again, in a different century and with a new chapter waiting to be written.

The neutrals were naturally thrilled at the prospect, but I didn't share their excitement. I wanted my team to win the Champions League, and the best route was to avoid Madrid at every turn and hope they got unlucky against somebody else. They say you have to beat the best teams somewhere along the line, but, of course, that's not always true.

By the time the first leg came around in early April, United had the Premier League all but won. Confidence was soaring on the back of a 7-1 hammering of West Ham, in which Paul Scholes helped himself to a hat-trick, and Ferguson had no major injuries or suspensions to concern himself for the trip to the Bernabeu. Things were going all too smoothly, and when they came away from Spain with a hard-fought 0-0 draw, notable for some excellent defending and a superb performance from Bosnich in goal, United were made odds-on favourites to advance to the semi-finals.

In the build-up to the second leg Ferguson talked wistfully of emulating Madrid, Ajax and Bayern Munich by winning back-to-back European titles. Madrid won five in a row from 1956 to 1960 and Ferguson said United should be aspiring to build a dynasty of their own. This was the rhetoric of a man ready to stand shoulder to shoulder with the greatest managers of them all, and for whom a solitary European Cup win was never going to be enough. Ferguson had visited the Promised Land, and now he wanted to build a home there.

But this time this script wasn't as kind, and the inspiration never arrived. Keane put through his own net after 20 minutes and Madrid doubled their lead just after half-time when Raúl was given the freedom of Old Trafford to curl a superb finish past Van der Gouw. The striker made it 3-0 inside an hour when he profited from an outrageous piece of skill by Fernando Redondo at the by-line, and United were on the rack. They pulled two back, but not even the introduction of Ole Gunnar Solskjaer and Teddy Sheringham could save them this time. United's Champions League defence was over.

The anti-United brigade relished every second of it. The tales of 1999 had been rammed down their throats for almost a year and United were well overdue a crushing disappointment. This was the team who were too important to play in the FA Cup – who'd spent two weeks in Rio promoting their global brand when they should have been respecting the oldest competition in world football. In Keane they had the greediest footballer in the country and in Beckham the most vain. And when you've won the Treble, resentment comes with the territory.

The stick was coming from all angles when I returned to work on Thursday morning, but there was no escaping the harsh reality. United had been outclassed by Vincent del Bosque's exuberant Madrid, who were more comfortable on the ball and played with a verve going forward that United never came close to matching. Ferguson's team harried and chased, but they never found their rhythm, and they were guilty of some woeful defending early in the second half that ultimately cost them the tie. It was United's first defeat at Old Trafford for 16 months, and after the heroics of 1999 it felt like a regression to Ferguson's failed European campaigns that had come before.

Some pointed to Del Bosque's decision to play three central defenders as the undoing of Ferguson's team. The formation allowed Madrid's wing-backs Roberto Carlos and Michel Salgado to bomb forward at every opportunity, and effectively marooned Beckham and Ryan Giggs without the support of their occupied full-backs. Ferguson was caught out by the approach and having said in a press conference he expected Madrid to adopt the more traditional attacking formation of 4-4-2, he was very publicly outwitted by his opposite number. 'They surprised us with the three at the back, but we really should have sorted that out very quickly,' he admitted after the game.

After all that talk of legacy building, Ferguson was left to deconstruct a disjointed performance from a team who looked a long way short of greatness at Old Trafford that night. Madrid once again won the hearts of the footballing romantics and all too predictably marched to a record eighth European title a month or so later – with none other than former Liverpool winger Steve McManaman bagging a brilliant goal in the final to rub it in for dejected United fans looking on from afar.

But we didn't stay down for long. Just three days after being humbled in Europe, United sealed an emphatic Premier League title with a 3-1 win at Southampton. It was Ferguson's sixth championship in eight seasons and it came with four games still to play. 'Wednesday was a terrible night for us but losing is part of the game. It's how you recover that counts,' he said. 'I'm lucky to have a collection of players who mirror my own hunger, but the drive comes from within themselves. This is a team full of players with inner drive.'

If Ferguson was still smarting from the European failure he wasn't showing it. He was overflowing with praise for his team and finished the press conference by honouring them with the ultimate accolade. 'I think this is a maturing team, they are getting better all the time,' he said. 'I think they are the best team Manchester United have ever had.' Giggs agreed, saying 'not only do I think this is the greatest team, I think it has the potential to get even better.'

I wasn't convinced. United might have been dominant domestically, but only once in Ferguson's six attempts had they succeeded in Europe, and at the death of the 1999/2000 campaign they were once again exposed on the biggest stage. To stand alongside the teams of 1968 and 1999 they would have to do better than that – no matter how emphatic their command of the league at home. The fans knew it and the manager knew it, but maybe denial was the best public course of action.

As a fan you didn't know how to feel. The league titles still brought cause for riotous celebration, but that night in Barcelona had changed everything. European glory was no longer the preserve of Best, Law and Charlton; it was ours for the taking. And every time we fell short under Ferguson you couldn't help but feel that the clock was ticking on the best generation of players Old Trafford would see in our lifetimes.

That's the problem with success. It's infuriatingly addictive.

CHAPTER 16
POWER PLAYS

It was more of the same in the 2000/2001 campaign. United completed a hat-trick of Premier League titles by a ten-point margin over runners-up Arsenal, but fell short in Europe and could only watch on as a resurgent Liverpool won the FA Cup, the League Cup and the UEFA Cup under Gerard Houllier.

Roy Keane once again dominated the headlines. United's captain labelled sections of the Old Trafford crowd 'the prawn sandwich brigade' after a home game against Dynamo Kyiv in November, and in April he launched into a horrific revenge tackle against Alf-Inge Haaland. Football's 'Mr Angry' also threatened to quit the international scene in protest at the Republic of Ireland's training facilities, and the fact the players were asked to sit behind the coaching staff on flights.

The 'prawn sandwich' slur was unquestionably the least damaging. If you were a true United fan you assumed he was talking about somebody else. And if you happened to be a frequenter of corporate hospitality at Old Trafford you probably couldn't have cared less what the mad Irishman was going on about. It was simply a case of 'pass the Moet', and 'let's get back to the canapés'.

But it was the disgraceful thigh-high lunge on Haaland in the Manchester derby that brought Keane the most publicity. Keane had never forgiven him for what happened in 1997, when Haaland accused him of play-acting when he suffered a season-ending cruciate ligament injury against Leeds. The media rightly assumed his assault was

Keane returning the favour, but it wasn't until his autobiography came out August 2002 that he revealed it was premeditated. 'I'd waited long enough. I f**king hit him hard. The ball was there (I think). Take that you c**t. And don't ever stand over me sneering about fake injuries,' he wrote.

It was a shocking revelation, but this was Keane we were talking about – a backstreet brawler whose fierce pride time and again undermined his discipline. United's captain had his own moral code and the more he grew in stature at the club the more he did what he pleased. We didn't care as long as we were driving United onto success, and Ferguson mostly stood back and let him get on with things, knowing full well the same animalistic drive was fundamental to the barnstorming midfielder who set the tone for his team's competitiveness on the pitch.

Censor the man and you risked censoring the player – and for that reason Keane was in the same category as Eric Cantona when it came to Ferguson's approach. His talent brought him licence to stray, and special treatment for a manager who made few exceptions. But thank goodness he did for those two – because without them United would never have achieved the success they did during the first 15 years of the Ferguson reign. Ferguson played favourites with Cantona and Keane, but he did so knowing their gifts would only be realised if he coaxed them out. It was brilliant man management, even if it went against the principles he set for the majority of his working life.

Perhaps some of the anger Keane took out on Haaland stemmed from United's failure in Europe. This time it was Bayern Munich who did the damage in the Champions League, the Germans exacting a modicum of revenge for 1999 with a comfortable 3-1 aggregate win in the quarter-finals. Bayern won 1-0 at Old Trafford and 2-1 in Germany, with all three goals the result of slack defending. Ferguson told a press conference before the away leg that his players were playing for their futures. 'Munich will make up our minds about a few things,' he said. But not even their manager's grandstanding could spark a performance worthy of the occasion.

You could argue the writing was on the wall when an impostor managed to sneak his way onto the pitch and into the team photo before kick-off. None of the genuine players seemed to spot the hoaxer and they were equally oblivious when Elber stole in unmarked at the far post to put Bayern ahead after five minutes. By half-time United were 2-0 down and they ultimately slipped out of the competition with barely a whimper. The dynamic, all-conquering force of the Premier League had once again gone missing in Europe.

'Maybe it is the end of the road for this team,' said Keane after the game. 'We have given our all and we're just not good enough. You have to face facts… It's no good winning the Premier League, we need to step up a level in Europe.'

It was quite a statement from the captain of a team who consistently annihilated the opposition in what was supposedly the best league in the world, but it summed up United's predicament perfectly. Domestic success had become a given to such an extent that the Champions League was now the only barometer of their progress worth reading. Europe was no longer the cherry on the cake, it was the cake itself – and unless United could translate their prolific trophy hunting at home to the plains of the Big Cup on a regular basis, they would be deemed a failure by not only large sections of the media, but a good number of the fans. We'd been spoiled rotten, and we were greedy as pigs for more glory.

Talk immediately turned to the players Ferguson needed to bring in to make a genuine challenge in Europe. The class of 1999 were still winning league titles, but the consensus was they'd run out of ideas and inspiration in the Champions League. United had gone stale, and the glorious night in Barcelona suddenly seemed a very long time ago. Patrick Kluivert's name once again peppered the gossip columns, as did that of Brazilian midfielder Rivaldo.

But as United prepared for their last game of the season at Tottenham, it wasn't their prospective signings that dominated the headlines – it was their manager. After 15 years of glittering success, Ferguson had announced the following campaign would be his last. His contract would run until May 2002, at which point he'd walk away from Old Trafford and presumably settle into a retirement filled with golf, horse racing and fine wine. Fans and players alike were devastated by the news, and from a personal perspective it was a jarring thought to contemplate life without Sir Alex, after 16 glorious years that had bridged almost my entire relationship with the club.

Ferguson's announcement came less than a year after Martin Edwards had stepped down as chief executive, to be replaced by his deputy Peter Kenyon. United would have new leaders in the boardroom and the dugout from the beginning of the 2002/03 season, and a new regime would be tasked with carrying the legacy of Ferguson's success forward. The stability that had facilitated United's dominance for a decade was under threat and, like the vast majority of United fans, I was seriously concerned at what was around the corner.

Kenyon's first high-profile act was a crowd-pleaser – he convinced Ferguson to stay at United in an ambassadorial role. He offered him £1 million a year to serve as a consultant for the club and sweetened the pot by upping his wages for his final season as manager to £3 million, making him the highest paid member of the playing and coaching staff. Ferguson's financial advisor Alan Baines greeted the news by saying, 'I am a great believer that a manager can't command respect from the changing room unless he earns more than the players.' It was a sentiment that had long been at the forefront of Ferguson's contract negotiations, but not until his final season would his wishes be realised.

Kenyon had bought Ferguson's favour and his generosity continued in the transfer market that summer. United broke the English transfer record when they paid £19 million for Ruud Van Nistelrooy, and smashed it to pieces when they shelled out £28.1 million for Juan Sebastian Veron a matter of days later. Goalkeeper Roy Carroll arrived for £2.5 million from Wigan and took United's spending in the build-up to Ferguson's final season to just under £40 million.

Carroll was brought in as cover for French international goalkeeper Fabien Barthez, who'd joined for £7.8 million the previous summer and made an impressive start to his United career. Barthez had been part of the France side that won the 1998 World Cup and Euro 2000, and Ferguson was attracted to his vibrant personality and lightning reflexes. He saw in him a player with the charisma and talent to take on the legacy of Peter Schmeichel, and United broke the British transfer record for a goalkeeper when they signed him from Monaco.

Barthez was an eccentric and the fans loved him for it. He would bring the ball out of defence and think nothing of sidestepping an onrushing attacker before distributing it. There was an exhibitionism to him that you rarely see in goalkeepers – a confidence that you might even compare to his fellow Frenchman Cantona. But ultimately he would come unstuck, and fall some way short of the standards set by Peter Schmeichel. The same eccentricities that made him a unique talent also made him vulnerable to rash errors of judgement and dips in concentration. He was a showman, and at times he could be brilliant, but he wasn't the long-term answer to United's goalkeeping problems.

Van Nistelrooy had come close to joining United 12 months' earlier, but a cruciate ligament injury sustained in training wrecked the deal and ruled him out for the majority of the season at PSV Eindhoven. Ferguson was prepared to wait. He met with the player regularly during his rehabilitation and maintained a relationship that would ultimately deliver United one of the most prolific goalscorers in the club's history. PSV resented Ferguson's regular visits to Van Nistelrooy, but the huge profit they made on him went a long way to easing their frustrations.

It was another example of Ferguson's willingness to go the extra mile for a player. He'd shown the same loyalty to Cantona during his suspension, and to David Beckham in the aftermath of his World Cup sending off against Argentina. There was a human touch to his approach that got the best out of the players he prized most, and fostered a sense of belonging at Old Trafford that was hard to find anywhere else. 'In spite of what has happened in the past year, my feelings for the club have never diminished,' Van Nistelrooy said on signing his deal. 'It has always been a dream of mine to play for United at Old Trafford.'

There was no doubt United needed a striker. Dwight Yorke had been a fading force since the Treble season of 1998/99 and his private life had spiralled into a very public embarrassment. Yorke's playboy lifestyle was the stuff of tabloid dreams and Ferguson's nightmares, and his relationship with glamour model Jordan took his notoriety to new lows. The pair had a child together, although it took a Jerry Springer style DNA test to prove it was Yorke's – a further indictment of his antics. FIFA vice-president Jack Warner called him 'a cancer' on the game, but Ferguson ultimately decided to give Yorke one more season to prove his worth.

Meanwhile Teddy Sheringham had returned to Tottenham on a free transfer. The veteran striker was named PFA Footballer of the Year for his performances in the 2000/01 campaign, but United were reticent to offer him the two-year deal he wanted and he decided to join his boyhood hero Glen Hoddle at White Hart Lane instead of signing a 12-month extension. It ended quite an adventure for Sheringham, who'd come to United to win trophies and suffered a barrage of abuse after ending his first season empty-handed. Four years later, Sheringham walked away from Old Trafford with three Premier League titles, an FA Cup win and Champions League triumph – and having contributed goals to two of the defining acts in an unprecedented Treble, at Wembley and, most famously, in Barcelona. 'Oh Teddy Teddy, he went to Man United and he won the lot,' we sang. And we were genuinely sad to see him go.

Sheringham was a thinking man's footballer, a player who always had time on the ball and whose passing nearly always encouraged a teammate to advance, rather than stopping him dead in his tracks, or forcing him to readjust. He was an expert in the air and had wonderful touch and poise, and in his final season at United he finished top scorer with 21 goals in all competitions. Such a return was mightily impressive for a player who was as unselfish as they come in striking circles. Sheringham's movement and vision made him a dream partner and even Cole, who claims he detests him as a human being to this day, profited handsomely from their forward union.

United fans said their goodbyes in a 3-1 defeat to his new club, but Sheringham was back at Old Trafford in the colours of England that October for a crucial World Cup qualifier against Greece. It was a game England couldn't afford to lose if they were to reach the 2002 finals in Japan and Korea, but they fell behind in the first half and were still trailing with just over 20 minutes remaining. Cue the introduction of Sheringham, on as a substitute for Robbie Fowler and greeted to a heroes' welcome by England fans desperate for some inspiration. He'd saved United in Barcelona and now he would save his country. And this time we didn't have to wait until the dying seconds for relief. Beckham won a free-kick on the left and his wicked curling cross was headed home by Sheringham at the near post with his first touch to bring Sven-Göran Eriksson's team level. It had taken him ten seconds to make a difference. 'My goodness, what a fairytale,' came the commentary. 'What a sensational substitution.'

But England conceded again almost immediately and for the final 20 minutes we watched on as a shaven-headed Beckham went about trying to save his team single-handed. For once he ignored Gary Neville's orders behind him and marauded around Old Trafford like a footballer possessed. It was a truly phenomenal, virtuoso performance. He tackled everything, went past players like we never knew he could and seemed to be in perpetual motion for the whole 90 minutes. England were practically a one-man team, with Beckham sprinting to take every free-kick and throw-in in sight – like the biggest kid in a school team.

It was the free-kicks that promised most. We'd seen him do it before and we prayed he could do it again. But time and again the crowd hushed and Beckham failed to find the target. He'd have one last chance. Sheringham was fouled 25 yards out in a central position and with the clock at 90 minutes captain Beckham stepped forward one last time. This time he struck the ball perfectly, into the net as sweetly as he had against Colombia in 1998 and, with the familiar fizz and dip of a Beckham special, England had its hero. We were going to the World Cup and the man who three years ago had been subject to death threats was now a messiah again. And Beckham was voted BBC Sports Personality of the Year a couple of months later.

However, not even the boys' own hero could do anything to save a hugely disappointing 2001/02 campaign for United. The start of the season had seen United fans met by the shock news that Jaap Stam would be leaving for Lazio. It was a deal that came out of nowhere and appeared to make no sense whatsoever in terms of United's ambitions, or the ambitions of their manager for his final season at the helm. The £16.5 million could at least be seen as a way of recouping some of the money spent on Veron and Van Nistelrooy, but if money was the issue surely one of those two deals should have been passed up to keep United's best defender at Old Trafford.

The speculation was that the contents of Stam's recently released autobiography were behind his exit. It featured damning allegations against Ferguson, including the fact that he'd made an illegal approach to PSV Eindhoven for his services. 'Ferguson fired me because he had problems about his own reputation,' Stam said in the wake of his rushed departure. 'He shouted at me, "What must the people think when they read your book and they read I told players they had to dive and that I flatten tables in the dressing room?"'

Ferguson played a straight bat. He totally rebuffed the suggestion that Stam's book had anything to do with the decision, and maintained United had made the sale based purely on football and financial reasoning. 'At the time he had just come back from an Achilles injury and we thought he'd lost a little bit,' he reflected some years later. '£16.5 million for a centre back who was 29. It was an offer I couldn't refuse.' There was also the suggestion Stam was not providing United's young defenders like Wes Brown, Mikael Silvestre and the Neville brothers with the nurturing influence they needed – that his communication skills were a problem.

Whatever the truth behind the deal, and I strongly suspect a power play on the part of United's manager was the defining factor, Ferguson now counts the sale of Stam as one of his biggest regrets. 'It was one of the mistakes I made – hopefully I haven't made too many – but that was one,' he said in 2010. 'I thought if we could get Laurent Blanc for a year or so and bring the young ones through – like Wes Brown and John O'Shea – but it backfired.'

Blanc's arrival was as curious as Stam's departure. The Frenchman was 35 years old and seemingly seeing out the twilight of his career at Inter Milan. He lacked pace and was as contrasting a physical specimen to Stam as you could possibly imagine. But Ferguson was convinced he was right for a one-year deal, worth an estimated £2.5 million. 'Laurent's experience will be vital to the young players,' he said, adding that he'd tried to sign him 'at least four times' before finally getting his man in time for the Champions League transfer window.

The deal reunited Blanc with his former international teammate Barthez, and treated United fans to the ritual of Blanc kissing his goal-keeper's head before every Champions League match. But the public displays of affection didn't make up for the fact that neither player was up to the task in the 2001/02 campaign. Blanc was off the pace and Barthez's once-endearing eccentricity began to present itself as mistake-laden fallibility. By Christmas United had already lost six times in the league and conceded three or more goals on seven occa-sions in all competitions – including 3-1 losses away at Liverpool and Arsenal, and a 3-0 home defeat to Chelsea. The New Year arrived with Ferguson's team fifth in the table, and the realisation dawning on all of us that perhaps his decision to leave was having a detrimental effect on his players.

There was still much to enjoy, not least a miraculous comeback against Glenn Hoddle's Tottenham at White Hart Lane. United trailed 3-0 at half-time, but goals from Andy Cole, Blanc and Van Nistelrooy brought them level inside 30 minutes of the restart. Veron then put them ahead with a fine finish, before Beckham completed a remark-able turnaround with a superb drive late on – launching into the same wild celebration we'd seen a few months before when he sent England to the World Cup. It was the kind of performance to galva-nise an entire season and it owed much to a baby-faced striker who didn't even get on the scoresheet. 'This was United's Headingley and in Ole Gunnar Solskjaer they had a Norwegian answer to Ian Botham,' wrote David Lacey in the *Guardian*. 'Solskjaer did not score but it was he who, Bothamlike, did more than anyone to retrieve an apparently hopeless situation by carrying the attack to the opposition.'

Solskjaer helped himself to a personal best 25 goals that season, filling the void as Yorke and Cole struggled with injuries and form. His prolific strike partner Van Nistelrooy did even better, emphatically justifying Ferguson's faith by scoring 36 goals in all competitions –

including a Premier League haul of 23. In the midst of that gluttony of goals the Dutchman set a new record by scoring in eight consecutive Premier League games. United were top of the league and still alive in the FA Cup and the Champions League when Ruud bagged the winner against Blackburn at Old Trafford.

But United weren't prepared to rest on their laurels. Three days later Uruguayan striker Diego Forlan completed a move from Independiente for £6.9 million. It seemed a lot of money for a relative unknown, but the 22-year-old came with a reputation as one of the brightest prospects in world football. He was quick and strong in the air, and could finish with both feet. Some were comparing him to a young Jürgen Klinsmann, and United saw enough potential to outbid Middlesbrough and pay through the nose for an unproven player who was yet to represent his country.

What nobody could know at the time was that it would take Forlan eight months, and 27 games, to open his account. In the intervening period the walnut-tanned, goldilocks South American blazed a million shots over the bar and left United's fans and their manager wondering if he'd been the victim of a horrible curse. They say you can't buy a goal, and in the case of Forlan they were right. But that didn't stop him trying... practically every time he got the ball.

This is the same player who left United in 2004 and embarked on insatiable goal binges at Villarreal and Atlético Madrid that marked him out as one of the world's best strikers. The same player who finished as Europe's top goalscorer in 2009 and scored both goals in the Europa League final a year later. And the same player who won the Golden Ball as the tournament's best player at the 2010 World Cup, finishing level top scorer with five goals as Uruguay reached the semi-finals. If ever there was a case of the bipolar footballer, Forlan was it.

But you couldn't fault his effort. Forlan might have played like a dog, but at least he worked like one. His earnest approach and unassuming manner made his plight strangely endearing, and when United were awarded a penalty the following season in a Champions League cakewalk against Maccabi Haifi, we rose as one to call for Forlan to take it. Beckham said he would 'have been hated by 67,000 people' if he'd not done the decent thing, and so came the moment we'd been waiting for. Up stepped Forlan to end the curse. 'If you put that amount of effort in you should get something,' said Ferguson after the game. 'Hopefully he will settle down now and get lots more.'

Thank goodness he scored. Had he missed you get the feeling Ferguson would have played him into his 50s, hailing his fantastic work ethic and making light of his 9,000 games without a goal. The United manager is that stubborn.

Forlan's plight reminded me of a teammate from my mini-minor days. An awkward and lumbering striker, he'd gone five years without scoring when his Forlan moment arrived. A cross floated over and he headed the ball home from a matter of inches. Every parent on the touchline was jumping up and down in wild celebration and the play-er's dad sprinted from the halfway line towards the goal waving his arms in the air and literally yelping with delight. It was a moment fit for a sentimental montage, an ode to the inclusiveness of sport, but it all came crashing down when the referee noticed the linesman's raised flag on the opposite side of the pitch.

United's 2001/02 campaign suffered much the same fate. Steve McClaren's Middlesbrough knocked them out of the FA Cup and Arsenal won their last 13 games in a row to take the Premier League title, with United third behind Liverpool. This time the Champions League quest reached the semi-finals, where Bayer Leverkusen came to Old Trafford and profited from some sloppy defending to get a 2-2 draw. United could only manage a 1-1 in the return, and the chance for Ferguson to take his team back home for the final in Glasgow was gone. It was depressing stuff, and it all had the feel of an empire in decline – in the last, fumbling throws of a once glorious dominance.

Arsenal also won the FA Cup, achieving their second Double under Arsène Wenger in the space of four years. The fact they sealed the league title with a 1-0 win at Old Trafford only added to our pain.

But amidst all the disappointment there was at least one cause for celebration. Ferguson had withdrawn his resignation and would fight another day at Old Trafford. 'It was really Cathy's idea,' he said of his about-turn. 'If she hadn't come up with it and the boys hadn't given full support, I wouldn't have considered a change of mind. But I do have to confess that maybe it was an idea I was hoping deep down she would come up with."

United fans reacted to the news by conducting a heartfelt rendition of 'Every single one of us loves Cathy Ferguson', at Charlton away, and with an enormous sense of relief. Ferguson had given us unprecedented success and a stability that suggested even greater things were around the corner. The last thing we wanted was a new manager coming in to derail the glory train and take United back to the dark days of the 1970s and early-to-mid 1980s. And with Wenger ensconced at Arsenal, building a potential dynasty of his own, this was not the time for United to go through a period of flux. For all we knew, such change could make us the new Liverpool.

Had Ferguson not changed his mind it's almost certain Sven-Göran Eriksson would have taken over at Old Trafford for the start of the 2002/03 season. The England manager had held informal talks with the United board and it was all but agreed he would step into the job after leading England at the 2002 World Cup. As Ferguson understood it Eriksson had 'shaken hands' on the deal with Kenyon.

Only Ferguson knows if the choice of his successor helped make up his mind to stay. 'I think Sven Eriksson would have been a nice easy choice for them [the United board] in terms of nothing really happens, does it?' he later reflected. 'He doesn't change anything. He sails along, nobody falls out with him. He comes out and says: "The first half we were good, second half we were not so good. I am very pleased with the result". I think he'd have been all right for United, you know what I mean? The acceptable face.'

From a man whose success was built on completely the opposite approach, it was hardly a ringing endorsement. The way Ferguson saw it upsetting people came with the territory of being a good manager. His was not a crusade for affirmation and good PR, but for winning football matches – and he strongly believed there were times you needed to follow your convictions whatever the consensus of the media, or the fans. It was for those reasons he'd doubted Brian Kidd's credentials as a future United manager. Kidd was too soft, and

Ferguson feared he didn't have the killer instinct you need to make important decisions. He clearly felt the same about Eriksson.

Fortunately for United fans we never got to see those fears realised.

PART THREE
(2002/03 TO 2010/11)

CHAPTER 17
GOOD MORNING NEVADA SMITHS

Manchester United have somewhere between 75 million and 350 million fans on planet earth. Taking the conservative estimate that's enough to fill Old Trafford a thousand times, and more fans than the entire population of the United Kingdom. Take the generous estimate and it's more than the population of the United States. There are at least 200 recognised branches of the official Manchester United supporters' club, spread across 24 countries, and in heavily populated areas we're like rats in London – you're never more than 20 yards away from one of us.

In 2005 the demographics were put before the public for the first time. Of the estimated 75 million, United said 23 million were based in Europe, with 4.6 million in the Americas and 5.9 million in South Africa. The largest base, by far, was Asia – where United reported to have 40.7 million fans. In countries like Malaysia, Thailand, China and Japan the Manchester United cult was spreading like a religion, or a horrible communicative disease – depending on your perspective. No wonder the club had visited for a pre-season tour before the 2001/02 campaign. It might not have pleased their manager, who blamed the exertions for the trophy-less season that followed, but it certainly made economic sense.

Whether we liked it or not, Manchester United plc was now a business first and a football club second. Martin Edwards had floated the club on the Stock Exchange in 1991, to a valuation of £18 million, and a decade later they were returning a pre-tax profit of £22 million. It was a return that made United the most valuable football club on the stock market. But what did it all mean for the soul of the club? Were United selling out? Had Old Trafford become a front for voracious corporate greed? Or was the whole exercise ultimately designed to ensure we – the fans – were served with the best players and the most success possible?

The record-breaking fees paid for Ruud van Nistelrooy and Juan Sebastian Veron suggested the latter. There were also generous new contracts for Ferguson, David Beckham and Roy Keane – with the club's wage control measures for elite players now just a quaint relic of a more innocent past. And then there was Old Trafford itself, by now a gleaming all-seater, prawn-sandwich serving facility that held close to 70,000 – and would ultimately be extended to take just over 76,000. If these were the fringe benefits of being a dastardly global brand, then maybe we could turn a blind eye to the rampant exploitation of the club throughout the world.

We'd have to put up with a good deal of stick along the way. Rival fans had long revelled in the notion of United's fans coming from anywhere but Manchester, and now their argument went global. There were stories of weekend tourists flying into Old Trafford from all corners of the earth, and of replica shirts turning up in remote jungle outposts that barely knew civilisation. The more popular United became, the more their games were televised throughout the world – and the more new fans they won over as a result. From a marketing perspective, United had stolen a march on virtually every football team on the planet. They were so far ahead they may never be caught.

I experienced United's global reach first-hand when I moved from London to New York in the summer of 2002. Having spent four penniless years working my way up from post boy to general dogsbody at Sony Records, I was handed the chance of a lifetime. It was goodbye to my hovel of a house in Streatham Common, sloppy, drunken nights in the Clapham Grand and my embarrassment of a love life, and hello to the coolest city on the planet.

It's not what you know, it's who you know – and in this case, who they know. When I told my chain-smoking, Newcastle United-loving boss in London I fancied a move to New York he said he'd make a call. A few days later he called me in to say that by a remarkable coincidence my identical job at Sony in Manhattan was available. I'd have to make a decision almost immediately. I'd be working on a record label called Legacy, dealing with producers and coordinating studio sessions for the re-mastering of classic old albums. Most of the artists would be dead, but I'd have a 58th floor corner office on Madison Avenue and be very much alive in New York City. I said yes immediately. And I felt like Ferguson the day he signed Eric Cantona.

Being an obsessive, one of the first things I did when I arrived in the Big Apple was look for a pub in which to watch United games. I knew there were plenty of ex-pats in the city and plenty of United-loving Irish – and I wanted to make sure I was among them when the season kicked off a month or so later. I asked around and it turned out Nevada Smiths, on the lower east side of Manhattan, had quite the reputation as New York's 'church' of football. It would prove the answer to my soccer-loving prayers.

Named after the 1966 film starring Steve McQueen, Nevada Smiths is best described as the sweat-and-beer drenched coming together of English football terraces in the 1970s and New York's east village hedonism. It's always packed, and as fans of all manner of nationalities and affiliations are thrust together there's a volatile chemistry at work that only adds to the excitement. The testosterone literally drips from the ceiling, and when you consider most of the games kick off at around 10 a.m. on a Saturday morning, and some as early as 7 a.m., that's quite an achievement.

The 7 a.m. starts were particularly memorable. As you piled in there was an equal mix of those looking like death from a heavy night before, and those who hadn't been to bed yet. The latter were unsurprisingly prone to hostilities, and on countless occasions the burly bouncers were forced to break up fights and lead away those whose brains were no longer connected to their mouths. At times you looked around and it felt like a scene from the film *From Dusk Till Dawn*, with crazed zombies looming over your shoulder and the very real threat of violence hanging in the air. The place stank of stale beer and antiseptic, but it felt like a sanctuary – a home from home for the football fanatics whose fandom knew no boundaries.

It was there I met United fans from all over the world, gathered together in the dark recesses of a bar that comes with the tagline, 'where football is religion'. It must have been quite a sight for New Yorkers out for their early morning jog as we filtered out onto the streets at 11 in the morning, under brilliant blue skies, like slit-eyed drunken moles. 'I knew you English soccer hooligans were crazy,' said one of my colleagues at work. 'But I didn't realise you were crazy enough to wake up in the middle of the night just to watch a game on TV.'

The American United fans were a revelation. Years of patronising abuse, not to mention the lingering embarrassment of Diana Ross's penalty miss at the opening ceremony for the 1994 World Cup, had prompted them to take in the game like they were studying for a doctorate. They came with an almost encyclopaedic knowledge of the cause and they ate stats for brunch. American Reds would reel off things like Ruud van Nistelrooy's goal ratio against teams beginning with L, or the correlation between Ferguson's gum chewing intensity and the number of free-kicks his teams conceded in the final third (I'm exaggerating slightly there but you get my point).

That's not to say they didn't occasionally get things wrong. There were still screams of 'shoooooot it!' every time a player got within 30 yards, and goals scored by 'awesome headed shots'. And they insisted on pronouncing Beckham as 'Beck-ham'. But it was all part of the New York experience and you certainly couldn't fault their enthusiasm.

I spent two heady years in New York and a good chunk of my weekend mornings watching United in Nevada Smiths. It was a Reds-centric venue, but not to the extent that opposition fans were wary of coming in. Liverpool, Chelsea and Arsenal fans arrived in large numbers to watch their team, and if two of the big guns went head-to-head you were guaranteed a healthy rivalry playing out across the room. Touring ex-pats only added to the intensity, pouring in straight from the late-night clubs and bars to the only place in town they could experience their team in the surroundings they'd become accustomed to.

The game that sticks out in my mind was a Sunday morning clash between Liverpool and United at Anfield in December 2002. I'd been out the night before and was running late when I squeezed my way into the heaving venue just after kick-off. There was large support for both teams and the banter was coming thick and fast. United won 2-1, with the rehabilitated Diego Forlan profiting from some terrible goal-keeping from Jerzy Dudek to grab both goals. As we emerged onto Third Avenue the United fans were in full voice, baiting the Liverpool fans as they trudged back to their apartments and hotels to spend the day in mourning. Brunch was particularly sweet that day – hangover cures don't come much better than that.

New York was also where I met my wife-to-be and the mother of my two children, a sweet southern girl living the dream in the big bad city. She knew nothing about football, but demonstrated her devotion in the purest possible way – by regularly accompanying her soccer-crazed English boyfriend into a filthy pit of unwashed men, who screamed at screens and drank beer for breakfast. She even brought some astute analysis to proceedings. 'How come that goldilocks guys always kicks the ball over the goal?' she said of Forlan. 'The guy with the long face is really good at scoring goals,' of Van Nistelrooy. And that, my friends, is a love that lasts.

Nevada Smiths worked for the weekends, but I needed a venue closer to my offices for United's midweek games. It came in the form of the Manchester Pub, a more upmarket alternative on Second Avenue between 48th and 49th Streets. It was there I watched United's Champions League campaigns of 2002/03 and 2003/04, mingling with the suited and booted executives who carried clips of $100 notes but whose happiness was still at the mercy of a team in red. Fortunately my boss at the time treated my football obsession like a genuine afflic-tion to cater for. 'You take as long as you need,' she'd say, as I bolted out of the office at 2.30 in the afternoon.

And there we were, United fans rolling with the same emotions as those 3,500 miles away inside Old Trafford. There was an inclusivity to it that gave ex-pats a feeling of belonging, and native New Yorkers a real sense of what it meant to follow a football team. All hail United's global brand I say, for without it none of this would have been possible, and I'd have spent those two years with nothing but text commentary to satisfy my love affair with United.

CHAPTER 18
THE BACKLASH

The 2001/02 season represented United's worst campaign of the Premier League era. It was the first time Ferguson's team had finished outside the top two, and it had the ever-hysterical media predicting the fall of an empire. But United's manager wasn't about to stand aside and let Arsenal do to him what he'd done to Liverpool.

'The disappointment of winning nothing will have a positive effect,' he told the *Daily Mirror*. 'Maybe it will be the kick up the backside we needed because I'm certainly not accepting it. We are going to have to do something about it. You have to say the only thing to worry about with the ability we have here is desire. Are the players hungry enough? Do they have that desire? I'm confident we will see that question positively answered next season.'

It was stirring rhetoric all right, and exactly what the fans needed to hear, but you couldn't help feel the sense of desperation beginning to creep in. Ferguson had been outmanoeuvred by Arsène Wenger at Arsenal, and his pride pierced by a season that had most experts suggesting a new manager for a new era which had left him behind. But while I feared the worst, I also knew Ferguson pushed into a corner was capable of doing just about anything to get himself out. Whatever happened next would be worth watching.

By this point Arsenal manager Wenger had become more than a slight irritant to Ferguson. 'Le Professuer' was being hailed as the mastermind of a more intelligent, cultured brand of football, and his side tipped to achieve a sustained period of dominance at United's expense. The contrast between the two men was striking. While Ferguson rallied his troops with roaring rhetoric, Wenger came with a calm self-assuredness that can only have infuriated Ferguson and everybody concerned at Old Trafford. 'They will be challenging but I don't expect a major backlash,' Wenger said of United on the eve of the 2002/03 season.

For arguably the first time in his reign at United, Ferguson had a worthy adversary. And much as he tried to play nice with congratulatory nods to the Frenchman's achievements, he wasn't fooling anybody. The challenge of Arsenal was a genuine threat to his legacy and he was all too ready to go to war for it – on and off the pitch. 'There is no player in the world who wouldn't want to play for Manchester United,' he said as quote grenades were exchanged between Highbury and Old Trafford. '[Patrick] Vieira would have loved to have come here last year, but they wouldn't let him go. We are, without question, the highest-profile team in the world. We have the best disciplinary record in the country, we score the most goals and we entertain the most.'

It was designed as a statement of supreme confidence, but it sounded like fear. And it sounded like denial. United had lost out on the title before under Ferguson, but there was always the sense among the fans that they'd get it back the next season. This time we weren't so sure. 'Previously, United folk could talk mockingly about their club lending Arsenal and Blackburn the title, as they had just twice in nine years of Premiership history,' wrote Nick Townsend in the *Independent*. 'Maybe Arsenal don't have the "profile", but the north London club possess the manager and the playing personnel capable of permanently damaging United's claim to English domination.'

Having reneged on his retirement, Ferguson's reputation was on the line. The media and the anti-United brigade were circling above, and there were plenty who questioned his credentials to go head-to-head with his younger, more forward-thinking opponent. Some said he should have kept to his word and walked away, others hinted at the possibility he wouldn't even see out the three years on his new deal. Personally, I was never in doubt he was the best man for the job.

Here was a man who knew the football club better than practically anyone else on the payroll, to whom losing ground to Arsenal was as unbearable a notion as it was to the fans. He cared like we did, and that fighting spirit was exactly what United needed.

One thing was for certain; for Ferguson to mount a response to Arsenal he'd need to be more astute in the transfer market than he'd been 12 months before. The relative failures of Juan Sebastian Veron and Laurent Blanc were defining factors in the 2001/02 campaign – and were being used to illustrate Ferguson's faltering judgement. Veron had shown only the faintest glimpses of his swaggering genius in the stifling midfields of English football, and looked a naive investment on the basis of his first season. Meanwhile Blanc, all too predictably, proved a little too old in the tooth for a turbo-charged Premier League baptism. Ferguson had gambled twice and lost both times, but fortunately there was still money in the pot.

United's pre-season was dominated by speculation surrounding the possible transfer of Rio Ferdinand from Leeds United. The 23-year-old was by now an England regular and had impressed alongside John Terry at the 2002 World Cup finals – which saw Sven-Göran Eriksson's team beaten by eventual champions Brazil in the quarter-finals. Ferdinand was an instinctive ball-playing centre-back in the mould of Bobby Moore, and a product of the same West Ham academy responsible for Frank Lampard and Joe Cole, among others. He was that rare commodity of a defender blessed with both composure on the ball and the physical attributes of speed, height and strength. Potentially, he was a once-in-a-generation talent.

United and Ferguson wanted him badly, but Leeds rebuffed their initial offer of £20 million and another a couple of weeks later, for £29 million. Their chairman Peter Ridsdale was not about to hand their bitter Lancastrian rivals the same kind of gift they received when Eric Cantona made the switch a decade earlier. He called the first offer 'derisory', and said 'we still have to receive a bid to the level that we would find acceptable,' after being faxed the second.

It was the stuff of endless, tedious speculation, and it seemed to drag on all summer. The numbers seemed to get bigger and bigger, until the time arrived when you began to wonder if United were about to put the keys to Old Trafford on the table, and start selling off silverware. 'If this Ferdinand is really worth 25 Cantonas, he's going to be some player,' a United fan said to me in the midst of the saga. 'And if Leeds want more than that for him, you better hope he can walk on water and piss lager.'

Leeds kept posturing, but they were in no position to miss out on the deal altogether. They were in financial meltdown and desperately needed a cash injection, so it came as no surprise when Ridsdale ultimately buckled. Some reported the fee as £30 million, some as £29 million – others at £29.1 million. Whatever the amount, it represented the third time in two seasons United had broken the British transfer record. 'I never thought in a million years I'd be playing alongside players like Juan Sebastian Veron and Roy Keane,' said Ferdinand on signing a five-year deal at Old Trafford. 'It was not an easy decision, but opportunities like this don't come around very often so I had to grab it with both hands.'

It was the second time in his career Ferdinand had been Britain's most expensive player, but Ferguson had little doubt he would prove a spectacular investment. 'I identified him many years ago. When you identify a particular great player you think, "How could I get him here?"' Ferguson said. 'That wasn't going to be easy but the board wanted him as much as I did and who wouldn't want him at Old Trafford? At 23 he has great potential. We're hoping he will mature here and develop into the best centre-half in the world.'

Once again Peter Kenyon had come good for Ferguson, the United chief executive having played a key role in the negotiations that brought Ferdinand to Old Trafford. Martin Edwards' successor was proving a valuable ally, and with the financial shackles well and truly off, he was giving his manager everything he needed to compete with the richest clubs in Europe. Little did he know that three years later Kenyon would have left for Chelsea and been implicated in under-the-table talks to steal Ferdinand away from Old Trafford.

The huge publicity surrounding Ferdinand's arrival allowed Dwight Yorke to slip out of Old Trafford relatively unnoticed. The striker left to be reunited with his old partner-in-crime Andy Cole at Blackburn Rovers, ending a United career that peaked in the Treble season of 1998/99 in which he and Cole scored 53 goals between them and conquered Europe. Yorke had become increasingly frustrated at life on the sidelines, and with the arrival of Ruud van Nistelrooy and Diego Forlan he sensed the time was right to move on. The fact that Ferguson hadn't even allocated him a squad number for the new campaign said it all. He was a fading force, and the desire Ferguson wanted from his team was not to be found in him.

Yorke was a hard player to turn against for the fans. That brimming smile, the infectious enthusiasm, the role he played in winning the Treble. But watching on it felt as if some of the desire was gone. He'd tasted the ultimate club success, and from there it was almost as if an inevitable slide into retirement awaited him. At times there were still glimpses of his brilliance, but there was no question his number was up at United.

The other big story in the build-up to the new season was Roy Keane's verbal assassination of his international manager Mick McCarthy at the 2002 World Cup – prompted by Keane's disgust at the training facilities afforded to the Republic of Ireland squad. 'Mick, you're a liar… you're a f**king w**ker,' he began. 'I didn't rate you as a player, I don't rate you as a manager, and I don't rate you as a person. You're a f**king w**ker and you can stick your World Cup up your arse. The only reason I have any dealings with you is that somehow you are the manager of my country! You can stick it up your b***ocks.'

The latest in a long line of highly publicised Keane explosions, it only exaggerated the Irishman's status as the untameable beast of British football. But United, and Ferguson for that matter, had been here before. Eric Cantona and David Beckham had both emerged from vilification with emphatic seasons on the pitch and Keane would do the same. The Irishman was the driving force as United chased down Arsenal in the second half of the season in arguably the most satisfying championship-winning campaign of the Ferguson era thus far.

But there was still time for plenty of controversy in the first half of the campaign. In United's third league game of the season, away to

Sunderland, Keane was sent off for elbowing his former Republic of Ireland teammate Jason McAteer. The pair had already clashed once in the game, with McAteer reacting brilliantly to Keane's frustration at a late tackle by telling him to 'go write it in your book', and miming to scribble notes. A furious Keane didn't see the funny side. He allegedly screamed 'I'll have you,' and as you'd expect was good to his word – connecting with the side of McAteer's head and knocking him to the floor to earn his marching orders.

The ever-loyal (blinkered) Ferguson initially defended his captain, but damning video evidence prompted a U-turn, and having called the elbow a weapon of 'cowards' in relation to an incident involving Patrick Vieira the previous season, he had little choice but to act. Keane was fined two weeks' wages by United, or £150,000, and suspended for three matches. It was the least he deserved, and it was smart for United to act of their own accord, rather than stand back and let the FA deliver what could well have been a sterner punishment.

As it turned out he might not have played the games anyway. A hip operation in September put him out of action for four months, during which time he was fined another £150,000 and banned for five matches by the FA for the account of the Alf-Inge Haaland incident in his autobiography. Not a great few months for Keane all things considered, and to make things worse, by the time he returned to United's starting line-up, for a Boxing Day trip to Middlesbrough, he found his team some distance behind Arsenal at the top of the table.

A dash of Keane was just what they needed, but it would take a game or two before he hit his stride. United lost 3-1 at The Riverside, with Boro manager Steve McClaren defeating his mentor Ferguson for the third time in two years. It was a game in which United dominated possession, but lacked inspiration in the final third and failed to capitalise on long periods camped in the attacking half. Keane and Veron should have dominated a midfield that included United rejects Jonathan Greening and Mark Wilson, but in truth neither player made an impact worthy of their salary. For Keane, the return from a long injury layoff was his justification. But Veron was running out of excuses. It was United's second league defeat in four days, and their fifth of a season that was coming off at the hinges.

Veron was my personal scapegoat, and I was beginning to seriously resent the sight of him in a United shirt. At a time when my team desperately needed some fire in their bellies, it looked to me as if the £30 million Argentine was prancing around like he was playing in a charity beach football tournament. Quite what Ferguson saw in him I couldn't tell – but whatever it was I was sure he'd left it behind at Lazio.

Thank goodness for Keane. The return of United's most devilish red sparked a devastating run of 18 Premier League matches unbeaten, from which Ferguson's team took 48 points from a possible 54 and left Arsenal wilting in their wake – just as Wenger's team had done to United in 1998. As the confidence flowed back into them, Ferguson's team began to express themselves – hammering Liverpool 4-0, Newcastle 6-2 and Charlton 4-1, as they overturned a seven-point deficit on Boxing Day to claim the title by five points from Arsenal.

Much was owed to the remarkable goalscoring of Van Nistelrooy, who collected 25 in the Premier League and 44 in all competitions, including hat-tricks against Newcastle, Fulham and Charlton. Time and again the Dutchman hung on the shoulder of the last man to collect a pass, shrug off a challenge and shoot home. And his swooping late runs were the perfect invitation for players like Beckham, Paul Scholes and Veron to lean on their technical abilities to find him. 'He could become one of the greatest strikers ever,' said Ferguson towards the end of the season. And I was beginning to agree with him.

Van Nistelrooy was a ruthless poacher. The six-yard box was his playground and he had an instinctive sense of where to be and when to get there. He was an assassin in the mould of Denis Law, Jimmy Greaves and Gary Lineker – a lone hunter who took care of business with the minimum of fuss. And there was no better indicator of his clinical approach than his penalty taking in the 2002/03 season. He scored 12 from 12, mostly drilling the ball low to the goalkeeper's right and burying the ball just inside the post. After a while the keepers knew which way to go, but it didn't make any difference.

And then there was the importance of the goals he delivered. Van Nistelrooy scored 13 times in United's last eight league games of the season, including two nerveless penalties in the home win against

Liverpool and a priceless goal against Arsenal at Highbury. Not since Cantona made a habit of deciding 1-0 wins had United's success been so linked to the goalscoring exploits of a single player. 'Ruuuuuud,' came the guttural call from the United fans as we hailed our new No. 10, and by the time he finished the season with a goal in a 2-0 win against Everton, Ferguson was running out of plaudits and the newspapers were running out of Ruud-related headlines. 'He's amazed us with what he's achieved this year... he's been exceptional,' he said.

But Ruud wasn't the easiest player for fans to relate to. He seemed to be cocooned in his own world, and there was little of his personality on show in interviews or on the pitch. It was as if he was a goalscoring robot, United's footballing Terminator sent down to put the ball in the net whatever it cost. I loved his goals, but it was harder to love Van Nistelrooy the man – a solitary character who seemed removed from the team dynamic, and didn't appear to take a great deal of enjoyment from fulfilling our childhood dreams on a weekly basis.

It was also a season to remember for Scholes, who scored a personal best 20 goals from midfield and was the only member of United's title winners included in the PFA Team of the Year (Thierry Henry and Alan Shearer somehow keeping Van Nistelrooy out). Scholes' performance of the season, and perhaps United's for that matter, came in the 6-2 win at Newcastle. He volleyed home a delightful first, crashed home a trademark show-stopper for his second and rounded off his hat-trick with a clinical finish at the far post, as United summoned an emphatic display to knock Arsenal off the top of the table.

Scholes was a throwback of a footballer, a refreshingly unaffected personality who eschewed the trappings of celebrity and fame as aggressively as others sought it. His was not a world of catwalks, clubbing and contract disputes – but of playing the game he loved and going home to his childhood sweetheart to escape the limelight afterwards. He might have been reckless in the tackle, but nothing we saw or read from the outside suggested an ounce of recklessness in the way he led his life away from football. He kept his opinions to himself and for that reason there was a universal appeal to him that brought admiration from even the most trenchant United haters.

United fans worshipped him. This was one of their own, a man who'd pay to watch Oldham on a day off, and would quite happily have played in the Sunday pub leagues had the club allowed it. He was a Bobby Charlton for the new generation, a straightforward and down-to-earth footballer touched by genius. He never once let his fame, or his talent, get to his head, and he set an example for behaviour off the field that unquestionably shaped the players who followed him into Old Trafford.

In the 2002/03 campaign Scholes was frequently asked to play as a support man to Van Nistelrooy, a position that afforded him a new freedom to get forward and influence things in the final third. His vision, creativity and shooting prowess used to lend themselves perfectly to the role, and he enjoyed arguably one of the most productive and influential seasons of his epic United career. Scholes had it all and we were beyond fortunate to have him. As a BBC reporter put it best, 'Ferguson got himself out of a hole by playing Scholes in one.'

United fans treated their local hero to a song as traditional and straightforward as the man himself. Scholes never overcomplicated things, and neither did we – and in the 2002/03 season there were plenty of opportunities to laud the man Spain's World Cup winner Xavi would later call the 'best midfielder I've seen in the last 15 to 20 years'. And so, to the tune of *Kumbaya*, we hailed the boy from Salford who never wanted anything more than to look back on his career and consider himself 'a half-decent player':

> *He scores goals my Lord, he scores goals*
> *He scores goals my Lord, he scores goals*
> *He scores goals my Lord, he scores goals*
> *Paul Scholes, he scores goals*

But for all his brilliance the ginger general still couldn't resist a rash tackle, and four years on from the heartbreak of being suspended for the 1999 Champions League final in Barcelona, he was at it again in United's quarter-final meeting with Real Madrid at the Bernabeu – the second time in four seasons the European giants had met in the knockout stages. Both Scholes and Gary Neville picked up bookings to put themselves out of the second leg at Old Trafford, and compound a miserable night for Ferguson, his team and every United fan on the planet.

It was a contest that saw Zinedine Zidane at his imperious best, conducting the defending champions to a comprehensive 3-1 victory that ultimately flattered United such was the dominance of the Spanish hosts. Luis Figo put Madrid ahead with a wicked curled shot from the corner of the penalty area, before Raúl helped himself to a clinical double – adding to the two goals he'd scored against United at Old Trafford in 2000. United were 3-0 down and reeling, but they snatched an away goal on 52 minutes through Van Nistelrooy and held out to give themselves at least a fighting chance for the home leg at Old Trafford.

In the build up to the second leg Ferguson focused on the positives and launched into mind games with his opposite number, Vincent del Bosque. 'The one thing that came out of Madrid was that the second half had them stretched,' he said. 'They knew they were in a game, no question about that. If we keep them at full stretch for 90 minutes we will get some benefit from it. Losing in Madrid was not a bad thing for our players; our defenders are all young lads learning all the time and this time they won't be sitting at the back, admiring the game. They will be doing something about it.'

The suggestion was very much that United would put the emphasis on good old-fashioned English physicality, and try to shake Madrid out of their comfort zone. Ferguson was not about to let the Spaniards come to Old Trafford and dictate the game as they had at the Bernabeu, and he called on his players to press with intensity and play the game at their pace. But Del Bosque wasn't ruffled. 'Our team is not made up of girls,' he said. 'If we have to play hard, we will do it. If that is the way the match has to be played, then so be it.'

One thing in United's favour looked to be the absence of Raúl, the player Ferguson had called 'the best in the world' after his exhibition display in the first leg. The United manager even joked about finding a way to stop him travelling to Manchester, before an aggressive bout of appendicitis did the job for him. When the media brought Raúl's name up at the press conference at Old Trafford, Ferguson couldn't help but smile. 'I do have some powers,' he said.

But as it turned out Real didn't need him at Old Trafford. This time their firepower came courtesy of Ronaldo, who scored a Roy of the Rovers-style hat-trick in a humdinger of a game that finished 4-3 to United, but saw them knocked out 6-5 on aggregate. The first came after just 12 minutes, with Fabien Barthez yet again found wanting in Europe as a low shot from 20 yards stole inside his near post to cancel out United's away goal. The second was a tap-in to culminate a brilliant team move, with the third an unstoppable drive from 25 yards that not even Peter Schmeichel in his prime would have stopped.

United had once again been beaten at their own game – a depressing realisation for all concerned that we'd lost ground in Europe. As Ferguson's team poured forward with abandon, Madrid picked them off with a ruthless efficiency that United never came close to matching. Del Bosque's star-studded team had reportedly been dubbed 'performing seals' by somebody inside the United camp, but they combined style and substance with devastating effect at Old Trafford. They were emphatically the better side, and the game was already up by the time Beckham came off the bench to score twice in the last 20 minutes, and lend some respectability to proceedings.

As a fan it was desperately disappointing, but you couldn't help but admire Madrid's modus operandi. Most teams would have come to Old Trafford and set out their stall to defend, but the visitors brought a swagger and ambition that made for one of the most entertaining European nights the stadium had known. This was football the way United fans dreamed it, only the opposition were more vivid in their imagination and more clinical in their application. Even Ferguson, smarting from yet another Champions misadventure, was forced to admit it had been a mighty spectacle. 'It was a pleasure to be involved in a game like that,' he said afterwards.

Watching on from the Manchester Pub in midtown Manhattan, I felt a strange mix of emotions. United were out, but had played a full part in a game for the ages. They'd been outclassed by the best team in the world – one peppered with once-in-a-generation players who most expected would go on to win a second successive European crown (we were wrong, they lost in the semi-finals, AC Milan were champions). There was something to salvage in that, a sense that sporting justice had been done and recriminations were futile. Losing to the might of Madrid on this kind of form was far easier to stomach than the exits to Monaco in 1998, Bayern Munich in 2001, and Bayer Leverkusen in 2002.

And there was still the title to celebrate, sealed when Arsenal capitulated to a 3-2 home defeat to Leeds. Ferguson may have been bested by Del Bosque in the Champions League, but the bragging rights were all his on the domestic stage. Wenger didn't expect a backlash, but a backlash he got. Arsenal were knocked clean off the perch they'd occupied for all of a season, and United proved they were a long way from a fading force.

Ferguson's eighth league title made him the most successful manager in English football history, but it wasn't long before his thoughts turned to the elusive prize that was beginning to haunt him. 'Now we have to get the big one again,' he said as AC Milan and Juventus prepared for a Champions League final at, of all places, Old Trafford. 'Winning it twice is not enough. We are not far away, believe me. Everyone was excited by the Real Madrid adventure. We want it again. It has become as important as anything you can think of in football.'

By the time United went after the Big Cup the following season, one of Ferguson's most important players would be in the colours of Real Madrid. And a new star would have arrived at Old Trafford in his place.

CHAPTER 19
No. 7s

Trevor Benjamin is an extreme journeyman footballer. At the time of writing, the imposing striker is plying his trade as player/manager at Northern League side Morpeth Town – the 27th club of a unashamedly promiscuous career that has stopped off at Cambridge United, Leicester City, Kidsgrove Athletic, Bedlington Terriers and Brighton & Hove Albion, to name but a few. And he's still just 32 years old. But perhaps Benjamin's most telling contribution to the game was the role he played in David Beckham's souring relationship with Sir Alex Ferguson – that ultimately led to his departure for Real Madrid.

It was Bonfire Night in 2002, and Benjamin came to Old Trafford with Leicester City, for a third round League Cup tie that few expected Beckham to play in. The England captain had been shaken by the news that a plot to kidnap his wife and children had been uncovered a few days earlier, and most expected Ferguson to give him the night off to be with his family. Beckham expected the same.

But Ferguson had other ideas. He not only named Beckham in his starting line-up, but made him captain for the evening. It was classic Ferguson psychology – designed to get Beckham's mind off the sensationalist circus and back on the business of playing football, and it worked. He scored from the penalty spot in a 2-0 win, and put in a focused performance that showed no signs of the emotional distress he was suffering at home.

But it came at a cost. With the clock running down and United coasting towards victory, Beckham went in for an innocuous challenge with Benjamin, who'd come on as substitute for the last ten minutes. The pair tangled and Beckham ended up under the full weight of his opponent, sprawling on the turf in agony. 'I was left there knowing something serious had happened,' he wrote in *My Side.* 'I could hardly breathe.' He continued to train for a few days, and even struggled through a Champions League clash with Bayer Leverkusen, before a scan revealed he'd broken a rib. He'd be out for four weeks.

Beckham decided to make use of his time off by booking a family holiday to Barbados, but before they jetted off there was the small matter of a drinks and canapés reception with the Queen for members of England's 2002 World Cup squad to attend. Beckham might have been injured, but as captain he felt obliged to go and was unsurprisingly centre stage in proceedings. He even found himself engaged in conversation with the Queen about matters arising from the much-publicised kidnap plot. 'She raised the subject of security and if anyone is going to know about that, it's the Queen,' Beckham said, with not a hint of irony.

The way Beckham tells it he returned to training refreshed and in buoyant mood. The exertions of a World Cup had taken their toll, and the enforced break was just what he needed to replenish his mental and physical reserves for the second half of the season at United. Optimism was through the roof, but when he walked back into United's Carrington complex, it soon became clear he'd invited the wrath of a manager who had grown increasingly tired of the celebrity trappings that came with the most famous footballer on the planet.

It turned out Ferguson was furious that Beckham had delayed his holiday by two days to attend the reception with the Queen. He saw it as yet another example of Beckham tending to his celebrity when he should have been concentrating on expediting his recovery from the broken rib, and he questioned his loyalty to United. The pair had clashed before over the incident that led to Beckham being dropped against Leeds, but this conflict ran far deeper. This was the culmination of months of frustration on the part of the United manager, who was clearly running out of patience with the Beckham circus.

In his book Beckham rightly argues that a rib injury is one of those you can do nothing about. It's four weeks to heal, no matter what you do, and therefore he sacrificed nothing by joining up with the England squad. He also makes the point that had he missed the reception there would have been a huge media furore – that would have provided a far bigger distraction to his recovery than his attendance. But to judge the situation in isolation, as with the fallout from the missed training session in 2000, is to pass over the underlying problem.

Beckham's celebrity lifestyle had been like a dripping tap for Ferguson. With every gushing magazine spread, hysterical public appearance and iconic new hairstyle, Beckham was fraying a bond they'd shared since he signed forms at Old Trafford as a teenager. He was beginning to feel like Beckham's fame was impinging not just on the player's ability to give his full commitment to United, but on his manager's ability to run the kind of everyman operation he'd spent 15 years cultivating. It's a great footballing cliché that no one player should be bigger than a club, but in this case no one player should be bigger than the manager either.

It was easy to sympathise with Ferguson's frustrations. From the outside, I was starting to feel like the Beckham circus was becoming an embarrassment to United. His fame was so overblown, so preposterous, that he was beginning to seem like a caricature of himself. And in his bubble of adulation he barely seemed to notice how ridiculous he often looked in the media, or how his public profile was threatening to overshadow the trade that made him famous in the first place. He was a footballer first, and a star second. And there were times when you wanted him to step away from the red carpet, and concentrate on the green one.

Beckham returned to action, and he and Ferguson continued to clash. Beckham was said to feel like Ferguson was 'torturing' him, such was his manager's lack of warmth in the wake of the Buckingham Palace affair, and that he was being unfairly singled out for a roasting when the team played badly. Famously, it all came to a head in the dressing room after United lost 2-0 to Arsenal in the fifth round of the FA Cup, when a furious Ferguson blamed Beckham for losing concentration in the build-up to Arsenal's second goal and kicked a boot in frustration. He might not have aimed for Beckham, but he caught him just above the eye and all hell broke loose.

According to Beckham's account, he had to be restrained by Ryan Giggs and Ruud van Nistelrooy as he lurched in for Ferguson. The frustrations of the last few months threatened to be released in a wild flurry of punches between the 27-year-old England captain and a knight of the realm. Had it kicked off it would surely have been difficult for either man to stay at Old Trafford – but fortunately Giggs and Van Nistelrooy were sharp enough to stop it happening. Beckham stormed off to the treatment room and sure enough news of the fracas seeped out of the dressing room and onto the front and back pages the following day.

Beckham arrived at training the following morning sporting a none-too-discreet Alice band, with the wound on show for every snapper and his brother to get the shots that dominated the news agenda. There was talk of him filing a personal injury lawsuit against Ferguson, and speculation that this was the final straw in a relationship that was already strained to breaking point. Ferguson's former players weighed in with stories of dressing room bust-ups gone by, of teacup tantrums and trolley traumas, and the press dug up the nickname he earned during his Aberdeen days, 'Furious Ferguson'. Only Gordon Taylor, the chief executive of the PFA, appeared to have the events in perspective. 'Things happen in dressing rooms that sometimes need to be kept in dressing rooms,' Taylor said. 'If I had a pound for every bust-up I've heard of in the dressing room, I would have a lot of pounds.'

When questions were asked, Ferguson, stubborn as ever, stopped a long way short of issuing a public apology. He seemed most annoyed at whoever had leaked the story from inside the dressing room, and was quick to make light of Beckham's injuries. 'Contrary to reports, David Beckham did not need to have two stitches. It was just a graze which was dealt with by the doctor,' he said. 'It was a freakish incident. If I tried it a hundred or a million times, it couldn't happen again. If it could I would have carried on playing. There is no problem and we move on... I have to stress whatever happens in the dressing room remains sacrosanct.'

The way many fans saw it, the whole thing was quite literally a storm in a teacup. We knew Ferguson was capable of exploding, and that Beckham had been pressing his buttons for months – and it could have been far worse. Was it right for the United manager to kick out at the club china? According to health and safety guidelines probably not – but it happens all the time. The fact the incident was leaked, and that Beckham appeared to play on it in the days that followed, would probably be identified as a psychologist as his 'cry for help'. Here was a man who'd grown up in fear of this father figure in his life, deciding to take a stand. Had he been happy at United, he would have brushed it off.

The way the incident played can only have inflamed Ferguson further. Beckham controlled the media agenda from the moment he stepped out in the Alice band to his public statement forgiving his manager three days later. It might not have been the way he intended it, but it felt once again like the David Beckham show. 'I want to assure all Manchester United fans that there is complete harmony and focus as we prepare for the Juventus game,' he said. 'The dressing room incident was just one of those things – it's all in the past now.'

Only it wasn't. The relationship between Ferguson and Beckham had become untenable, and by April it was beginning to look like United were making plans for life without their one-man global brand. Ferguson dropped Beckham for the crucial Premier League meeting with Arsenal at Highbury, and a week later for the second leg of the Champions League quarter-final against Real Madrid. Both times he justified the decision by making an argument for Ole Gunnar Solskjaer's superb run of form, but not even the baby-faced assassin's parents thought he merited a place on the right flank at Beckham's expense.

Beckham came off the bench and scored twice against Madrid, channelling his frustrations in a blistering 20-minute cameo that had United fans bemused as to why he hadn't been on the pitch from the outset. Ferguson refused to concede he'd made a mistake, but responded by starting him in United's final three league games of the season. They won all three, with Beckham scoring at Old Trafford against Charlton and away at Everton on the last day of the season. As it turned out, his wicked, curling free-kick past Richard Wright at Goodison Park proved to be his last act in a United shirt.

On 18 June 2003, after nearly a year of incessant speculation, United released a statement to the London Stock Exchange that confirmed what most of us had known for weeks. Beckham was going to Real Madrid, in a deal worth around £25 million. His relationship with Ferguson had run its course and it was time for both men to go about their business at different football clubs.

But as one superstar walked out of Old Trafford that summer, so another goose-stepped precociously in. His name was Cristiano Ronaldo, an 18-year-old wunderkind who had risen from nowhere to a value of £12.2 million and the very top of United's shopping list – and all in the space of just one season, 31 appearances and five goals in the colours of Sporting Lisbon. 'He is an extremely talented footballer, a two-footed attacker who can play anywhere – up front, right, left or through the middle,' Ferguson said on completing the deal for the Portuguese player in August 2003.

United had been monitoring Ronaldo since he broke into Sporting's first team aged 17. He was the kind of player Old Trafford was made for, an extravagant attacking talent with devastating pace and unflinching self-belief. When he put in a virtuoso display in a friendly against United that summer, Ferguson was in little doubt he'd uncovered a future star. 'After we played Sporting last week the lads in the dressing room talked about him constantly, and on the plane back from the game they urged me to sign him. That's how highly they rated him. He is one of the most exciting young players I've ever seen,' Ferguson said.

Watching the highlights of that game again today, it's easy to see why. Ronaldo lacked the bulk he would later add to his physique, but his raw pace and dribbling ability left United mesmerised. Time and again he ran at them, dipping a shoulder and offering a feint, before changing direction with devastating effect. He could run the flank, or cut inside, and looked to shoot at every opportunity. Here was a precocious talent with pretty much everything covered, and the most prized attribute at his disposal was his fearlessness. Taking on the most famous team in football, he appeared to be relishing the contest like a schoolboy in the playground. There was a revelry in everything he did, and a boldness that set the tone for his years to come at Old Trafford.

The secret was out, and with Europe's finest beginning to circle, Ronaldo signed a five-year deal at United and committed himself to what he called 'the best team in the world'. In the space of a season, the puck-faced teenager from Madeira had gone from a promising teenager in the Portuguese first division, to the most hyped prospect in world football. It was little wonder he requested the No. 28 shirt at United to avoid the pressures of following George Best, Bryan Robson, Eric Cantona and Beckham in the famous No. 7. But Ferguson wasn't having any of it. He told Ronaldo the shirt would provide extra motivation and the subject wasn't up for discussion.

The fans mostly reserved judgement. There were a good number who resented the departure of Beckham, and blamed Ferguson for forcing him out. And the ill-advised signings of Laurent Blanc and Juan Sebastian Veron had left others beginning to doubt Ferguson's acumen in the transfer market. Had he given Ronaldo the No. 7 to spite the man who no longer wore it? Or because he genuinely believed this relatively unproven teenager was the next messiah, and a player worthy of the shirt?

On 16 August 2003, at Old Trafford, we got the answer. Ronaldo came off the bench in a 4-0 win against Bolton and put in a 30-minute display that had the English newspapers falling over themselves with plaudits. His combination of searing pace, jutting angles and feather-light touch made him an instant 'get-off-your-seat-when-he-gets-the-ball' type. Here was a player stripped of inhibition – that rare breed of raw, exhibitionist talent that arrives almost perfectly formed. 'A star is born,' read the headline in the *Sunday Telegraph*. 'Ronaldo is an instant legend', said the *Mail on Sunday*. 'Who needs Beckham?' led the *People* – who were clearly in Ferguson appeasing mode.

The verdict was unanimous. United had unearthed a player who not only promised greatness, but whose arrival could ultimately make light of Beckham's move to Madrid. For Ferguson it was the perfect tonic after a summer that had seen his relationship with England's favourite son dominate the back pages and his leadership qualities once again doubted. Beckham had moved on, and so had he. But most importantly, so had United. There were those who said Ferguson's time had passed, but in Ronaldo he appeared to have uncovered the future.

And while Beckham bathed in the adulation of the hysterical fans in Madrid, and took his global profile to ever more dizzying heights, United were able to focus on the potential of the man who replaced him. It was too early to make a comparison, but there were already those suggesting Ronaldo had the attributes to outshine the superstar he followed into the No. 7 shirt. He was certainly quicker, and more adept at beating his man, and there was even the argument he possessed two good feet to Beckham's one.

We were getting carried away, but we weren't the only ones. 'Just this once all the hype and hullabaloo could be justified,' read the match report in the *Sunday Times*. 'This precocious 18-year-old's mesmeric feet are destined to give a few defenders twisted blood as they used to say of the No. 7 par excellence, George Best.' As compliments go, they don't come much better than that. And it was impossible not to get picked up in the hysteria. Football fans are always on the lookout for their club's next great player, and it was fast becoming the consensus that his name was Ronaldo.

But the cocksure winger could do nothing to stop Arsène Wenger's Arsenal achieve the remarkable feat of going unbeaten for an entire Premier League season. The so-called 'Invincibles' won 26 and drew 12 of their 38 games, to finish 15 points clear of United and celebrate the third title of the Wenger era. The defence of Lauren, Sol Campbell, Kolo Toure and Ashley Cole took up the mantle of legendary Arsenal back four Lee Dixon, Tony Adams, Martin Keown and Nigel Winterburn, and simply refused to be beaten. While in attack, the brilliant Thierry Henry helped himself to 30 goals in the league, and deservedly won every award going.

The Arsenal-United rivalry had by now escalated into a searing hatred, on and off the pitch. In September 2003 the two teams squared up in what has become known as 'The Battle of Old Trafford'. An otherwise laboured game sparked in life late on, when Patrick Vieira was sent off for kicking out at Ruud van Nistelrooy. United went in for the kill, and when the veteran Keown was harshly adjudged to have fouled Diego Forlan in the dying seconds, Van Nistelrooy had the chance to win the match from the penalty spot, and send United to the top of the league. But the Dutchman smashed his effort against the bar, and when the final whistle sounded moments later, the jubilant Arsenal players surrounded him like a baying mob – claiming he'd cheated to get Vieira sent off.

Keown jumped up and down in front of Van Nistelrooy like an unhinged ape, kick-starting a melee that soon became a riot. Ronaldo and Ryan Giggs were handed small fines for their part in the unrest, but most pundits agreed the antagonists had been Wenger's Arsenal. The club issued a formal apology, but were still handed a record £175,000 fine by the FA, with Lauren, Keown, Vieira and Ray Parlour given individual punishments of fines and suspensions. Amazingly, despite the ruckus at Old Trafford, they still went on to win the Premier League's Fair Play award that season.

The battle lines had been drawn on the pitch, and now it was time for the managers to exchange pot shots. Wenger's reaction to the mass brawl was to label Van Nistelrooy a cheat. 'His attitude is always to look for provocation and (an opportunity) for diving,' he said. 'He's a nice boy, but I think on the pitch his behaviour is not always fair.'

Ferguson's complexion took a turn for the red when he watched the playback of the interview. 'As far as I'm concerned I can defend Ruud van Nistelrooy. I've heard Arsène Wenger's comments and I'm really disappointed,' he said. The way the United manager saw it, Van Nistelrooy was guilty of a foul, but nothing more. He hadn't dived to avoid Vieira's donkey kick – he'd simply got his body out of the way. Ferguson added that he'd leave it up to the referee to pass comment on Arsenal's discipline at the final whistle, but refused to accept United had done anything wrong. 'I think my players have behaved perfectly,' he said. And with all that to go on, the newspapers had a field day.

You had to hand it to Ferguson for his absolute denial that United had anything to answer for. He'd been standing a matter of yards away in the dugout when most of his team rushed in for pushing and shoving duties, yet the way he saw it, United were as clean as a whistle. Such a partisan take on proceedings brings managers the kind of resentment that Ferguson and Wenger have invited throughout their careers. When your modus operandi is to deny everything and cast blame elsewhere, controversy is never far behind. But the fans didn't care – we loved Ferguson for his blinkered loyalty, as Arsenal fans did Wenger.

When it's 'us against the world', you need every possible advantage. It's all part of the game.

United fans were left with a bitter taste in their mouths as Arsenal marched to the title – but at least this time they didn't win the Double. United and Arsenal squared off at Villa Park to recreate their famous FA Cup semi-final of 1999, and once again it was Ferguson's team who rode their luck and found the slice of inspiration to advance.

Paul Scholes got the winner in the first half, smashing a trademark drive past Thomas Lehmann from just inside the box. Arsenal looked tired, and with their talisman Henry reduced to a cameo from the substitutes' bench, they were some way short of the standard they'd set the rest of the season. Three days later they were out of Europe too – beaten over two legs by Chelsea – and for all the talk of matching United's famous Treble, Wenger's 'Invincibles' were left with only the title to show for a season that promised everything.

United got a trophy of their own, albeit the one they coveted least, in a one-sided FA Cup Final. They eased to a comfortable 3-0 win over First Division Millwall at the Millennium Stadium in Cardiff, and Ronaldo was the catalyst – rising to the occasion with a scintillating display that consolidated his burgeoning reputation. The 19-year-old rolled out his full array of flicks and tricks in the sunshine, and gave the United fans reason for optimism at the end of a season in which their team had finished third in the league, and once again fallen short in Europe – beaten by eventual champions Porto in the knockout stages.

The league position was particularly galling. It meant United would have to negotiate the qualifying rounds of the Champions League, and brought into focus the emergence of a new adversary on the domestic stage. Arsenal were no longer the only team in London with designs on knocking United off their perch. Cash-rich Chelsea had joined the party, and having spent tens of millions on new players for the 2003/04 season they'd not only beaten United to runners-up spot in the Premier League, but also reached the Champions League semi-finals.

As the battle between United and Arsenal intensified, so a new enemy threatened to outflank the both of them.

CHAPTER 20
FERGIE'S FURY

The day after this book became available for presale, I received an email from a 50-something United season ticket holder. 'Can't wait to read your book, but just promise me you'll mention that bloody horse,' he wrote. 'He's behind everything that's gone wrong at our football club.'

The horse was Rock of Gibraltar, a pedigree colt so good at winning races that experts suggested he could make £9 million a year when he retired to stud. As a three-year-old he won a record seven Group One races in a row, and earned his owners over £1.2 million in prize money. And he did it all running in the colours of Manchester United.

'The Rock' was a United horse through and through – and as fans we never stopped hearing about him. Trained by the Coolmore stable of shareholder John Magnier, he was co-owned by Magnier's wife Sue and United's manager Sir Alex Ferguson. Success on the football field was being mirrored on the racetrack. Ferguson and the Magniers were getting a nice little piece of the action, and looking on it seemed like an extension of a relationship that could only bode well for boardroom politics at Old Trafford.

I always thought the horses were therapeutic for Ferguson. They offered a release from the stresses and strains of running the biggest football club in the world, and every time you saw him in the winners' circle he looked ten years younger that he did in the dugout. Racing was still business, but you got the sense he could relax and unwind at the track – which is more than he ever managed on United duty. Would racing be the distraction he needed to leave football behind? It certainly looked that way for a while, and countless column inches have been devoted to predicting Ferguson's next life as a full-time race-horse owner. This was a man who needed a vocation, and an element of competition in his life. Racing seemed the ideal alternative to a life in slippers, tending to the roses.

Then it all went wrong. 'The Rock' went to stud and Magnier contested Ferguson's rights to a 50 per cent split of the fees. United's manager was so enraged he took one of the club's major shareholders to court, and the pair embarked on a bitter feud. Ferguson claimed astronomical damages, while Magnier publicly questioned his leader-ship credentials at Old Trafford, and called for an investigation into some of the transfer dealings on his watch. It looked for a while like United wasn't big enough for the both of them – and you weren't sure which one would blink first.

It was a worrying time for United fans. Ferguson might have had the power in the dressing room, but the boardroom was an exercise in wealth and influence – not footballing acumen. Magnier had the chips and the harder Ferguson pressed him, the more likely it seemed he'd be forced out of the famous gates. This was a fight like no other Ferguson had taken on before it. And it angered me more with every article I read, and every news bulletin I watched devoted to it. As fans, we just wanted it to go away, and to concentrate on the business of winning football matches. But the story was forced down our throats for months.

Magnier was getting death threats, but it didn't stop him increasing his shares in the club. And as his company, Cubic Expressions, took their holding to 28.89 per cent, talk of a takeover move grew louder by the day. If it happened, it seemed certain Ferguson would be removed from his duties and a new manager bought in to replace him. It was the last thing the fans wanted, and the hostilities towards Magnier forced him to take on 24-hour bodyguards at the height of the battle.

Thankfully a settlement was reached in March 2004. Ferguson's lawyers backed down from an original claim of £110 million, and accepted a one-off payment of £2.5 million. Ferguson called for calm from the supporters who were demanding Magnier's exit from United, but it was hard to believe the wounds of their relationship would ever truly heal. The following summer Magnier sold to Malcolm Glazer, and the boardroom war that threatened to bring down United's greatest ever manager was resigned to history.

But there was considerable collateral damage. The transfer dealings at United were put under the microscope, and a 2004 BBC documentary called *Father and Son* cast Ferguson's son Jason as an unscrupulous agent using his dad's reputation to further his business interests. Ferguson was so enraged at the film that he hasn't spoken to the BBC since.

The business with 'The Rock' and the BBC proved Ferguson is not a man who likes to back down – ever. He'd proved his stubbornness in his dealings with Paul Ince, David Beckham and Jaap Stam at United, and his combative streak in the way he'd gone at rival managers like Kevin Keegan and Arsène Wenger. But now he'd taken his fight to two infinitely more powerful opponents. You had to admire his fighting spirit.

Magnier was a hugely influential businessman, with a highly influential share in the football club that employed him. The BBC was the national broadcaster with rights to the richest league in the world, and close links to some of the most powerful people in politics. But Ferguson wasn't interested in appeasing either of them. When it came to settling a dispute, Ferguson had been raised to stand up for his convictions and fight tooth and nail for his pride.

The boy from Glasgow has never suffered fools. And he's never played anybody's game but his own. He can be opinionated, bad-tempered and a ferocious adversary, but without that stubborn streak it seems unlikely he'd have stayed the course at a club like United.

CHAPTER 21
THE OLIGARCH
AND THE SPECIAL ONE

The power base of English football is forever shifting. There will always be periods of dominance, and the rise of dynasties at Liverpool in the 1980s and United in the 1990s are the perfect examples, but the sporting laws of nature decree that soon enough a new force will emerge to redress the balance. As Ferguson had promised, United had knocked Liverpool 'off their f**king perch', and now Arsenal were taking aim at United. But neither could have foreseen the second coming of Chelsea, half a century after the club's one and only league title in 1955.

The uprising from SW6 was less of the plates shifting, and more of a spectacular earthquake that transformed the English football landscape overnight. In the summer of 2003 a Russian billionaire called Roman Abramovich bought a controlling share in the club, and set about spending £111 million on new players. He bankrolled £17 million for Damien Duff, £16.8 million for Herman Crespo, £16 million for Claude Makelele, £15.8 million for Adrian Mutu, and £15 million for Juan Sebastian Veron – who had somehow maintained his market value despite a largely underwhelming couple of seasons flouncing about in United's midfield. Ambramovich was just getting started.

Having spent just £500,000 on a little known teenager called Felipe Oliveira in 2002, Chelsea had gone from the 29th biggest spenders in

England to the most extravagant shoppers in world football, in the space of 12 remarkable months – taking their pick of the most desirable players on the planet and throwing the kind of salaries around that turn agents into whoremongers. They outspent United four times over in 2003, and accounted for 40 per cent of all spending in the English transfer market, according to research conducted by the *Daily Telegraph*. It was jaw-dropping stuff, and the implications for United were obvious.

'You can't buy the title,' was the knee-jerk response from United fans when talk turned to Chelsea's millions and their shiny squad of world-class players. But deep down we knew they could. Blackburn had done it in 1995, and while their success had gone away when the money dried up, Ambramovich's spending power was in a different league to that of Jack Walker. This was not a local businessman made good with a few million quid to throw around; Ambramovich was a 36-year-old billionaire with designs on decades of global domination and the capital to make it happen. He could have bought every club in the league if he wanted to.

If United needed any convincing they faced a serious threat to their ascendancy, it came with the news Chelsea had poached Peter Kenyon from Old Trafford to be their chief executive. Ambramovich offered him a package said to be worth £2 million a year including bonuses, which roughly tripled the figure he was on at United. 'Chelsea represents a different sort of challenge and that's why I was ready to change,' said Kenyon on completing the deal in September 2003.

Ferguson publicly wished him well, adopting the same 'United goes on without him' motto he'd become well versed in delivering in the wake of the Beckham transfer. But there was no mistaking the fact Chelsea had achieved a notable power play in extracting the man responsible for revolutionising United's corporate empire. It was a bold move that said everything about Ambramovich's ruthless ambition, and it caught practically everybody at United, including Ferguson, by complete surprise. 'First Veron and then Kenyon,' wrote Sam Wallace in the *Daily Telegraph*. 'Resisting this shift of power could prove more trouble than any resistance Arsenal have offered.'

Chelsea now had an oligarch owner, the Premier League's most forward-thinking executive and a squad of the best players on the planet. But despite the talk of overnight success, their manager Claudio Ranieri was pleading caution. 'Rome wasn't built in a day,' he said. 'I am working very hard to build a Rome. If I remember well, Sir Alex Ferguson had seven years, more or less, to win his first title... For me, it's very, very important to build the team first.'

And with that the likeable Italian was pretty much a dead man walking. The man who replaced him would forever change the way we see footballer managers. His name was Jose Mourinho, and he attracted a huge contract at Stamford Bridge a month after leading Porto to the most unlikely European triumph of the modern era. In two seasons at the Portuguese club he'd won back-to-back league titles, the domestic cup, a UEFA Cup and, most recently and most remarkably, the 2003/04 Champions League. He was the hottest property in world football and nobody knew it better than he did.

'We have top players and, sorry if I'm arrogant, we have a top manager,' Mourinho said. 'I'm not a defender of old or new football managers. I believe in good ones and bad ones, those that achieve success and those that don't. Please don't call me arrogant, but I'm European champion and I think I'm a special one.'

United had experienced the Mourinho factor first-hand when Porto knocked them out of the Champions League at Old Trafford. Having lost the first leg 2-1 United went ahead through Paul Scholes to draw level on aggregate, and were heading through on away goals with a minute left on the clock. But a mistake by Phil Neville conceded a free-kick on the edge of the box, and when United's new goalkeeper Tim Howard failed to hold it, Costinha stole in to give the Portuguese side a famous victory. The enduring image of the night was Mourinho sprinting down the touchline in delirious celebration, with his designer coat-tails flapping wildly behind him.

It was a victory for exuberance against experience, both on the pitch and in the dugout. In the build-up to the game journalists asked Mourinho what he thought of Ferguson's claim his players had dived in the first leg. 'You say, "mind games?"' he replied, underplaying his strong hold of both the context of the question and the language he would soon be asked to master. 'Yeah, they are no problem to me.' And with that the tone was set for the battles to come between the seasoned master and the precocious apprentice. Mourinho dismissed Ferguson's comments as fear, flippantly waving away the kind of tactics that had long since poisoned the relationship between Ferguson and Wenger. It was a typically bold response, and Ferguson would ultimately respect him for it.

The feeling went both ways. Mourinho had admired Ferguson from afar long before the pair came together in the Champions League, and his admiration for the godfather of British football was only enhanced by the events at Old Trafford. Ferguson and Gary Neville came into the Porto dressing room after the game and shook every one of the Porto players' hands to congratulate them. The United manager then invited Mourinho to share a bottle of wine in his office – beginning a ritual between the two that continues to this day.

'He started it, he always had one in his office,' Mourinho is quoted in Patrick Barclay's *Football: Bloody Hell.* 'So I decided it could not always be him and brought one myself, a good one, Portuguese. And that started a competition. Who would bring the best bottle? Who would bring the most expensive? He came with a fine Bordeaux, I would retaliate – always with a Portuguese wine – and so it went on.'

Watching on, you could tell the pair shared a mutual respect – as if both felt they were working on a higher plane to the managers around them. Ferguson knew Mourinho was the future, and he knew he'd met an adversary who'd relish taking him into battle. For Mourinho, there was the chance to exchange blows with a manager he considered one of the best in the business. It was a fascinating clash of cultures and styles of management, but it was underpinned by the unflinching belief and ambition that both men had shared since they first entered a dugout. As a United fan, there was a part of me that looked on Mourinho as a man whose personality would fit perfectly at Old Trafford – and maybe Ferguson did too. Perhaps both men believed at some level that Mourinho would ultimately be the man to take Ferguson's legacy forward? It could still happen.

As the fixtures gods would have it, the pair didn't have to wait long to renew wine tasting rivalries the following season. United were drawn away to Chelsea on the opening day, and with the Ambramovich spending now at £200 million, the subject of finance predictably dominated the pre-match build-up. 'I still think we can compete aggressively in the transfer market for the right players,' said United chairman David Gill. 'But most sensible fans will clearly understand that we cannot compete with Chelsea. They have written off a lot of what they spent last year and then spent about £90 million this summer. I mean, no other club can do that.'

Mourinho had been given carte blanche to make the team his own. In came his former Porto defenders Paulo Ferreira and Ricardo Carvalho, for a combined fee of around £32 million, goalkeeper Petr Cech (£7.1 million), strikers Didier Drogba (£24 million) and Mateja Kezman (£5.3 million), and midfielders Tiago (£10 million) and Arjen Robben (£12 million). Robben had looked destined for United, and even visited their training ground in readiness to sign, before Chelsea offered an inflated fee to PSV Eindhoven, and the Dutch winger bigger wages. And while the nouveau riche pretenders were cherry-picking the best of European talent and effectively pricing everybody but themselves out of the biggest deals, the rest of the Premier League were left to lean on their romantic pull to entice players, or simply go for the ones Chelsea didn't want.

Alan Smith and Gabriel Heinze were in the former category. Leeds striker Smith was a self-confessed lifelong fan of United's Yorkshire rivals, but he desperately wanted to come to Old Trafford. Ferguson paid £7 million for a player he called 'one of the most promising youngsters' he'd ever seen, and next added Paris St Germain's fiery Argentine defender Heinze for an almost identical fee. Both men talked up United's rich history and their status as one of the world's best clubs. United also signed promising 22-year-old Celtic midfielder Liam Miller – a man tipped to be 'the next Roy Keane', and another who had long dreamed of putting on a red shirt.

For United fans there was something to embrace in that. Chelsea were rolling in roubles and competing in their very own trophy auction, but they would never have United's rich tradition. Theirs was a squad of mercenaries, guns for hire who came to south-west London because money was flowing through the club, not because they'd spent their formative years dreaming of scoring a goal at Stamford Bridge. Chelsea's fast-assembled team of all-stars seemed soulless in comparison with the likes of United, Liverpool and Arsenal. And while United fans resented Chelsea's sense of entitlement, their spending power, and the overnight nature of their success, we were never jealous. It was always a case of 'What we've got, you just can't buy', and 'what you've got, we don't want anyway'.

There was also a fringe benefit to Chelsea's second coming – they were now competing with United for the title of most hated club in the country. To some, the megalomania of Abramovich felt like a vulgar exercise in cheapening the Premier League and boiling it down into a spend-off, and it nurtured a strong anti-Chelsea sentiment across the nation. But at least they had Mourinho. He brought personality and charisma to the cause, and while he was around there were always plenty of things to talk about besides money. Whether you loved him or loathed him, you couldn't help but be captivated by his every press conference. For a while we hung on his every word, and it seemed like everything he touched turned to gold.

The game at Stamford Bridge got him off to the perfect start. Mourinho's team went ahead through Eidur Gudjohnsen early on, and enjoyed a relatively untroubled stroll to a 1-0 win. In fairness United were without Rio Ferdinand, Wes Brown and Heinze in defence, Cristiano Ronaldo in midfield and Ruud van Nistelrooy in attack – but there was much to make of the relative depths in their squads and Ferguson was forced to give Miller his league debut, and use Roy Keane as a centre-back. While Chelsea's bench boasted the likes of Carvalho, Kezman and Mutu, United's replacements were the soon-to-be-sold Diego Forlan and a handful of unproven youngsters.

But United were about to make a Chelsea-esque move of their own in the transfer market. After a summer of endless speculation, it was announced they had beaten Newcastle United to the signing of 18-year-old Everton and England striker Wayne Rooney. The fee was in the region of £25.6 million, and it represented a bold statement of intent, not to mention a PR coup. Here was arguably the most coveted young player in the country, and he'd chosen to stake his future on United. 'They'd won loads of pots and I would, I expected, win lots more,' said the youngster in his book *Wayne Rooney: The Way It Is*.

As it turned out he'd have to wait a while. Chelsea romped to their first Premier League title with a record points total of 94. They lost just once all season, away at Manchester City, and conceded only 15 times in 38 games. Mourinho's team were treated to a guard of honour from United players when they visited Old Trafford in the penultimate fixture of the season. And if that wasn't humbling enough for the likes of Keane, Scholes and Giggs – players who'd become accustomed to taking the plaudits themselves – they were subsequently beaten 3-1 in a game that emphasised a gulf in class Ferguson had been trying to deny all season.

Chelsea fans milked every second of it. They chanted the name of Hernan Crespo, who was out on loan at AC Milan and had scored two goals to knock United out of the Champions League. And they sang 'Channel Five, Channel Five, Channel Five,' in reference to the station that would most likely show United's Champions League qualifying games the following season. But hardest of all to bear was the chant that followed Joe Cole's goal that sealed their victory. 'That's why we're champions,' they sang as most of Old Trafford fell silent. And they were absolutely right. As for the battle of the managers, it was now Mourinho 3-0 Ferguson.

United's season ended the way it began – with defeat to Arsenal at the Millennium Stadium. The FA Cup Final finished 0-0, with United somehow failing to score, despite dominating virtually the entire game. It all came down to penalties, and when Scholes missed, it was left to United hate figure Patrick Vieira to ensure Ferguson ended the season without a major trophy for the first time since 1997/98.

There was more misery to follow in the 2005/06 campaign. Chelsea once again ran away with the title, and had the pleasure of despatching United 3-0 at Stamford Bridge to make it official. And this time United didn't even get past the group stages in the Champions League, losing away at Benfica and Lille, and recording just two wins from their six games. The FA Cup ended in a fifth-round defeat to Liverpool, and a League Cup final triumph against Wigan did little to lift the impending sense of doom surrounding everybody concerned with United.

The mood was captured perfectly by Roy Keane, who criticised his teammates in an interview for MUTV following a 4-1 loss to Middlesbrough. The footage was pulled, but the contents of his rant made it to the back pages and made a lasting impressing on United fans who were already beginning to doubt their team's application. Keane questioned the desire and commitment of United's younger players – giving special attention to Keiron Richardson and Rio Ferdinand – and he cast doubt on the credentials of the club to challenge for major honours. It proved the beginning of the end for the Irishman, who left for Celtic in December, after nearly 13 years at United.

From the outside it was starting to look like Ferguson's empire was collapsing around him. 'Just as the glory years of 1992 to 2001 will only fully be appreciated in 20 years' time, so will Ferguson's subsequent failure,' wrote Rob Smyth in the *Guardian*, in a ferocious attack that labelled United's manager 'incompetent', and suggested the club would continue their plummet from grace if he stayed in charge. He highlighted Ferguson's growing tactical ineptitude, his increasingly lightweight squad and his seemingly ever-decreasing standards. It was as if the greatest manager in the country was guilty of a dereliction of duties. 'In years gone by he would never have given a game to someone like John O'Shea, whose sole use is to put the podge in a hodgepodge midfield, or someone as meek as Darren Fletcher,' wrote Smyth.

Smyth's was a vicious and provocative attack, but some of the sentiments rang true – and the truth hurt for the fans. United's new crop of youngsters were clearly no match for the generation of Giggs, Beckham, Scholes and the Neville brothers, and Ferguson had unquestionably made some ill-informed moves in the transfer market. There were tactical issues that hit a nerve too – such as his persistence in using Rooney as a wide player, and the suggestion he was transforming Ronaldo 'from the world's most thrilling talent into a run-of-the-mill winger' every time he put on the United shirt. But the most damning of all was the accusation that Ferguson was out of touch with a shifting player culture at the club. Smyth wrote of the 'Merc berks' – the likes of Ferdinand, Richardson and Wes Brown – to whom 'playing the field seems as important as playing the game'.

If Ferguson had let a disruptive culture like that develop, then it stood to reason his powers were on the wane. This was the man who walked into Old Trafford in 1986 and laid down the law like a sergeant major. Lee Sharpe wouldn't have got away with it, so why should Ferdinand? Ferguson's was a regime of discipline and order, where distractions should be kept at a minimum and focus was everything – that was the blueprint for his success. But the ever-inflated wealth and celebrity of his players appeared to have blurred the lines.

Change had arrived in the boardroom too. In May 2005, American tycoon Malcolm Glazer gained a controlling interest in United, and a month later Manchester United had a new owner. Ferguson objected with a brief entry in the United programme, but it was left to United's fans to get across the sentiment at the heart of the football club. We saw a once financially stable football club suddenly shouldered with £650 million in debt, and in the hands of an American with little interest or knowledge of the club we lived our lives by. It's hardly surprising many fans continue to protest the situation to this day.

Some blamed Ferguson for not making more of a stand against Glazer, and Daniel Taylor's book *This Is The One* gives an account of United fans taking him to task on the subject in the middle of a crowded airport. One way or another, by the end of the 2005/06 season, United's manager was getting it from all sides, and there was even the suggestion he was considering retirement again. But this is Sir Alex Ferguson we're talking about here – and it would take more than an oligarch, a special one, the Invincibles, the loss of his captain, a controversial takeover, a dearth of young talent and three years without a Premier League title to dampen his enthusiasm.

It was time for red revival.

CHAPTER 22
ROONALDO

Cristiano Ronaldo returned from the 2006 World Cup in that grand tradition of United players under Ferguson – as the most vilified man in the country. David Beckham had started the trend by getting sent off against Argentina in 1998, and Roy Keane followed suit with his hysterical rant at Mick McCarthy in 2002. But Ronaldo's controversy threatened to bring more complications to Old Trafford than the two of those acts combined. His was a crime not only against England, but also against one of his United teammates.

Sven-Göran Eriksson's England had reached the quarter-finals in Germany, where they faced a Portugal side who'd won all four of their games and beaten Holland in the second round. Ronaldo was to the Portuguese as Rooney was to England – a precocious young prodigy with the potential to set the tournament alight. But neither player could assert his authority in a tense game that was still locked at 0-0 after an hour's play. And when Rooney appeared to tread on Chelsea defender Ricardo Carvalho, it looked like a frustrating evening had got the better of him.

What happened next threatened to have serious repercussions for United. Rooney was sent off, and once again England would be reduced to ten men by virtue of the ill discipline of one of their own. It felt like Beckham on Simeone all over again, only this time there was a more sinister villain for a nation to focus its hatred on. Ronaldo had run the length of the field to protest to the referee, and when Rooney was duly shown the red card he'd called for, he turned to his teammates with a broad grin and winked at them. His actions were caught for eternity by the cameras, and the watching millions in England – including a good number of United fans – were baying for Ronaldo's blood.

'What a winker,' came the headline the following day, after England's World Cup had once again gone the way of a penalty shootout heartbreak. And the 21-year-old, now officially the most hated footballer in the country where he made his living, seemed certain to be on his way out of Old Trafford. 'After what happened with Rooney I can't remain there,' he told Spanish newspaper *Marca*. 'I don't think I've got the support of the owner or the manager. Neither of them has backed me… [I] will have my future sorted out in a couple of days and I want to join Real Madrid.'

But a week passed and nothing happened. Meanwhile, United issued a statement saying Ronaldo was not for sale, and Eric Cantona leaned on his considerable experience as a pantomime villain to urge Ronaldo to stay at 'the greatest club in the world', and tell him there was no better place to develop his talent. Ferguson tasked his Portuguese assistant Carlos Queiroz to relay the same message to the player, and it gradually seemed possible that Ronaldo would indeed stay at United. In truth, Ferguson refused to countenance anything else.

When he returned to the fold, it quickly became apparent there was no lingering rift between Ronaldo and Rooney. The pair were implicit in United's opening day 5-1 blitz of Fulham at Old Trafford, which saw them four up inside 20 minutes. Rooney scored twice and set up another for Ronaldo, and the pair celebrated each other's goals as wildly as their own. It was an afternoon of pure release, and it was just what United needed after yet another difficult summer.

When they weren't vilifying Ronaldo, the press had been mostly revelling in the Ruud van Nistelrooy situation. It turned out the Dutchman had reacted angrily to being dropped for the Carling Cup final and was beginning to feel like he was no longer a priority. When he was named on the bench for the last game of the season against Charlton, which some suggested was the result of a training ground bust-up with Ronaldo, Ferguson claimed Van Nistelrooy walked out of Old Trafford in protest. Whatever the truth of the matter, the relationship between the striker and Ferguson was stretched at best – and untenable at worst.

In late July he was sold to Real Madrid for just over £10 million, and United had lost the man who'd scored 150 goals for the club in just 218 appearances since joining from PSV Eindhoven in 2001. That he came to United in the first place owed everything to Ferguson's persistence and his faith in a player he said could be a United great. But as was the case with Jaap Stam's departure, Ferguson never let talent stand in the way of his convictions. Van Nistelrooy might have been United's best player, but he'd broken ranks and he had to go.

The fans were bemused that he wasn't replaced. United would start the new season with a threadbare strike-force of Rooney, Louis Saha and the now 33-year-old Ole Gunnar Solskjaer – and there was a serious question mark over whether Ferguson's team could produce the kind of goal tally they needed to challenge for honours. When you consider the only major addition to his squad that summer was Tottenham midfielder Michael Carrick, there was an argument to be had that United began the campaign weaker than they'd ended the last. Carrick's potential had been brought for £18.6 million, but he was never expected to bring the value of Van Nistelrooy in his first season at Old Trafford.

At least at the other end of the pitch things were starting to come together. Defenders Nemanja Vidic and Patrice Evra had arrived midway through the 2005/06 campaign, and the dependable Edwin van der Sar was beginning to look like the long-term solution to United's goalkeeping problem. Gabriel Heinze was also growing into his role as an Old Trafford cult hero – marauding down the left flank and entering into every challenge as if he was defending the honour of his family. Ferguson had also brought in South Korean Park Ji-Sung, a neat and effective midfielder, who some wrongly suggested was no more than a cheap marketing exercise.

Four games in and United were top of the league with a perfect record, having enjoyed their best ever start to a Premier League season. Much was owed to the resurgence of a 33-year-old Ryan Giggs, who scored winners against Watford and Tottenham and appeared to be revelling in what we wrongly thought was the twilight of his career. The Welshman was named Premier League Player of the Month for August, and was now being used in all manner of roles by Ferguson. Along with his customary berth on the left, there were now times he played in the centre of midfield – either holding or pushing on, and even as a striker – as he did alongside Saha at White Hart Lane.

But not even the evergreen Giggs could touch the soaring heights achieved by Ronaldo, who scored 23 goals from midfield and played his part in countless more, displaying the kind of virtuoso talent Ferguson always knew he was capable of. And what's more, he did it all in the face of fierce provocation and intimidation at every stadium he visited. The more they booed him, the better he played. Like Cantona, Beckham and Keane before him, Ronaldo reacted to infamy with an emphatic season on the pitch.

Watching Ronaldo in the 2006/07 season was to get a sense of what earlier United fans must have felt watching George Best in his pomp. There was a marriage of joyous expression and ruthless execution that made you believe he could beat a team on his own – and frequently he did. Over Christmas Ronaldo scored six times in three games to see off Aston Villa, Wigan and Reading, as United began to pull away from Chelsea at the top of the table. There had always been step-overs and lollipops aplenty, but now they were justified. The showboat had a destination, and United had arguably the best young player on the planet.

And for all the talk of their World Cup feud, Rooney and Ronaldo dovetailed brilliantly. Rooney matched Ronaldo's haul of 23 goals in all competitions, and the pair both featured in the Premier League top ten for assists at the end of the season – as did the renaissance man Giggs. Saha and Solskjaer also proved their worth to Ferguson, making light of the hole left by Van Nistelrooy with double-figure goal tallies.

Meanwhile, United's back four of Gary Neville, Rio Ferdinand, Vidic and Evra were showing the potential to be Ferguson's best ever defence. Ferdinand and Vidic appeared to offer the perfect blend of poise and power, and the Serbian was making a name for himself as an uncompromising defender who'd put his body on the line for the cause. Neville was the same old Neville we'd always known, while Evra gave United a fresh impetus on the left, and made the collective a physical force to be reckoned with. The four were all named in a Manchester United-dominated Premier League team of the season, which also included Van der Sar, Scholes, Giggs, Rooney and Ronaldo.

It was starting to feel as if United had entered a bold new era, and you couldn't help but be excited at the possibilities. The defence was at times impenetrable, and our attacking options boasting two of the most exciting players in the world. United had evolved, and once again managed to catch up with what the game was doing around them. We now had a squad fully equipped for more physically demanding times, and capable of morphing from the traditional 4-4-2 on which Ferguson had built his reputation, to the 4-5-1 that was increasingly bringing results in Europe, even against the toughest Premier League opposition.

United were six points clear at the turn of the year, and they would not be caught. When Chelsea failed to beat Arsenal with two games remaining, Ferguson had achieved the ninth Premier League title of his career and arguably the most satisfying. 'Some years ago I used to always have an obsession with winning in Europe but it's been overtaken by the demands of the Premier League,' Ferguson said. 'I think it's the highest league in Europe now and to win it is a big, big achievement.'

Ferguson and his team had been written off before the season, but they'd answered their critics with the most emphatic of campaigns. And just as Chelsea's empire began to show signs of strain, with the breakdown of the relationship between Jose Mourinho and Roman Abramovich, United mounted a response to the revolution of which few had thought them capable. Ferguson's men had excelled in all areas of the pitch, and their manager once again dispelled the notion that he was a fading force. And as for Van Nistelrooy, it said everything that they didn't really miss him.

This time it was Chelsea's turn to roll out the guard of honour when United visited for the penultimate game of the season at Stamford Bridge. But Mourinho would have the last word, as his side beat United in a tired FA Cup Final at Wembley courtesy of an extra-time winner from Didier Drogba. It proved to be the last celebration for the Special One, who walked out on Chelsea 'by mutual consent' in the early throes of the 2007/08 season. In his place came Avram Grant, who had the misfortune of walking into a Rooney and Ronaldo-inspired red blizzard.

United picked up where they left off the following season, and Ronaldo – remarkably – managed to be even more dominant, and even more prolific. He scored 42 goals in all competitions, and finished as Premier League top scorer with an incredible haul of 31 from 34 appearances. Ferguson had signed a loan deal for Carlos Tevez on the eve of the new campaign, and the Argentine not only provided an instant return with 19 goals, but also became an instant cult hero with the fans – with his overflowing Latino passion there for all to see. Tevez was an all-or-nothing, all-action hero, and he played as if he would have killed people for a victory. Little did we know he'd swap red for blue in years to come.

United had also strengthened in midfield. The Brazilian Anderson, Portuguese winger Nani and England international Owen Hargreaves were added to Ferguson's squad, and all three would play their part in a season that saw United once again beat Chelsea to the championship, and finally end their wait for a second European title under Ferguson. In the space of two years, United's manager would go from dead man walking to the king of Europe – and his team would reinvent themselves yet again.

CHAPTER 23
MOSCOW IN FELTHAM

After spending a couple of heady years in New York, getting my United fix with the boozy ex-pats and the soccer extremists in Nevada Smiths, I spent six months chasing United bars around Asia. And it was there I somehow came upon my vocation. I was 25 years old and whatever I did next would define at least the next 40 years of my life – and probably more – so it made sense to do something I was at least vaguely interested in. I'd tried music, and that didn't work. And there weren't really jobs to be had in *Star Wars* or sandwiches. Sport was the answer.

As with most sports writers I was never nearly good enough to actually compete on the pitch and get paid for it. My football career peaked at 16 and has continued to spiral downwards since, from the heights of Horsham Town, to the village warfare of Barns Green, and Sundays playing for the brilliantly named Ajax Kings Arms. In fact, reading my footballing CV is a bit like reading a list of Lee Sharpe's clubs after he left United – only some of mine you might have heard of.

So it turned out sports journalism was the only option. I applied for a course at university, and duly immersed myself among a brood of giddy alcoholics who shared my dream. At the end of the day, when they slunk away to drink copious amounts of snakebite and play a game they called 'Edward Ciderhands', I returned to the wife who was supporting me. Removed from her country of birth, she had married a poverty-stricken student, so there was a huge motivation to pull my finger out and actually earn some money.

After two years of practising match reports and agonising over shorthand (don't bother, waste of time), I managed to chance myself a job. I called the British Eurosport office, and was fortunate enough to be put through to a chirpy Australian called Buffy in Human Resources. Bizarrely she entertained my enquiry, and a couple of weeks later I opened my junk mail to find an email from the editor of the Eurosport-Yahoo website, inviting me in for a writing test. In I went, and lo and behold – having sub-edited a fictional match report and attempted a sports quiz – I was offered gainful employment.

Three months later I was reporting on the Champions League final between United and Chelsea. But it wasn't as good as it sounds. The two main football writers at the website were both Reds, and both had plans to watch the game in a bar. And with the third choice away on holiday, it was left to yours truly to provide the build-up to the action and the live text commentary of the game itself. It was United's most important game for nine years, and I would be watching it in the dark recesses of an office in Feltham, with no alcohol to soothe my nerves, and nobody for company. If United won it would be bearable, but if they lost the journey home promised to be one of the most depressing of my life.

On the day of the game the pressure was seriously taking hold. I filed a feature on 'Champions League Drinking Games', which provided some light relief, but otherwise was left to tick over the usual nuts and bolts of the build-up to a big game. Not only was I dealing with my team facing their destiny, but also with the looming responsibility of turning round a minute-by-minute text commentary and an extended 'on-the-whistle' match report. The thought of beginning my report with, 'Chelsea were crowned champions of Europe for the first time in their history…' was enough to make me feel physically sick.

When the teams were announced I was pleased to learn United would go into the game with a three-pronged attack of Cristiano Ronaldo, Wayne Rooney and Carlos Tevez. Ferguson had used 4-5-1 for much of the campaign, but it was important United set the tone for the final. They'd been here before, and on that basis had to be favourites. Avram Grant's Chelsea were in unchartered territory, and to that end they had to be vulnerable to an early blitz from United.

The game itself proved a surprisingly open and entertaining spectacle. United went ahead through a Ronaldo header on 26 minutes, his 42nd and final goal of the season, before Frank Lampard capitalised on a deflection to bring Chelsea level on the stroke of half-time. Both sides went for the jugular in the second half, and Chelsea came closest when Didier Drogba's shot hit the upright, but into extra-time we went. By now the Feltham office was empty but for the occasional appearance of the commentators who were working on a ski jumping show. And one of them was a Chelsea fan.

As the tension mounted Chelsea were once again denied by the woodwork when Lampard's shot beat Van der Sar. Then substitute Ryan Giggs looked to have won it, only for John Terry to put his head in the way of his shot. It was unbearable stuff, and with nobody around to share it with I was at breaking point. I was contemplating a penalty shootout, and at the same time having to ready a match report that could go either way depending on the result of it. Then Drogba got himself sent off for raising his arms at Vidic, and added another couple of paragraphs to the already epic account of the night's action.

The penalty shootout was almost unwatchable. Tevez and Michael Carrick scored for United, but Ronaldo – of all people – missed. And suddenly up leapt a man at the end of the Eurosport office with the kind of celebration Feltham had surely not often seen. Throwing his arms in the air and stamping his feet in delight, he yelled, 'F**k off, Ronaldo, you f**king c**t... have some of that, you absolute f**king w**ker!' And with that he shook himself off, nodded his head towards me and sat back down in his chair to continue watching the action. No wonder the other guys had wanted to watch the game in a bar.

Nine penalties in, and nobody but Ronaldo had missed. It meant Chelsea's Chelsea-loving captain Terry would step up with the chance to complete the most famous triumph in Chelsea's history. And I would have little choice but to kill the bloke at the other end of the office. But he missed. In possibly the cruellest penalty shootout moment in history, Terry lost his footing and hit the post with the goal gaping. Van der Sar had gone the other way, but it didn't matter. Somehow, I stayed silent.

Into sudden death we went. Anderson scored first for United. Salomon Kalou replied for Chelsea. Then Giggs passed the ball calmly into the bottom corner to put the pressure on once more. By this time the rain was coming down in sheets in Moscow and the players of both teams were in various states of mental breakdown on the half-way line. Some could barely watch, some weren't watching at all. A few were holding onto their teammates for dear life, waiting to hear what happened next. Up stepped Nicolas Anelka, that most mercenary of footballers with a reputation for sulking. Van der Sar guessed right, and the man at the other end of the office stormed out in disgust. 'Back luck mate,' I said. 'Terry must be pretty gutted I'd imagine.'

I was all on my own in a remote office in the backwaters of Feltham, with a report to file and a train to catch, but I couldn't have been happier. Nine years after Dad and I had watched them win in Barcelona, United were back where they belonged. I rocked back in my chair and picked up the phone. And as it rang, I started to type: 'Manchester United were crowned European champions for the third time in their history after a dramatic sudden-death penalty shootout victory over Chelsea in Moscow…'

CHAPTER 24
NEW ARRIVALS, LOOMING DEPARTURES

The summer of 2008 was all about Cristiano Ronaldo – which was just the way he would have liked it. United's world-beating winger spent most of June and July winking provocatively at Real Madrid, talking up a 'dream' move to the Spanish megalomaniacs and treating the club that paid his wages, the reigning champions of Europe no less, like a haggard fish wife he'd been forced to suffer while waiting for a more attractive model to come along.

Ronaldo played the situation spectacularly badly. In the heady aftermath of United's Champions League win against Chelsea, he pledged his future to Old Trafford. A matter of days later, as thoughts turned to his Euro 2008 duties with Portugal, he began openly talking about a move to Madrid. The big-spending Spanish giants responded by publicly stating their desire to make Ronaldo their next 'Galactico', and before the perma-tanned Roy of the Rovers could so much as summon a step-over, a few tears or a sprawling swallow dive, a deal for a mooted £80 million looked as good as done.

United were furious with Ronaldo, but they channelled their contempt at Madrid. The club went to FIFA and demanded an investigation into what they alleged was a deliberate attempt by the Spaniards to influence a player under contract until 2012. But Madrid's president Ramon Calderon said United had 'no evidence' to back up their claims, and the dark lords of the game agreed. Sepp Blatter even went so far as to say United were treating Ronaldo like a 'slave', suggesting the club should free the 23-year-old from an 'uncomfortable' life spent earning millions of pounds kicking a ball around for one of the greatest footballing institutions on the planet. It was another Prince Philip moment for FIFA's preposterous president. 'If this is slavery, then give me a life sentence,' said Sir Bobby Charlton, capturing the mood of reaction perfectly. Blatter later claimed his comments had been taken out of context, but he was the same man who'd said women's football would be improved by tighter shorts – and was by now well on his way to becoming the least popular man in the world game.

Ultimately, Ronaldo was kept in chains. The saga ran for two months, although it felt like a decade, and by the time Ferguson confirmed he'd be staying at United for another season there were a good number of fans who wished he'd left. He might have been a precocious, match-winning talent to stand comparison with the likes of George Best and Eric Cantona, but it was now abundantly clear he lacked the respect for the red No. 7 shirt we demanded. Nobody could blame Ronaldo for desiring to join the club of his boyhood dreams, but to dismiss the pride of the fans who adored him was to betray our trust. 'That [the fans' resentment] will pass. A couple of good goals and people will be happy,' he said. But I wasn't convinced.

Ferguson, publicly at least, dealt with the situation in typically no-nonsense fashion. He returned from holiday to schedule a meeting with Ronaldo in Portugal, and emerged to emphatically state his best player was going nowhere – doing so in a manner that suggested there was barely an issue to deal with at all. 'It's not a difficult position,' he said. 'I was on my holiday and I was not going to interrupt my holiday, believe me. I wasn't panicked because the player is under contract so the strength and the rights are with Manchester United.' It was classic Ferguson, choosing attack as the best mode of defence. The gathered press pack dared not challenge him.

Fortunately for fans of anything other than endless speculation over Ronaldo's future, the want-away winger would be absent for the start of the new season after undergoing ankle surgery. It was something of a relief for United fans not to have to welcome in the new campaign with pictures of his grinning mug celebrating a winning goal at Old Trafford – or by hearing him pledge his undying love for the club in a post-match interview. Time heals all wounds so they say – but we needed a bit more of it to resume glorification duties on the precocious youngster. The whole affair had the feel of a couple welcoming back the son-in-law who cheated on their daughter. Awkward.

A welcome distraction arrived with the capture of Tottenham's rakish striker Dimitar Berbatov, who signed late on transfer deadline day for a fee of £30.75 million. In light of United's anger at the Real-Ronaldo situation, there was more than a hint of irony in the accusations from Spurs that United had spent the last 12 months tapping up the Bulgarian, but ultimately the two sides were happy enough to agree a cash-for-no-questions arrangement, and Berba was a Red. It would have given Ferguson no shortage of satisfaction that the two suitors he beat to deal were Manchester City, disgustingly flush with cash after a takeover by the Abu Dhabi United Group, and Real Madrid.

Berbatov was a sumptuous proposition for the fans. At Spurs he'd earned a reputation as an intelligent forward of exquisite technique, with a reading of the game that drew comparisons to Teddy Sheringham and Cantona. Like Sheringham, he made up for what he lacked in pace with an acute awareness of where to operate and what was going on around him. He appeared the ideal foil for the blossoming talents of Wayne Rooney and a bespoke fit for Ferguson's United. 'This is a key signing,' Ferguson said. 'Dimitar is one of the best and most exciting strikers in world football. His style and ability will give the team a different dimension and I'm sure he will be a popular player with the fans.'

Berbatov wasted little time earning our approval – firing a timely snipe at the nouveau riche boys in blue across town. 'I would not even have thought about Manchester City. My only goal was to come to United,' he said. 'I heard about the offer City made and the money they want to spend. It did not make any difference to me. I just wanted to come here.' And to make things even sweeter, while we bathed in a victory for United's rich history over City's overflowing coffers, they went and paid a British transfer record £33 million for Robinho instead.

By the time Berbatov made his debut, away at Anfield on 13 September, United had already beaten Portsmouth to win the Charity Shield, lost to Zenit St Petersburg in the European Super Cup final and collected a win and a draw from their opening two Premier League games. When you consider we'd been talking about Ronaldo since June and spent July watching them on pre-season duty in South Africa and Nigeria, it's no wonder the season already felt like a long one.

From a personal perspective, the start of the new campaign washed over me in a sleep-deprived haze. A month after that fateful night covering United's Champions League triumph from a bunker in Feltham, my wife had given birth to our first child – a boy we named Henry – and it made for sweeping changes to my fandom. Overnight, United were relegated to third on my priority list, and making time to watch their games became a complex political operation. Forget what happened before; when you've got a baby 'It's only a game' always wins.

But while a two-month-old might not be the ideal companion for an afternoon at Old Trafford, what with all that processed meat, lager and swearing to get through, a sleeping Henry on my chest turned about to be a free pass for watching endless hours of football on television. If I could work his naps around key fixtures, Henry and I would be able to give United's quest to match Liverpool's 18 league titles, win a third Premier League on the spin, and claim a fourth European Cup our full attention. Nappy changes and feeds at half-time; mum sleeps during the games. Easy street.

Let's just say it was a hit and miss operation. There were times when we sat through entire games to our mutual, blissful content. And there were times when I spent the full 90 minutes jogging a pushchair around the block, trying desperately to get the little guy to close his eyes and give up on the spirited wailing that betrayed the commitment of a barnstorming Roy Keane. Worst of all were the self-inflicted howlers – the stifled yelps of joy that met important United goals, and would unfailingly wake the little master from his slumber. When Ji-Sung Park scored against Chelsea, Dad and I screamed at such volume it's a wonder Henry isn't traumatised by the sight of the South Korean to this day.

But while a good number of United's games in the 2008/09 season were spent with Henry attached like a tree frog to my torso, a good deal more were watched in the testosterone-infused man pit that doubled as the Eurosport-Yahoo office in Feltham – fuelled by half-pints of espresso to counteract my nappy-frazzled mind. It was there I watched Berbatov's debut against Liverpool, a game that saw Ferguson go bold with Rooney, Carlos Tevez and Berbatov in a three-pronged attack against a Rafa Benitez team shorn of Steven Gerrard and Fernando Torres – the two key players in what was increasingly looking like a two-man Liverpool team.

The game kicked off at 12.45 p.m., and by 12.48 p.m. United were ahead. Berbatov took three minutes to make his first telling contribution, collecting a pass from Anderson and running at Jamie Carragher, before teeing up Tevez to fizz a shot home in front of the Kop. It should have been the launching pad for an afternoon to relish for United fans, but Liverpool equalised through a comical Wes Brown own goal, and Ryan Babel profited from a rare lack of concentration by Ryan Giggs to score the winner. It was the first time Liverpool had beaten United at Anfield for seven years, and the result saw United fall six points behind their resurgent rivals at the top of the table.

Ferguson's team were criticised for a shambolic defensive performance, and the manner of their defeat – out-manned in a physical midfield battle – was enough for some to suggest they were a waning force. 'We never won a tackle and you have to hand it to Liverpool,' Ferguson admitted. 'They deserved the victory. When you have bad days, the big thing is to get something from them but we conceded two goals that were absolute shockers. People will say that it is some Conference team defending when they see us on television. It was shocking stuff. The first was a really scabby goal to lose [an expression he must have remembered from the 1980s] and the second was a shocker.'

If United needed a tonic after their Anfield debacle it arrived in the return of Ronaldo to the starting line-up ten days later in a 3-1 League Cup win against Middlesbrough at Old Trafford. All too predictably he opened the scoring, heading home a Giggs corner, and duly helped himself to another in a 2-0 league win against Bolton four days' later. Rooney was also on target that day, bagging his first of the season to lend the scoreboard a reassuring glean of quality, and remind us all of the Rooney-Ronaldo axis of power that had conquered Europe the season before. By the time Berbatov got off the mark with a Champions League double against Aalborg at the end of September, United had emerged from their early-season stupor and were beginning to look like the genuine article again.

Berbatov had started slowly, but now began to purr like the classic sports car United had paid all that money for. He marked their next Champions League outing with a double against Celtic, putting in a sublime shift that drew heavy praise from his new manager. 'It was fantastic, a marvellous performance from Dimitar again,' Ferguson said, as his team collected their sixth straight victory. 'He's bringing that composure to the final third of the field... I also think the other players are beginning to understand what type of player he is. You always feel he can produce a pass that means something and his weight of pass on three or four occasions was superb. He has got five goals for us already and that is a terrific contribution.'

With Berbatov firing, Tevez found first-team opportunities hard to come by. The blood-and-guts Argentine was now fighting to justify his selection as part of Ferguson's Manchester United 'Lite' in the League Cup. To his credit he did just that with a fourth-round winner against QPR and four goals in a 5-3 win against Blackburn in the quarter-finals. All the while, speculation was rife that Manchester City were planning a cross-town raid for the striker, whose complicated loan arrangement was due to run out at the end of the season. Tevez's 'advisor' Kia Joorabchian was the architect of his bizarre predicament, and had placed a £30 million price tag on the player's head for a permanent deal. With United powerless, all they could do was offer him a deal and hope he accepted.

At the start of the season Joorabchian said a move to City was out of the question, that Tevez was committed to United and he fully expected his player to be at Old Trafford for the foreseeable future.

But as the campaign unfolded, and Tevez found himself a somewhat peripheral figure in the shadow of Rooney and Berbatov, the temptation of becoming a focal point once again in the blue of Manchester City – twinned with the promise of a quite incredible wage package – clearly made up his mind. Ferguson later claimed the deal was done as early as in January, but the Tevez saga would not be finally put to bed until the following June.

For long-suffering City fans, the speculation alone gave them reason to believe they were on the verge of mounting a serious challenge to United's supremacy. By the close of the January window City had spent well over £100 million on new players, and for most commentators it was now a question of when, and not if, they would translate their financial power to the football pitch – and finally win the club a long-awaited trophy. It might have been 32 years since City lifted the League Cup in 1976, but the fact a United player was even considering swapping red for blue in 2008, left us in little doubt the club would be reunited with silverware in the near future. They would have bought their success, but that wouldn't make it any easier to take from the vantage point of Old Trafford.

But for all their spending Mark Hughes and his City slickers remained light years behind United in the 2008/09 season. After recovering from a shaky start, Ferguson's team put the boosters on for a fine run into Christmas and capped a vintage year by winning the FIFA Club World Cup in Japan (not that we cared half as much as FIFA wanted us to). United returned from their travels to win 11 Premier League games in a row, beat Tottenham on penalties to win the League Cup final, and burn past a Liverpool side who had topped the table at Christmas. The run put to bed any lingering doubts over United's defending – with Edwin van der Sar managing a remarkable 1,113 minutes without conceding a league goal – and had us dreaming once again of the Treble.

Trust Liverpool to bring us back down to earth again. This time they won at Old Trafford, inflicting a humiliating 4-1 defeat in March that represented United's first Premier League loss since the previous November. It was a glorious double for Benitez's team, and an inglorious one for Nemanja Vidic – who made it two red cards in two games against the enemy, and was treated to a roasting by Torres that once again raised questions about United's defensive fallibility against quality opposition.

But despite suffering his biggest Premier League defeat in 17 years, and United's worst home loss to Liverpool since 1936, a resolute Ferguson managed to maintain a sense of perspective. He even claimed United had been the better side at Old Trafford, before calling on his team to channel their disappointment next time out against Fulham. 'Now the thing is to respond,' he said. 'It always is at this club – you lose a game and you respond. We always do.' But this time it didn't happen. United lost 2-0 at Craven Cottage, in a game that saw Rooney and Paul Scholes sent off and gave the impression Ferguson's team were in danger of collapsing before the finish line.

The next league game was at home to Aston Villa, and with United 2-1 down with ten minutes left we began to think the unthinkable. In the very season we were set to draw level with Liverpool's once seemingly untouchable haul of 18 titles, the Scousers were threatening to snatch the prize from under our noses. It was time for a 1999 moment, and United duly delivered one. First Ronaldo produced a trademark cut inside and low drive to bring us level on 80 minutes. Then, in the dying seconds, a little-known 17-year-old Italian striker called Federico Macheda summoned a delightful curling winner to send Old Trafford into raptures.

That Macheda was even on the bench was something of a shock. The teenage trainee had been due to fly back for a game in Italy, before Ferguson made a late decision to use him as a substitute – with Rooney suspended and Berbatov injured. It was a 'gamble' that paid off, said Ferguson. 'We take risks but risks are part of football.' Watching on as a fan you couldn't help think it was just the spark of inspiration United needed to ignite their run-in. Whatever it was, Ferguson still had it, and by the time his team came back from 2-0 down to beat Tottenham 5-2 at Old Trafford, the title race was as good as over.

The magic number of 18 was confirmed after a 0-0 home draw with Arsenal, and Ferguson became the first manager to twice lead his team to three successive titles. For some managers it would have been enough to equal Liverpool's record and walk off into the sunset, but the fight and ambition Ferguson had leant to United since his arrival in 1986 showed no sign of receding. 'I am already thinking about next year. You have to do it here,' he said. 'There is nothing else for it. You just drive on. I do take a lot of pride from equalling Liverpool. When I came down here they were the top guns. My job was to try to change that. I never thought we could get 11 titles – never in a million years.'

By now the Treble was dead in the water, shot down by a penalty shootout loss to Everton in the FA Cup semi-final at Wembley, but dreams of Europe loomed large. Having beaten Inter Milan, Porto and Arsenal to get there, United would take on the might of Barcelona in a Champions League final that had the neutrals practically frothing at the mouth with excitement.

To Rome they went, hoping to conquer a Barcelona outfit considered the most technically proficient and vibrant attacking force on the Continent. Pep Guardiola's team was built on a spine of players who'd led Spain to glory at Euro 2008, and they displayed many of the same characteristics. Barca had made possession an art form and, with Xavi and Andres Iniesta conducting their midfield, had inflicted their brand of 'tiki-taka' torture on just about every opponent who dared stand in the way. It was a strange position for United to be in, but most agreed they were underdogs that night. Sadly, they were proved emphatically right.

Things might have gone differently had United capitalised on an early blitz, that saw Barcelona visibly shaken and betray a vulnerability that had us wondering for a brief period if we might just thump them 5-0. But from the moment Samuel Eto'o scored from their first attack on nine minutes, the game was up. From there on in it was regulation Barca brilliance, with passes fizzing across the turf this way and that, and United's midfield hopelessly outclassed by what would ultimately be viewed as one of the greatest teams of all time. Lionel Messi finished United off with a headed second on 70 minutes, the diminutive genius capitalising on some woeful defending to bag a deserved goal and cap a humbling and hugely anti-climactic night for Ferguson and his team.

'The better team won and there's nothing you can do about that,' Ferguson said afterwards. ' ... Could be it was an off night. Could be it was a mountain too big to climb.'

From a fan's perspective, it was clear United faced a new challenge in this Barcelona team – one that they'd need to meet with an injection of youth and a reinvention of the kind Ferguson had masterminded so brilliantly in years past. The likes of Giggs – who'd produced a vintage season to win PFA Player of the Year aged 35 and would go on to be named BBC Sports Personality of the Year – Gary Neville, Van der Sar and Paul Scholes wouldn't be around forever, and United needed to come up with a contingency plan sooner rather than later. Perhaps it was exactly the kind of challenge that kept Ferguson from retiring, a nagging question for which he simply had to find an answer.

Ferguson was determined to use the Barcelona defeat as a catalyst for success, just as he had the 4-0 hammering they inflicted on his team back in 1994. But by the time he'd have the chance to lead his team on a redemption mission, Ferguson had lost two players whose looming departures had hung over the club all season. First Ronaldo left for Real Madrid, for a world record £80 million. Then Tevez did what United fans had been pleading him not to all season – he joined City and they seized the moment by producing a giant poster of the striker wearing blue, accompanied by the slogan, 'Welcome to Manchester'.

The loss of Tevez was hard to take for the fans. Here was a player who had given every ounce of himself to every minute he'd spent in a red shirt. There was a ferocious hunger in him and we loved him for it. Whether Ferguson had failed to do enough to convince him to stay, as he claimed, or Tevez had made up his mind in January to go – as Ferguson would have it – may never be known. But the fact he joined City gave them the kind of ammunition they'd been courting for decades.

As for Ronaldo's departure, United had unquestionably been shorn of their best player – and there was widespread dismay among the fans that the club appeared to have little ambition to find a worthy replacement. Having arrived a naive but precocious teenager at Old Trafford, Ronaldo left United as arguably the second best footballer on the planet behind Messi. He picked up three Premier League titles, a Champions League win and a Ballon d'Or in that time – scoring a bucket-load of goals and treating United fans to the kind of virtuoso performances we would sorely miss in the following campaign. He might have been a poser, but he was a hell of a player.

United undoubtedly suffered his loss through a lukewarm 2009/10 season. The performances of his countryman Nani and new arrival Antonio Valencia were notable positives of the campaign, but ultimately United dropped too many points as a result of their lack of penetration in the final third. They lost out on the Premier League title to Chelsea on the final day, as Carlo Ancelotti's team walloped Wigan 8-0 before going on to complete the club's first Double with an FA Cup triumph at Wembley. United did manage to defend their League Cup crown, beating Aston Villa in the final, but it was scant consolation for a season that promised the holy grail of a 19th league title.

In Europe, United looked a decent bet to reach their third straight Champions League final after a Rooney-inspired 4-0 demolition of AC Milan in the second round, but a brilliant Arjen Robben volley at Old Trafford saw them knocked out by Bayern Munich in the quarter-finals. Ferguson was furious at the 'typical Germans' for their part in the sending off of young Brazilian full back Rafael that night, but ultimately his team was guilty of surrendering a 2-0 aggregate lead at half-time through a combination of poor defending and mental frailty. Even with ten men they should have had enough, but somehow you felt the players themselves didn't believe they had the stuff this time around.

This being a season in which United failed to win the title, the all-too predictable 'Fergie to retire' rumours followed like clockwork. The man himself was having none of it. According to Patrice Evra he asked the United players whether they really believed he would walk away to a life spent 'sitting in his house watching the TV, listening to the radio and doing nothing'. They all knew the answer. 'No chance,' Ferguson said. 'I have worked all my life and I will work until I die. This is my victory. I cannot walk away from this.'

And that was that. Ferguson would 'die on the bench' read one football website, and for United fans there was great comfort in that.

Now United's longest serving manager, the most successful leader in British football history, had given up any notion of retirement, and at 68 years old was as passionate and pragmatic as he was the day he walked into Old Trafford in November 1986. 'Next season we'll go again and bring back the title to the best place in the world,' he said. 'We'll come back next year, that's exactly what Manchester United do.'

CHAPTER 25
19 AND BEYOND

Most pundits expected Chelsea to make it back-to-back titles in 2011, and when Carlo Ancelotti's team started the new campaign with ravenous 6-0 wins against West Brom and Wigan, it was easy to see why. The Londoners looked ominous, with Florent Malouda and Frank Lampard on the rampage from midfield, and the prolific Didier Drogba in the form of his life. The Ivorian was the Premier League's top scorer with 29 in the 2009/10 season, and he looked odds on to repeat the feat with a clinical hat-trick on opening day.

Meanwhile, the man who'd finished runner-up to Drogba in the scoring charts the previous season, Wayne Rooney, was in danger of imploding. United's best player had returned from a miserable World Cup with England to tabloid allegations that he'd cheated on his pregnant wife with two prostitutes. Rooney's reputation had first been undermined by his tepid performances on the game's biggest stage in South Africa, and now by the notion he was a sex-crazed, morally bankrupt footballer – like a good number of his England teammates. It was a PR disaster for United, and Ferguson was said to be furious at the way it reflected on the club that had made Rooney a multi-millionaire, and a global superstar.

Rooney was not a happy man, and his frustrations stretched beyond his worrying dip in form and his troubled private life. The 24-year-old felt United had shown a lack of ambition in the transfer market, failing to replace the departed Cristiano Ronaldo and Carlos

Tevez, and that Ferguson was playing him out of position and not allowing him to roam in the central areas he felt would bring the best out of him. And when Ferguson left him out of games against Valencia and Sunderland, citing an ankle injury, their relationship reached breaking point. 'I've not had an ankle injury all season,' Rooney said, in a bold act of defiance. When asked why Ferguson would have claimed he did, Rooney shrugged his shoulders and replied, 'I don't know'.

It was not long before the news we all feared finally arrived. After six years at the club, Ferguson said Rooney had told him he wanted to leave United. 'We're as bemused as anyone can be because we can't quite understand why he'd want to leave a club that no one can deny is the most successful in British football,' Ferguson said. 'We've won 40 major trophies, countless cup finals, have a fantastic history, a great stadium, great training arrangements – a platform for anyone to take up the challenges here. We don't understand it.' If that wasn't bad enough, Rooney's most viable destination was Manchester City – who were prepared to up his wages and put together a package that Rooney's agent thought too good to turn down. The *Guardian* said such a deal would represent the 'most rancorous and staggering transfer of modern times', and that was barely the half of it.

But just two days later, and somewhat miraculously from the perspective of everybody from the outside looking in, Rooney made the sharpest turn he'd managed all season. On 22 October, it was announced he'd signed a new five-year deal at Old Trafford. He and Ferguson were pictured, arms around each other, smiling as if nothing had happened. 'I'm signing a new deal in the absolute belief that the management, coaching staff, board and owners are totally committed to making sure United maintains its proud winning history – which is the reason I joined the club in the first place,' Rooney said, labelling Ferguson a 'genius'.

It was a remarkable change of mind, influenced not just by the advice of Ferguson and the United board, but arguably in part by the fans' rabid reaction to the idea of him leaving. 'Join City and die,' read the graffiti scrawled on Rooney's Nike poster in Manchester city centre. Forty or so irate fans descended upon his family home to launch a more targeted protest, and Rooney was left in little doubt of the public sentiment he'd face were he to swap red for blue. It was hard enough watching Tevez make the switch, but to watch Rooney follow his lead would have been a rusty knife through our hearts. Much as his recent behaviour made us squirm, his talent remained the focus of this United team. To lose him would have been a devastating blow.

Ferguson had played the situation in typically proud fashion. Rather than bow to Rooney's demands and beg him to stay, he stuck to his guns and once again made it clear that no player was bigger than Manchester United. If that meant Rooney leaving the club for City, then so be it. Ferguson had a regime to protect and a club ethos that had seen bigger names than Rooney jettisoned in the past. That said, as with his dealings with David Beckham, Eric Cantona and Roy Keane, there were allowances made for Rooney that would not have been made for a lesser talent. Ferguson was prepared to fight for him, and that alone was a privilege of his ability. He was also prepared to forgive. Theirs was a father and son relationship much like the one he had with Beckham, and as such able to withstand the kind of defiance for which a player other than Rooney would have been buried.

By the time Rooney, the born-again Red, returned to the starting line-up in late November, United had drawn level with Chelsea at the top of the table and were on an unbeaten league run that would last until the following February. The goals of Dimitar Berbatov were a defining factor, with the enigmatic Bulgarian now very much back in favour after an unconvincing 2009/10 campaign. Berba would finish the season as the Premier League's joint top scorer, and there was no better example of his genius than the hat-trick he scored in a 3-2 win against Liverpool at Old Trafford. Rooney hogged the headlines on his return, scoring a Champions League winner against Rangers, but it was back to Berbatov for a five-goal masterclass in a 7-1 slaughter of Blackburn three days later.

United's attacking ambition was furthered by a 21-year-old Mexican who went by the name 'Chicharito'. The third generation of his family to play for his country, Javier Hernandez had been on United's radar for two years before they agreed a £7 million deal with

Guadalajara to bring him to Old Trafford – just in time to watch him sizzle at the World Cup and see his value skyrocket in a matter of days. Ferguson saw huge potential in the wide-eyed, lightning fast striker, but he fully expected Hernandez to need at least a season or two to find his feet in English football. At it turned out, the Little Pea needed nothing of the sort. By May he'd relegated Berbatov to the substitutes' bench, and was widely considered the buy of the season.

Hernandez delivered 20 goals, and a good number of them were delivered with impeccable timing. It was Hernandez who snatched a late winner against Everton to maintain United's hold on the title race in April. And Hernandez again who eased United's nerves as Chelsea came to Old Trafford looking to force an uncomfortable, and potentially disastrous conclusion. He was equally as potent in the Champions League, scoring twice as Marseille were beaten 2-0 in the second round and getting United's first in a 2-1 win against Chelsea in the quarters. It was little wonder the Little Pea drew comparison with Ole Gunnar Solskjaer.

For a time it looked like the title race would go to the wire, but a combination of Arsenal's all-too predictable crumbling, and a Chelsea unable to recover from a miserable winter of discontent, meant United travelled to Blackburn on 14 May needing just a point to secure a record 19th title. It was left to Rooney to fire the decisive blow, scoring a second-half penalty to earn his side a 1-1 draw and Ferguson his 12th Premier League title in a remarkable quarter of a century at Old Trafford.

Most agreed they were far from a vintage Ferguson crop, and fell a good way short of the standards set by the teams of 1994, 1999 and 2008 – they might even have been the poorest of his dozen champions. But with criticism of United's 2011 team came an acceptance that Ferguson's genius was still a defining factor in the English game. If this squad really was as weak as people said it was, then surely Ferguson had masterminded one of the great achievements of his career. 'This is a particularly special one because it means we've won the title more than anyone in the country,' Ferguson said. 'It's history and it's great for the tradition of this club… it was Liverpool's time in the 1980s; it's our time now.'

With the title won, United turned their attentions to European matters – and the chance to avenge Barcelona in the Champions League final at Wembley. By this time, Barcelona were an even stronger force than that which had given Ferguson's team a footballing lesson in Rome two years before. Their Spanish internationals had added a World Cup triumph to their experience, and from that team Barca had added David Villa to work in tandem with the by-now incomparable talents of Messi. Pep Guardiola's pass masters had been untouchable all season, and it seemed unthinkable that Ferguson's team could challenge their authority in what one newspaper called 'a game for the ages'.

Ultimately United were once again out-passed, and outclassed, by the greatest team of their generation – and perhaps the greatest of them all. Messi skipped past tackles and opened up Ferguson's team at will, and the midfield pairing of Andres Iniesta and Xavi made Ryan Giggs and Michael Carrick look pedestrian by comparison. There was brief hope when Rooney's instinctive finish drew the game level at 1-1, but from the moment Messi skimmed a shot past Edwin van der Sar the contest was over. Villa's exquisite finish made it 3-1, and if anything the scoreline was kind of United. It was a crushing loss to match those inflicted by Barcelona in 1994 and 2008, and it left Ferguson facing up to the monumental task of overhauling the greatest opponent he'd come up against in nearly four decades of management.

I was on in-laws duty in America for the final, holed up in a soulless Ruby Tuesday's chain restaurant in Clinton, North Carolina with only my willing brother-in-law for company. Even as a relative novice of Champions League football, he could see as well as I could just how superior Barcelona were. It was a strange, detached experience to watch the biggest game of the season with the volume down, on one of six screens showing everything from lacrosse to women's softball – but by half-time I felt relieved to be so far removed from the fans who cared like I did. Dad was on the other side of the Atlantic, and this time it was just as well. After a game like that, there's really nothing left to say.

'Nobody's given us a hiding like that but they deserve it,' Ferguson said. 'They play the right way and they enjoy their football. In my time as manager it's the best team I've faced. It's [taking on Barcelona] not going to be easy, but that's the challenge. You shouldn't be afraid of a challenge. The one thing we have shown is that we are consistent in Europe. This may be the kind of stepping stone that we had some years ago when we got beaten 4-0. We improved after that and we want to improve after tonight.'

And with that the 69-year-old obsessive went back to work. Twenty-five years after taking over Ron Atkinson's 'social club' at Old Trafford and turning it into a trophy factory, Ferguson was preparing to do it all over again. As Van der Sar, Paul Scholes and Gary Neville called time on their playing careers, and with Giggs now 37 and hanging on, the time had come to breathe new life into this United team. And if United needed to be reborn, then who better than the man who'd re-imagined them so many times before to make it happen again? He'd taken over a lumbering, booze-addled relic and dragged United up through two decades of spectacular success – and now he'd go head-to-head with the greatest team on the planet. It would be one hell of a battle – but like the teenager who roamed those Govan streets all those years ago, Ferguson wasn't about to back down.

As a fan you couldn't help think United's humbling at the hands of Barcelona marked the beginning of the great man's last chapter at Old Trafford. From wide-eyed eight-year-old boy, to married 30-something with two kids and a mortgage, Ferguson has been there all along in my United obsession – but he won't be there forever. And if the next couple of seasons truly are to be his final throes then we can only hope he bows out in a style to befit his remarkable reign. A slow decline wouldn't detract from his legacy, but if Ferguson can somehow build another great team and conspire to win a third Champions League, no accolades will suffice. Immortality beckons – and you wouldn't bet against him getting it. Maybe it's time to knock Barcelona off their f**king perch.

SIR ALEX FERGUSON'S ACHIEVEMENTS AT MANCHESTER UNITED (1986–2011)

Premier League titles: 12
1992/93, 1993/94*, 1995/96*, 1996/97, 1998/99**, 1999/2000, 2000/01, 2002/03, 2006/07, 2007/08, 2008/09, 2010/11

FA Cup wins: 5
1989/90, 1993/94*, 1995/96*, 1998/99**, 2003/04

League Cup wins: 4
1991/92, 2005/06, 2008/09, 2009/10

UEFA Champions League wins: 2
1998/99**, 2007/08

UEFA Cup-Winners' Cup wins: 1
1990/91

Other: UEFA Super Cup (1991), Intercontinental Cup (1999), FIFA Club World Cup (2008)

* Double winners (Premier League and FA Cup)
** Treble winners (Premier League, FA Cup and UEFA Champions League)

ACKNOWLEDGEMENTS

Writing my first book was always going to be a learning experience, and one in which I was to lean heavily on the support of the experts around me – not to mention those closest to me – who've suffered my obsession for the best part of a year.

I'd like to thank John Pawsey, firstly for giving me the opportunity to tell people I've got an agent – but more importantly for his support and guidance throughout the project. It was John who saw the mileage in the book, and John who put it out there and ultimately got us the Holy Grail of a book deal. I can only apologise for the thousands of pitches that filled your inbox until I got one to stick.

The book as you read it now would have not been possible without the input of two key people. Firstly, that of Charlotte Atyeo at Bloomsbury – whose remarkable diligence and patience in the line of duty has ensured you're reading the most coherent work possible, from an author now well versed in the difference between brought and bought, and thrown and throne. That said, I still think the line about David Beckham s***ting rainbows should have made the cut. Secondly, the meticulous eye for detail and good humour of Julian Flanders, the editor who put the final touches to the book. There will doubtless be some criticism of what's in these pages, but not half as much as there might have been had Julian not played the sweeper role with such elegant efficiency. Thirdly, I'd like to thank my dad – and for a good deal more than tirelessly trawling through the text and checking every score, transfer fee and attendance figure. You gave me United, and in return you've been forced to share hundreds of games with a son who continues to sulk when they lose. I couldn't have hoped for a better companion in the stands, or in the living room. And if Barcelona is the legacy of our relationship, then I can think of far worse stories to tell your great, great grandchildren.

As for my wife, she hates football and always will. But the book would not have happened without her unswerving love and support. We had our second child a month before the deadline, and she juggled a toddler and a baby with the skill and endurance of Bryan Robson, to make sure I met it. I can't thank you enough, and I can only hope the impending United fandom of our two boys will see you converted before it's too late.

Finally, a word for the United players who've lived the last 25 years and contributed to the story of Sir Alex Ferguson's remarkable reign. To Robson, Olsen, Whiteside, Hughes, Sharpe, Giggs, Cantona, Scholes, Bruce, Keane, Beckham, Schmeichel, Ronaldo, Rooney and beyond. Thanks for the memories.

As for Sir Alex himself, here's hoping we're back here in five years celebrating 30 years at Old Trafford with a re-issue.

INDEX

The letters AF refer to Sir Alex Ferguson and the letters MU refer to Manchester United. References to countries, cities etc are to teams, unless otherwise indicated.